EVERYBODY'S DAUGHTER, NOBODY'S CHILD

Jane Lapotaire

BBC
LARGE
PRINT

First published 1989
by
Macmillan Ltd
as *Grace and Favour*
This Large Print edition published 2007
by
BBC Audiobooks Ltd
by arrangement with
Little, Brown Book Group

UK Hardcover ISBN 978 1 405 64863 9
UK Softcover   ISBN 978 1 405 64864 6

British Library Cataloguing in Publication Data available

Printed and bound in Great Britain by
Antony Rowe Ltd., Chippenham, Wiltshire

To the memory of Grace Elizabeth Chisnall,
and to foster mothers everywhere

ACKNOWLEDGEMENTS

To Kyle Cathie of Macmillan for listening to *Desert Island Discs*, and for following up Michael Parkinson's interest in my childhood, and prompting me to find the courage to put all this down on paper. To Judith Gollings for her support, encouragement and hard work. Without Judith, this book would have remained a bundle of notes. To Kate Jones, my editor at Macmillan, for her unflinching belief in my writing and long hours spent out of the office taking me through the manuscript. To my friends in Ipswich—the Kerridges, Whitmans and Haywards, Pat, Doug, Doris and Russell—my thanks for the kindnesses shown me as a child. To my London friends—Lis, Maurice, Carmen, Maureen, Marty and Marcia— my thanks for reading excerpts and putting up with me wittering on about this book for nearly two years. And to my son Rowan, who never read a word of it before it was printed—my thanks for just being around.

FOREWORD

This is not a formal autobiography, rather a collection of impressions and experiences seen through the eyes of a child. Other people in my story may have seen it differently: this is how I saw it.

Quand il ne se passe rien écrit pour le dire.
Ciceron

Fancy tellin' 'em all your business.
Gran

CHAPTER 1

She had a lump of veined skin that sprouted hair above her top lip, and another on her forehead. One of her thumbs had a nail that had been shut in a window; the skin behind it grew in two separate sections. I liked running my finger along the join. Or I'd sit on her knee and suck my thumb and play with her ear. The lobes were fleshy and large enough for me to set up a comforting twisting motion with my fingers, but I only did this when her ears were cold; warm ones didn't have the same soothing feel. I'd put my face into her neck where her wrinkled skin fell in folds, and smell her smell. It made me feel safe and good. Carried away to the point where I would almost double up the ear, she'd shift me off her knee with a ' 'ere now, that's enough of that' in her broad sing-song Suffolk accent.

She had an ill-fitting pair of false teeth with bright orange gums that food stuck to, and when I riled her she'd dislodge the bottom set and make her lip bulge menacingly. 'No you can't have any money for sweets, thass all I've got till pension day,' she'd say, thrusting her open, empty purse at my enquiring face.

I loved her more than anything else in the world. It didn't matter that she was old. Not at first. It didn't matter that she had whiskers that stuck into my nose when she kissed me. It didn't even matter that she made me take treacly black malt every morning. 'Come on, open wide, this'll build you up. All war babies have to have it now.' I'd gag as the

1

gluey bitter taste hit the back of my throat. 'From The Clinic,' she'd say emphatically as if that were reason enough to endure it, but she'd follow it with a glass of orange juice from a bottle with a turquoise label from The Clinic too, that tasted good.

Sometimes if I hadn't made too much of a fuss she'd give me one of her 'Milady' toffees from a crumpled paper bag that she kept in the sideboard drawer in the living-room amongst the ration books, rusting metal hair curlers, and bones that she'd taken out of her corset because they hurt.

I loved her. I thought she was my mother. I didn't know any different until I was six. I never questioned what she told me. 'We din't have anywhere to put you. You slept in a drawer after you was born. One of them drawers from the chest in the front bedroom.' I thought it funny. Couldn't picture myself sleeping amongst her felt hats with their straggly bits of net and large pearlised hat-pins, or the half-empty box of Christmas crackers. 'Don't be daft,' she'd say. 'I put blankets in the drawer first.'

I was special. She told me so. 'I do things for you I never did for the other girls.' They were always 'the other girls'. I knew they weren't my sisters. They weren't even sisters to each other. Edna and Gladys had gone by the time I was old enough to ask questions. But Pat and Doris were still there. 'You're spoiled rotten,' Doris would say to me. 'She never asked *us* what we wanted for tea; we got what we were given, and we sat there till we ate it.' I liked Doris; she had dark hair and twinkly eyes and she laughed a lot. She wore cotton dresses, sticky-out skirts with splodges of bright flowers all over

2

them, 'dirndl' she called them, and wide elastic belts that jumped out of her hands when she tried to fasten the metal buckle. I thought she was very pretty. 'There's ten years between you and Doris,' Mummy Grace said, 'and ten years between Doris and Louie.' I didn't know who Louie was, but I knew Mummy Grace's face changed when she spoke of her. 'Louie's abroad,' I heard her say disapprovingly. 'With some French bloke.'

Doris had lots of boyfriends. She'd take me down to the park with them sometimes, and they would give me chewing-gum, and let me wear their peaked hats with braid and buttons on them. Most of them talked in a soft blurry way that I liked, but Mummy Grace didn't.

'I don't want them Yanks in here.' I'd hear her raise her voice to Doris if I were in the other room.

'Oh, don't be so silly, Mum, there's no harm in it, and we've got Jane with us.'

'Well, I don't like it,' Mummy Grace would reply. 'What will the neighbours say, with Louie carrying on the way she did an' all . . .'

I didn't know what Yanks were. Doris threatened to do that with my baby teeth if one of them was loose and she saw me wiggling it. 'I'm going to put a piece of cotton round that tooth and tie it to the handle of the kitchen door. One quick yank and it'll be out.' My face would fall and then she'd laugh.

Had Pat said it, I would have run to Mummy Grace. Pat was huge and smelled of sour sweat. She had hair that poked out from under the short sleeves of the lacy pullovers that she knitted for herself. She was always knitting when she wasn't at work. Her needles whirled and clicked much faster

3

than Mummy Grace's. She could knit without looking, while she read *True Romance*. She would unpick Mummy Grace's knitting, working backwards along the row, almost as fast as she worked forwards. She bought me *Sunny Stories* every week on her way home from the laundry where she sweated in the steam while she pressed sheets. She was always hot, perhaps that was why she never wore things with sleeves; even in the winter her arms were always bare and their great bulk wobbled in time with the needles. I liked the Enid Blyton stories in the *Sunny Stories* comic, but I didn't like Pat. Fat Pat I called her when she wasn't there to hear. 'She'll catch you one of these days, you tinker,' said Mummy Grace, 'then you'll get what for.'

Doris didn't like her either. 'You're always squabbling, you two. You'll give me blood pressure.' Mummy Grace worried a lot about having blood pressure. I'd hear her shout over the garden fence to Mrs Whitman at number 81, two doors away: 'If you're goin' into the town, pick us up a bit of haddock for tea. I don't get out much now what with me hearttroubleandbloodpressure.' I thought they were one illness. 'Thass no good askin' the girls to do anything. They're always gallivanting about, after one thing or another.'

'The girls' had a fight once. I didn't know why. Mummy Grace pushed me into the front room before I had a chance to find out, but Pat had Doris's finger marks, that bled at first, then turned into bruises, on her arms for days after. I felt sorry for Pat, for a while. I thought it was very exciting to hear them shouting, as long as they weren't shouting at me.

4

'I'll take the rolling pin to you lot,' Mummy Grace threatened. 'Oh, sort it out between you,' she said, shutting the kitchen door on them. 'And don't stand there gawpin', Jane. Git along with you into the front room.' She always called me Jane when she was worried or I'd done something wrong. Other times she called me Nanie, my baby word for myself.

I didn't like the front room. Nobody went in there except the doctor or the minister from Alan Road Methodist Church. It was always cold and smelled of Brasso from the brass fender round the fireplace. It had an aspidistra on the table in the bay window. It wasn't 'the biggest aspidistra in the world' like the one Mummy Grace used to sing about in a wobbly high voice like someone called Gracie Fields on the wireless. Then she'd wheeze and laugh and her whole body would shake. She didn't laugh often but I could make her chuckle with a rhyme she taught me:

> Patience is a virtue
> Virtue is a grace
> Grace was a dirty girl
> Who never washed her face.

But I didn't like it when she chanted back at me:

> There was a little girl
> Who had a little curl
> Right in the middle of her forehead
> When she was good
> She was very very good
> But when she was bad
> She was—Jane.

5

We used to sit in the front room on Sunday after I'd been to Sunday School and watch the people go by. Mummy Grace liked this because she could say rude things from behind her net curtains about the people who were walking up the street.

'Look at that mawther, she's got a new hat on agin this week. Who *do* she think she is? She weren't nobody afore she married. She were only a Catchpole. They had one of those jerry-built houses on the Nacton Estate. I'm not proud, but this in't a council-house.'

There were three pictures on the walls of the front room. One of shaggy red bulls with long horns eating grass between Scottish mountains and two matching pictures called 'Betrothed' and 'Wedded Bliss'. The man wore sandals and a skirt like the pictures from the Bible on the walls at Sunday School, and the lady wore a floaty see-through dress and flowers in her hair. He had his arm around her in 'Betrothed' but they were standing far apart in 'Wedded Bliss'. 'They've got them the wrong way round, Mummy Grace.'

'Well, I don't know about that,' she'd say. 'My Walter was taken from me after only a year, then I had to have radium needles . . . you know, down there.'

Perhaps that's why she liked Gracie Fields so much. She sang another song, 'Walter Lead Me to the Altar'.

'Finish up your Spam then we can have the fruit, thass pineapple tidbits this week.' I loved tinned fruit and the evaporated milk that went with it even more, but she made me eat bread and butter with it too. 'It'll make it go farther,' she'd say. I didn't see

6

why the lovely taste of mandarin oranges or crunchy peach slices had to be spoiled with white Co-op bread. 'Waste not want not. Think of the poor children in Africa.' We sang 'All round the world there are little brown children' at Alan Road Sunday School, but I'd never seen a real one. Jesus in the picture on the wall above the piano had brown children in the crowd around His feet. So I supposed it must be true. But Jesus wore a dress and a beard. He didn't look at all like Mr Holden at number 87, or Mr Kerridge at number 83, and they were the only men I knew.

Till Doris married John. But they went to live in Trimley St Martin on the road to Felixstowe so I didn't see him often. I thought he was ever so good-looking. He had blond hair too and blue eyes, but Mummy Grace didn't think much of him. ''At takes all sorts I s'pose,' she sighed. 'If he keep her out late like this, night after night, she'll have one of her fits.'

I almost saw Doris have a fit once. She was sitting by the fire in the living-room talking, then the words stopped and came in spurts which didn't make sense. I sniggered, because I thought she was trying to make me laugh and she sounded funny; gurgling staccato sounds came from her throat. Then I saw her eyes. Or rather I didn't. They had rolled back into her head. All I could see were the whites. 'Mummy Grace, Mummy Grace, come quick. Doris has gone all trembly and stiff, and I can't see her eyes.' My world stopped as I stood transfixed watching her body go into spasm.

'Oh, you girls'll be the death of me,' Mummy Grace said, pushing a strand of grey hair out of her eyes. 'She's been doin' too much lately. Don't just

7

stand there, bang on the wall for Joan Holden.' She wiped her hands on her pinafore. 'Wouldn't you know it—I've just mixed a bowl of starch for your school dress. That'll set stiff in the basin now. Go on, bang on the kitchen wall, then run and see if Holdy's sitting in his shed. Tell him Doris has been took bad . . .'

Joan Holden was as big as Mummy Grace. She smelled of cigarette smoke. Mrs Holden, her mother, had arthritis so Joan was used to lifting people. 'Go on, dear, up you go to your room now,' she said as I let her in the front door. I knew it must be very serious, she never called me 'dear'. I went reluctantly up to the little back bedroom, carefully leaving my door open so I could hear what was going on. There was a lot of banging and scuffling. Then everything went quiet, apart from the murmur of Joan's and Mummy Grace's voices in the front room.

I got bored sitting on my bed. It was cold in there too. There was never a fire in the small black lead grate, except as a treat when I was ill. Sometimes the frost made lacy patterns on the glass inside the window. I thought I'd creep downstairs, which wasn't easy because the stairs creaked when I walked on them, especially the third one from the bottom and sometimes if the brass stair rods hadn't been slotted back properly into their rings they'd work loose and go crashing down on to the floorboards at the sides of the hall carpet and make a terrible noise. The front room door was slightly open but I couldn't see round it, so I peered in through the crack near the hinges.

Doris was rolled up inside the best fireside rug. I couldn't see her arms. Only her face. Her eyes were

8

closed and she looked very white. A toothbrush stuck out of her mouth. I was shocked. Why had they done this to her? Poor Doris, she looked like one of those cocoons that butterflies come out of, all bundled up like that. And how could she talk with that silly brush sticking out of her mouth? I wasn't at all surprised that Joan Holden had done this, but Mummy Grace was just standing with her hands on her hips watching.

'Bin burnin' the candle at both ends,' I heard her say. 'They'll be the death of me, these girls, I swear to God.'

She said that a lot and it worried me. I didn't want Mummy Grace to die because if she did I'd have to go into a Home. She said so. 'If it weren't for me, you'd all be in a Home.' I knew it was true. She'd got Pat and Doris from a Home, and Edna and Gladys and that girl called Lillian who only stayed with us for a while, and had mumps which made her happy because she missed her exams. 'Louie' had come from the same Home too. Barnardo's they called it, in Stepney, wherever that was. It wasn't near Ipswich because it wasn't on the map on Class 5's wall, which had a face of someone called Wolsey on it wearing a funny flat hat, and a man called Constable who didn't look at all like a policeman. I sucked my thumb and that made me feel better. Perhaps that's what Mummy Grace meant when she'd flop down on the kitchen chair, her face all red from bucketing the water into the copper for our bath, 'I don't know how to put one foot in front of the other, I wish God 'ould take me Home.' Perhaps she wanted to go into a Home to get away from all of us. Then I'd be left with Pat. I didn't like that idea at all, except for Doug, Pat's boyfriend.

He'd call round on his way home from work and have a wash in the kitchen sink. He'd scrub and scrub at his hands that were covered in splashes of whitewash; his overalls were dotted all over with paint too, and sometimes he'd find a small lump of putty in the pocket which he'd give me to play with. I could squeeze it into all sorts of shapes and see the lines that my fingerprints made on it. It smelled dry and floury. 'It's not chewing-gum, you know. Put that in your mouth you won't be able to speak for a week. Oh, I don't know, that's not such a bad idea, the rest of us could get a word in edgeways then.' He'd laugh and grip my knees as he passed me where I sat on the kitchen step, making me squeal. 'Come on out of the way, sparrows' kneecaps, let a bloke through.'

I thought he was good-looking too, and couldn't understand why he was marrying Pat. She was getting bigger and bigger all the time. 'Well, 'at's not what she eat, she only pick at her food—'at must be her glands. Course, it probably run in the family, only we're not to know that . . .' I had heard her mutter something about Pat's dad having run foul of something. So that's why Pat had been put in a Home, I thought. But then I didn't have a dad either so what had my dad done?

Pat could hardly read, and her spelling was atrocious, even Mummy Grace said so. 'Oh, Pat! That's not how you write margarine. Give me the order book.' I promised myself I'd learn to spell really well at Cliff Lane, just in case that had something to do with being put into a Home . . .

Cliff Lane Primary School was about ten minutes' walk from Levington Road, at the bottom of a steep hill. Margaret Whitman and I went there every morning. She was a mouse of a girl with a pudding-basin haircut, like her mother's, and a red face like her mother's too. She was as shy as I was garrulous. I used to have to put my hand up when she wanted to be excused, as she didn't dare. It wasn't really a chore as it meant I could blackmail some of her sweets off her, or bully her into buying some of my favourite Horlicks Tablets with her money when Mummy Grace's purse was empty. She'd suck her gobstoppers really slowly while I crunched mine quickly down to the hard bit in the middle, not bothering to watch them change colour.

We played together when we weren't at school, mostly in the old Anderson shelter in our back yard. We couldn't play in hers, because her mother kept her mangle in it, and as she took in washing, which made her face even redder, their shed was always cluttered up with large tin buckets full of neatly folded damp sheets. When Mrs Whitman wasn't washing sheets, she was washing Margaret. Her face shone with her mother's vigorous flannel work.

'No, you're not washing me,' I said to Mummy Grace. 'I don't care what Mrs Whitman does, I'm not Margaret.'

'Oh, you botty little mawther—don't care was made to care and don't care was hung and don't care was put in a pot and stewed till he was done. Well, you make sure you have a proper stand-up wash then,' said Mummy Grace, pouring hot water from the stained brass kettle into the plastic washing-up bowl in the kitchen sink. 'We may be poor but we're clean.'

11

We had a bath once a week. The old tin bath hung outside on a nail on the wall near the coal-shed. Mummy Grace bucketed cold water from the kitchen tap into the copper that was built into the corner of the kitchen wall, lit the fire under it after I'd gone to school in the morning, and by the time I came home, the water would be hot. The bath would be carried in, wiped free of brick dust and shrivelled-up spiders, and the hot water bucketed into it. It took up the entire length of the kitchen floor.

'Now don't you go slopping water all over the lino,' Mummy Grace would say, giving me half a precious Cussons Apple Blossom bath cube to crumble into it. Although it was good to feel the hot water creep up my skinny body, and comforting to know that at least I had it first (the privilege of being the youngest; Pat and Doris, while they still lived with us, had to take their turn), I never really relaxed in it. I was never sure whether the grit under my person was the grainy bath cube that left a ring of grey scum at the water's edge, or escaped brick dust, or worse.

I'd run, scattering Avon talcum powder as I went (Pat was an Avon representative), into the warmth of the living-room where Mummy Grace put my pyjamas and slippers, turned inside out, to warm on the fender by the fire. Sometimes if I dawdled getting dry, there would be faint scorch marks on my clothes, but not as bad as the marks on her legs. She sat too close to the fire throughout the winter, once her work was done, listening to *The Archers* on the wireless in the evenings, or to *Workers' Playtime* while she waited for my dinner to cook. The small fire only gave out enough warmth to heat the area around the fireside, so I'd move the old utility chair almost into the grate when I listened to *Children's Hour*, or, if she was sitting in it, I'd creep up behind her and take out the pole that supported the back and it would slide slowly towards the window and lodge itself against the sill, leaving her at a precarious angle.

'You'll do that once too often, my girl,' she'd say crossly, 'and I'll go through that window and that would be a fine lookout! Now put that chair back straight, and go and get the Vick. I'll rub some of that on your chest before you go to bed.' The biting Suffolk easterly winds made me chesty in winter. As unpleasant as the Vick was—it made my nose run and my eyes water, but was rubbed on my chest, then covered with a piece of soft material that was lodged inside my liberty bodice—it was better than the torture of her holding my head covered in a towel over a jug of steaming hot water with friar's Balsam in it. 'Now, come on, git up those stairs quick, and don't forget to say your prayers.'

They weren't the same prayers that I said at Sunday School. Mr Keen was the Sunday School superintendent. He said our prayers with us on special occasions. He wore a tall black hat and a long black jacket with tails at the back. His shoes were covered with black felt gaiters that had shiny buttons all the way up the legs, like the eyes on teddy bears. We sang 'Hear the Pennies Dropping' as the collection plate was passed round. Sometimes I had a silver sixpenny bit to drop inside, like the ones I found inside the Christmas pudding, but mostly it was a brass-coloured threepenny piece that made the palm of my hand green if I held it tightly. Miss Reynolds, who had wavy permed hair and small grey eyes behind her pale pink glasses, played the piano while we sang 'Jesus Wants Me for a Sunbeam'. I liked Sunday School. I could wear my best outfit and Miss Reynolds sometimes smiled at me and said, 'Poor little dear.' I didn't know why she said it, but it made me feel good. It was the only time I ever went out. We murmured the Lord's Prayer with our hands clasped tightly in front of our noses, squeezing one eye open just to check if anyone else was brave enough to look up at Mr Keen and giggle.

But with Mummy Grace standing by my bed I said a different prayer, one that she'd taught me, that I didn't really understand.

> 'God bless Mummy Mummy Grace,
> Pat and Doris and all kind friends
> And please God make Jane a good girl
> For Christ's sake, Amen.'

I thought it odd that I had to repeat Mummy Grace's name twice. But then talking to God was odd anyway. Perhaps there was a rule about repeating yourself at the beginning of a prayer, just to catch His attention. I dismissed it. Grown-ups had such odd rules, and this must be one of them.

CHAPTER 2

Margaret Whitman liked playing mothers and fathers with tea-sets in our shed. I didn't. I didn't know what fathers did, but it didn't worry me. Mr Whitman sat with his feet in a bowl of hot water and mustard when he wasn't at work on the Eastern Counties buses reading *The News Chronicle*. Margaret Whitman had *I Spy* books because he read *The News Chronicle*. On Sundays he read *Reveille*. His conductor's hat left a red ridge on his forehead even when he took it off. I didn't want to be him. It was much better playing doctors and nurses. I could keep Margaret all wrapped up in one of Mummy Grace's old blankets so she couldn't move, and boss her around for hours, till she got bored and ran grizzling home to her mother.

'Oh, why can't you two git on? You're always squabbling. I'll bang your heads together one of these days! Now go on, git out from under my feet while I get the dinner on.'

I'd learned early to distract. 'Oh, let me lick the bowl out first.'

'No you can't. There won't be enough left for the pudding.'

'Oh, please.' Lovely creamy steamed pudding mixture with lots of sugar at the bottom.

'Now go on, run along and play in the shed.'

'It's no fun in there on my own. It's dark and horrible.'

'Oh, don't be so daft.'

'I don't believe you went down there in the war.'

15

'Well, we did.'

'What, under the floor?'

'Well, it wasn't filled in with earth then, daft! I had steps going down. We used to sleep down there when the doodlebugs went over.' That name made me laugh. Fancy grown-ups being frightened of something with such a silly name. 'When the siren went you had to go, or you'd have the air-raid warden after you. Course, towards the end, we couldn't get old Nana down there any more.'

Mummy Grace's mother. I remembered old Nana. Just. I'd been allowed to sit on the pillow behind her head and comb her thin grey hair when I was very small. She was always in bed and the room smelled of something they called methylated spirits. 'To stop her getting bed sores,' Mummy Grace said. She'd shared half a large yellow fruit with me once. I'd never seen one like it before.

'It's a grapefruit,' she said in her thin squeaky voice. 'Here, open your mouth and have a taste.'

'You'd rob Jesus Christ of His shoe strings,' said Mummy Grace coming into the room. 'That was for Nana.'

'Oh, leave the child alone, Grace, she's not doin' no harm.'

'Well, that's all the coupons for this week, that grapefruit. They don't grow on trees, you know, we in't got no more.'

Old Nana's father had been a miller at the flour mill in Wickham Market but we'd never been there. I could imagine the big sails going round and round like the pictures in the books at school. But I couldn't imagine Mummy Grace sleeping under the floor of the shed. 'Wasn't it dark?'

'We'd take down a little oil lamp like the one in

the privy.'

'I wouldn't have gone.'

'You *had* to go. Din't have no choice. Everyone had to go. 'Cept Louie of course. She thought she knew better. But then she always did . . . You take after her.'

I felt chastened but I didn't know why.

I'd play in the garden till the night came, shining a torch up at Margaret Whitman's window if she'd gone to bed before me, or stealing currants from Holdy's garden and eating them till my stomach swelled and ached.

If I was lonely, there was always the blue fairy. She lived by the white rose bush Walter had planted in 1912; it was the only flower in the garden of long grass and weeds, apart from the spindly lilac bushes right at the bottom that straggled along the fencc of the house in Hatfield Road. Mummy Grace wouldn't let me cut the purple blooms and put them in a vase because they brought bad luck. Crossed knives did too, and shoes on the table meant that we were going to have a row, and if I used scissors on a Sunday she'd say, 'You'll have the devil with you all the week.' Sometimes the rose had a flower or two and they seemed beautiful amongst the knee-high grass and stinging nettles.

My fairy was beautiful too. She had blue gossamer wings and a floaty dress that I could see right through. She was always there when I wanted her. She didn't go grizzling home to her mother. She always wanted to play with me. She liked me all the time not just some of it, and she always came when I called her. She was magic, she could take me wherever I wanted to go and she never got

17

cross even when I blamed her.

'Come on in now, your tea's ready. You'll get your death of cold out there, and my suet dumpling'll go heavy. Who are you jawing to at this time of night?'

'The blue fairy. She says I can go with her wherever I want. Far away. Even further than Ipswich.'

'Oh, I don't know who put these ideas into your head, I really don't. Your tea's ready, and don't you walk dirt all over my clean coconut matting.'

I went to bed as usual that night. The hot water bottle had been placed in my bed and the pot under it. The stairs were dark, narrow and steep and I couldn't go up them alone unless the landing light was on. I'd undressed downstairs by the living-room fire as usual, my liberty bodice and navy-blue Cliff Lane knickers folded on the stool in front of the fire, my stubby plaits released from the snare of the elastic bands.

'Ouch, that hurt.'

'Oh, don't be so wet. Pride must bear a pinch.'

Mummy Grace panting behind me, almost as wide as the stairs, stopped halfway up to catch her breath.

'Come on quick or the bogey on the landing will get me.'

'Don't be so daft.' Her stock reaction to my excitability.

The blessed oasis of warmth where the hot water bottle was, and the chill of the flannelette sheets where it wasn't. I shivered from the cold of the unheated hall and bedroom.

'Move your legs up and down quick; that'll warm you up.' The wooden bedhead creaked as I did,

18

and the worn-out metal springs twanged.

'That's enough of that, you'll have the bedstead on the floor. Now don't forget to say your prayers.' A wet kiss, the hairs from her moustache tickling my face. 'And ask God to forgive you for all the bad things you've done today.'

There were so many. Little spiteful nasty things I knew I'd done. But the ones that no one spoke of frightened me the most. I had begun to feel them in the air. Snatches of conversation whirled in my head.

Joan Holden saying, 'If she spoke to me like that I'd slap the back of her legs, but of course, it's not the same if she's not your own.'

Carol Jones saying in the playground, 'I'm not coming to school next week. It's my Dad's holiday. We're going to Walton on the Naze.' That wasn't fair. Mummy Grace never had a holiday so I could never have a week off school. I'd pulled Carol's pigtails and pushed her. I'd have to speak to the angel about that too.

The angel lived in the dark ceiling above my bed when the light went out. It had a great book with everyone's name on a page. My page was covered in black marks. Always almost full. Something unspeakable would happen to me when it was. Of this I was sure. I'd have to pray again for a clean page. It was the most important thing in the world to start tomorrow with a clean page. A growing sense of unease that I was different because of something I'd done wrong. But how could I ask the angel if I didn't know what it was I'd done? What was it? Why didn't they tell me? I knew they knew. If only I could remember.

'Speak when you're spoken to, you tinker.'

19

'What?'

'I said, "Night night, Nanie".'

'Night night, Mummy Grace.'

She left the bedroom door ajar, the light from the hall spilling in at an angle that made the old washstand with its bowl and jug into a distorted eerie shadow on the wall. The angel stayed as stubborn as ever. However hard I tried to will a clean page, the black marks stayed. I slept.

It felt like the middle of the night. The shaft of light from the door was wider but the overhead light hadn't been switched on. Perhaps they didn't want to wake me up completely, and as they didn't, what followed is rather a haze.

'Ja-ane, Ja-ane, come on, wake up!' Mummy Grace pushing my shoulder, pulling my wrinkled wet thumb out of my mouth. 'Wake up, it's your mother.'

Two shapes in the darkness of the room. A shape above me. Too small for Pat. A large wide-brimmed hat? Or hair dark like mine? An unfamiliar face white in the blackness. Hands with long red pointed nails and many shiny rings stroked my face, then pushed my hair back. I'd never seen hands like those. Mummy Grace's were chapped and red from the washing soda and Sunlight soap that she used to scrub the clothes on the draining-board. She only had a wedding ring. And the smell. Such a sweet heady smell. She was the most beautiful lady I had ever half-seen. She must have kissed me but I don't remember. She must have said something that I don't remember either. Mother. Mother. The word tumbled around my befuddled brain. I don't remember how long she stayed, but I do remember Mummy Grace tucking

20

me up again, because she was more brusque than usual and she pulled the sheets in so tight, I could hardly move. She knew I didn't like them like that. Why had she done it? Why was she cross?

'Come on, Louie, let the child get some sleep.'

There was a small green suitcase by my bed when I woke in the morning. A doll's suitcase. Inside was a set of doll clothes that made me gasp. A little grey corduroy coat with collar, cuffs and pockets and a matching corduroy beret complete with the most beautiful pheasant feather. I stroked it with my fingers and it fell back into shape. And the smell. The suitcase had that smell from the night before.

It was my best treasure. I even took it to school with me. I spurned the knitted pink lacy jackets that Pat had made for Josephine. This coat was better than anything anyone had at school.

I was better too. I felt better in the playground, better enough to boast.

Mother, Mother, said the voice in my head. My mother was beautiful and smelled good. Better than Mrs Whitman or Joan Holden or even Mrs Murrills who lived in Cliff Lane and collected Mummy Grace's pension on Tuesdays. I liked her because I could tell that she liked me and for some reason there weren't many who did. But Mrs Murrills had permed hair and wore no make-up. She had a kindly face, but my mother was beautiful. Mummy Grace's lined face danced in front of my eyes. (I wanted to ask her so many questions.) I pushed the face away and felt bad. I couldn't let her know I thought my mother beautiful. Somehow that was wrong. So what I didn't dare ask, I made up.

21

'My mother made these doll clothes for me.' The word tasted odd in my mouth.

'Oh, yeah? That old lady who waits outside the school for you sometimes?'

'No, daft, my *mother*,' as if that were explanation enough.

'You can't have two mothers, silly.'

'Well I *have*.' I knew I was different; here at last was the proof.

'You're soft, you are. Nobody's got *two* mothers. Where is she then, your *other* mother?' Giggles.

A small crowd had gathered round me. I felt cornered against the rough wooden boards of the playground fence.

'She's abroad,' I said, panicking, the word dropping into my head from somewhere. I didn't know what it meant and worried in case they asked.

'Why in't she here then?'

I hadn't bargained for that. I didn't know.

'My mother's French.' Where did I get these ideas from? I felt as if bits of jigsaw were falling into place, but I was inventing the pieces. That couldn't be right.

'Go on then, say some French!' Jeers.

'I can't yet but I will next time she comes.'

'When's that then?'

Panic.

'Next week.'

Silence.

'Your name in't French. Burgess in't French, is it?'

'Perhaps you're like me,' said Lurline Golding quietly, 'perhaps you're adopted.'

'Well, of course I am,' I said roughly, not knowing what that meant either, but cross with her

22

because she did, although underneath I felt so grateful to her, which made me doubly bad. I promised myself she would become my best friend. Margaret Whitman could ask to go to the lavatory by herself from now on. She'd stood silently at my side, her round eyes wide with unspoken disbelief at what I was doing.

'I'm adopted, so there.'

They went away answered at last.

'Did she bring you the doll with the clothes as well?' said Susan Inskip gently.

'No, she couldn't bring it this time, she had too much to carry but she will . . .'

I tried to squeeze Josephine into the clothes.

Josephine, much-loved, battered, rag doll Josephine, who somebody had won at the Co-op fête in Christchurch Park, with her sewn-on mask of a face and her hairless head that curved into a funny triangular shape, her stuffed body with its stick-out arms and legs, that ended in round pads. Josephine was half as big as me; she couldn't fit into these clothes. Josephine was retrieved from under the shelf in the living-room cupboard where Mummy Grace kept the bread out of the reach of the mice in the kitchen pantry, and was reinstated in my affections. Why had this lady brought clothes to fit a doll I didn't have? Thinking of her as 'this lady' made me feel safe again.

I sat on Mummy Grace's knee twirling Josephine's pointed head in my fingers and sucked my thumb.

'Mummy Grace, Mummy Grace,' I said over and over again into her neck. That made me feel better too.

'What?' she said.

'Mummy Grace, Mummy Grace, Mummy Grace.'

'I don't know what's got into you today,' she said. I hugged her hard.

'Don't do that, you'll have my corsets digging into me. I can't sit here all day. The fire needs stoking or this room'll be like Greenland's icy mountains.'

I giggled.

'I'm adopted, aren't I?'

'No, you're darn well not,' she said roughly. 'Who put that idea into your head?'

'Well, why aren't I?'

'She wouldn't let me, that's why.' She was getting riled now. I wished I hadn't asked. 'Anyway, they won't let you adopt if you in't got a husband, and God saw fit to take my Walter Home. We were only wed a year.' Her eyes misted over. Now I knew it was wrong to have started the questions.

'Come on, get down. I'm getting flustered by this fire. The coal-scuttle won't fill itself.'

'Don't cry, Mummy Grace. If you *do*, I'll cry. I *will*.'

'Oh, we are a pair,' she said, wiping her eyes with the edge of her apron. 'C'mon, pull yourself together. You've got a face that'd turn milk sour. If the wind changes you'll stay like that.'

I managed a smile. 'It's Wilfred Pickles tonight, isn't it? Oh, please, let's listen to it, please,' I asked with more enthusiasm than I felt. 'Let's "have a go, Joe".' She smiled.

> 'Another spot of homely fun
> Bringing the people to the people
> With Mabel at the table . . .'

24

'Oh, I don't know what I'm going to do with you I'm sure,' and she laughed. I liked making her laugh. I wouldn't ask any more questions. Not for a while.

I put the green suitcase in the sideboard and forgot about it. It seemed best that way, then we could go on as before.

CHAPTER 3

We didn't go on holiday because there wasn't any money. Mrs Whitman and Margaret had free Eastern Counties bus tickets to relatives in Swindon or they'd stay in Ipswich and go on a Runabout ticket on the trolley buses. I thought that was boring. Mummy Grace couldn't get up the narrow winding stairs as the bus lurched forward and the front seat on the top deck was the only place worth being. With all that glass in front it was like not being part of the bus at all. I'd stand up and holding on to the window rail I could imagine myself driving it alone. Speeding down Bishop's Hill was best. I could only do that with Mrs Whitman and Margaret though, when we went to Christchurch Park. We walked to see her grandmother. It seemed such a long way. She was grey and bony and sat all day in a chair by the fire. Her voice was laboured and thin and it made my shoulders ache watching her struggle for breath. Her house was dark and smelled of camphorated oil. She kept a black plastic tube in a jam-jar on the sideboard that had an odd-shaped head on it which fitted over her mouth and helped her to breathe. It frightened me rather, and I didn't like watching so I didn't go every time I was invited. I'd make up an excuse. 'A white lie,' Mummy Grace called it.

Anyway, trolley buses often broke down. There'd be a crackle overhead as one, or both, of the long arms that went from the roof of the buses to the overhead wires became disconnected and bounced feebly up and down in mid-air. Then the bus would stop, the conductor would have to get out and stand in the middle of the road with the long wooden pole that was kept outside the bus when not in use, and re-attach the arms to the wires with the aid of the hook at the end of the pole. Then off the bus would lurch again. It was fun to stand and watch them go along the Nacton Road, at the end of our street, in winter, when the frost on the wires made a spitting sound and small blue sparks marked the bus's passage along the network that joined Nacton Road to Clapgate Lane.

We walked round the docks sometimes on Sunday afternoons in summer. I liked the docks with their railway tracks that ran round the edge of the water. The grains of corn that had been spilled on the quayside crunched under our shoes. Mummy Grace would pick up small lumps of coal, spit on them for luck, chuckle, and wrap them carefully in a handkerchief and put them in her handbag. I liked the huge boats docked in the muddy water. They made me dream of far-away places with their foreign names and strange flags. We'd sit on a bollard and stare out to sea or at least across the mud-flats to Pin Mill which seemed so far away on the other side of the Orwell.

                    *   *   *

Sometimes Mummy Grace would shout over the Kerridges' fence to Mrs Whitman as she stood hanging out her washing in the garden on the line between the apple and the plum tree.

'Mrs Whitman, Mrs Whitman.'

'Come into the garden, Maud,' I'd snigger under my breath. A man on the wireless sang about her in a plummy voice in a show with a man called Mantovani.

'Ssh, you tinker. 'At looks as if thass goin' to be nice then agin today, 'at make a change, don't it?'

And Mrs Whitman would mumble something like: 'Yes, 'at do look pretty settled.' It was often difficult to understand what she said because she kept her teeth in a glass on the draining-board and her rubbery lips seemed to cave into her mouth without them. She only wore them for best. But she always wore a hat to hang out the washing.

'Ja-ane, Ja-ane, run down to Fowlers and get me some eggs. We're goin' to Felixstowe for the day.'

I didn't have to be asked twice. I flew down to the corner, jumping the cracks in the pavement, singing all the way, 'Oh, I do like to be beside the seaside.'

The eggs would be hard-boiled, chopped and spread between thick wedges of Co-op white sliced bread. Sometimes there'd be corned beef too, or Shiphams Potted Meat Spread, all carefully wrapped in grey crackling sheets of greaseproof paper.

'Can I have some fizzy orange?'

'No, you can't, dear, I in't got the money for

27

train tickets and for pop as well.'

'That's all right, it's Saturday, the Corona man goes to Mrs Whitman's on a Wednesday. Bet they've got some left. I hope it's Vimto. I'll just go round and make sure they bring it.'

'You've got the cheek of the devil,' she said, smiling as she rolled up my shirred elastic swimsuit in a towel.

' 'Ere, before you dash out, let me have a look and see if your feet are clean. We don't want no performance like last time.'

She hadn't forgotten the shame of my being sent home by Mrs Whitman one hot day in summer, when, after endless pleading and whining, Margaret and I had managed to persuade her to fill one of her small tin baths with water so we could paddle in it in their back yard and cool down. We weren't allowed to paddle in the shallow paddling pool in Holywells Park because we'd catch something that sounded like 'empytigo'. Neither Margaret nor I knew what it was and no one bothered to explain. We were sure it was just another of the excuses that grown-ups made when they didn't want to stop their housework and take us out. Mrs Whitman had finally given way, taken the round tin bath out from underneath the mangle in the shed, and we'd filled it with icy cold water from a standpipe in the garden. I pulled off my heavy black lace-up shoes without undoing them, tore off my white ankle socks, their tops all wavy where the elastic had gone, and stood on the cold concrete of their back yard, stretching my toes with the pleasure of it. Margaret and her mother stared down in silent horror at my feet. The ankles were caked with dust, little balls of black fluff and dirt

28

were caught between my toes and the nails were black with the dirt that was trapped underneath them. Of course it must have been nearly a week since I'd had my bath and I'd lied about having a proper stand-up wash when Mummy Grace had shouted from the living-room to ask. Two basinsful had taken me as far as my middle, then I'd forgotten the rest.

'You dirty little tyke,' said Mrs Whitman. 'You'd better go off to Mrs Chisnall and get her to wash your feet afore you put them into any tin bath of mine.'

'You little beggar,' Mummy Grace had said, pouring hot water from the kettle down into the washing-up bowl on the kitchen floor, 'I won't be able to look the Whitmans in the face again. People'll say I don't look after you properly.'

'Oh, I do like to be beside the seaside,' I screeched, flinging my arms round her wide middle, 'Oh, I do like to be beside the sea.'

'You'll have my glasses off in a minute—don't get so wound up, there'll be tears before bedtime . . .'

We walked to the Felixstowe Road, past the shops, past the Royal Oak pub that smelled of sour beer with its Suffolk Punch horses stamping their huge legs impatiently by the gaping hole in the pavement edged round by wooden casks of beer waiting to be rolled down the plank into the darkness.

'Let's cross to the other side, we don't want to get tangled up with the drunks falling out of there,' said Mummy Grace. It was early. The place looked deserted. From the other side of the road it was easier to see the brightly coloured toucan advertising Guinness on the hoarding. Past Newsteads Bakery where I was sometimes sent to buy two lemon curd puff pastries for a special tea, and Jacksons, the pie shop next door. We didn't have Jackson's pies often enough. I loved their straight sides with the fluted tops that fitted so beautifully, that were stained with mutton gravy. When I stole one from the bag and ate it on the way down Levington Road it was difficult to eat it without the whole pie caving in and the gravy and minced meat running down my arm. I should have waited until we sat down properly at the living-room table after they'd been heated up in the oven. But they never tasted so good somehow.

'I said get four, there's only three here.'

'I've eaten one already.'

'You little tinker. 'At's common, eatin' walkin' down the road. People'll think you've been brought up in a pigsty.'

Past the Co-op yard and Derby Road School to Derby Road Station. Margaret and I running on ahead, me in front wanting to get there first, wanting to beat her. The bridge over the tracks that led to the platform and the ticket office halted me soon enough. There was another way round continuing along the road and turning a corner into the gravel track that led into the back of the station; that took longer so the bridge had to be faced. It had uneven wooden slits through which I could see the railway tracks underneath. The sense of nothing stable under my feet gave me a horrid kind of thrill that I disliked as much as I liked. Sometimes if we were bored playing in the street we'd walk up to the station, although we weren't allowed that far away, and play dares there. They

30

knew how frightened I was of the bridge. I was never collected enough to hide my excited terror and consequently my dare was always to have to walk from one side of the bridge to the other looking down through the boards. There was a strange-looking black pole to one side of the track, with a wide rubber chute hanging from it that dripped water and flapped in the breeze. That frightened me too.

I screeched with terror and delight at the prospect of having to face the bridge again and hovered on the pavement long enough for Mummy Grace and the Whitmans to catch me up, and say from somewhere behind me, 'Nobody's forcin' you to go that way. Come with us, round by the road. Calm down, you'll have everyone lookin' at us if you carry on like that.'

But across I went, slow and terrified, my heart beating hard against my ribs.

The train chugged along like the poem I couldn't quite remember from school:

Past all the hedges past all the ditches
Something and something and faster than witches
And travelling along like troops in a battle
All of the something and horses and cattle.

I couldn't see any horses. Just fields and fields of sugarbeet and Ransomes Sims and Jeffries farm machinery standing like prehistoric monsters in dark ridged fields. I could catch sight of puffs of smoke from the engine if I pressed my nose up against the grimy glass. I wasn't allowed to touch the leather strap that let down the window although I ached to stick my head out and feel the

31

wind rushing past my face that would make me gasp for breath, but in a thrilling way. Not like when I had bronchitis.

'You'll get smuts in your eyes if you do,' warned Mrs Whitman, dabbing at the spittle that collected at the corners of her mouth when she didn't wear her teeth, 'and that'll be a right lookout.'

The shopping bags rustled with the movement of the train in the luggage net above our heads. We always sat in a carriage marked 'Ladies Only' if there was one.

'Oh, why can't we go up the front near the engine?'

'We don't want no men poking their noses in. Better off in this one,' said Mrs Whitman, smoothing her summer dress over her knees and folding her hands neatly in her lap.

Orwell, Trimley, Felixstowe Town, and at last Felixstowe Beach.

'I can see the sea, I can see the sea,' I chanted.

'Ooh, she never stop, do she?' ventured Mrs Whitman.

Margaret sat silently sucking the same sweet.

'Well at least she in't got her thumb in her mouth,' said Mummy Grace, always ready to take my part. 'C'mon, out we get, and mind that step.' The air smelled different on the platform, the train heaved quietly as if recovering its breath.

Impatient with their slow pace, I ran ahead leaving Margaret to walk obediently beside her mother. Past the shops with their buckets and spades stacked outside, and the rubber rings hanging by strings from striped awnings that bumped into each other in the wind. Plastic windmills on sticks making a clicking sound as they

32

spun backwards and forwards in the breeze. Past the Peters ice-cream stand. Almost. I turned, filling my lungs with air that tasted salty on my tongue, preparing to shout.

'No, you can't have one,' shouted Mummy Grace, pre-empting my question, her voice travelling sideways on the wind.

I had to wait at the main road that had to be crossed to get to the beach for them to catch up. I cast a longing glance at Butlins fun fair to my right. Girls were screaming on the Big Dipper as the cars plunged down its turquoise, trellis-like slopes and disappeared from sight behind a row of beach huts. As the screaming grew louder I could hear music from the Dodgem Cars mingled with distant bumps and crashes. 'In Gilly Gilly Ossenfefer Katzenellan Bogen, by the sea-ee-ee-ee-ee,' sang Max Bygraves. People walked past me eating bright pink clouds of candy-floss that were almost lifted off their paper tubes by the wind, dark pink sugary stains round their mouths.

I shivered. It was always cold at Felixstowe, but I didn't mind. We walked along the prom till we saw a place on the beach that wasn't too crowded.

'That'll do, over there, look, that'll do.'

'Ooh, you'll be in a hurry to get to your own funeral, you will. We don't want to sit near the pier, 'at get cold by the pier. Let's go up the Pavilion end away from the noise.'

They meant away from Butlins, so my hopes of having a go on the painted brass horses that danced jerkily up and down on wooden poles as the roundabout went round were dashed.

'When it's spring again, I'll bring again, tulips from Amsterdam,' continued Mr Bygraves from an ever-increasing distance. I stopped running and looked across the grey choppy vastness of the water. Holland was over there. They said so at school. Difficult to imagine girls in those funny starched white hats and yellow wooden clogs like on the cheese labels that Margaret and I collected and did swaps with, clattering along a beach like this on the other side of all those waves with foaming crests. The water seemed to go on for ever. Its greyness not the greyness of the sky. Such a long way away, further than I'd ever been. Yet it was difficult to see the join.

The beach was stones. Shingle they called it. Odd. That was something that Mummy Grace got when she was worried about money, then she couldn't sit near the fire because the heat made the red bumps on her arms and legs itch and she would get more and more irritable the more she scratched. No time for thoughts like those today though.

I ran down the concrete steps to the beach, leaping and jumping as best I could, over the stones that made a crunching sound under my sandals and slowed me down, straight to the water's edge where I screamed as I dodged the waves as they fell on to the narrow strip of sand and powdered shells that loosened dangerously under my feet and made a sucking noise as the water retreated over it. I screamed some more and laughed and hopped up and down, released by the hugeness of the space, throwing stones into the swell until my arm ached, then ran back to where they'd settled out of the wind by a stone breakwater fringed by seaweed, my sandals caked in sand drying into white tide marks around the punched-out stencilled flower pattern.

'People'll think you're potty, carryin' on like that. They'll think you've just been let out of Foxhall Road for the day.' That was where mad people went. It was on the heath near the speedway track. Doug had taken me to speedway once. The whine of the tinny engines made me cover my ears. The noise hurt, but I liked the spray of churned-up mud that curved out behind the back wheels of the motor-bikes. The smell of diesel oil clung to my nostrils and made me sniff the air for more.

The sea air stung my face, caught my breath and dried my lips. My tongue tasted salt everywhere: on the egg sandwiches, the Victoria plums from the Whitmans' tree and on the bar of Fry's mint chocolate cream from the bottom of Mrs Whitman's Home & Colonial Stores' shopping bag.

I ate everything that came my way and burped, while Margaret dipped slowly into her bag of crisps. 'Manners,' said Mrs Whitman, which always made me smile. I didn't know whether it was a request or a remonstrance. Mummy Grace and I said 'Pardon.'

I wished my greed hadn't got the better of me when I said, 'Come on, Margaret, I'll race you into the sea,' and Mummy Grace replied, 'Not if I have anything to do with it you won't, my girl. S'posin' you got cramp out there, I in't a comin' in to get you.' She couldn't swim. Neither could Mrs Whitman. 'You in't a goin' in that there sea till you've digested your dinner and that's a fact.'

So I contented myself with popping seaweed blisters and trailing a stick behind me in the wet sand, and gazing longingly out to sea. That space set up such a yearning inside me. Margaret sat obediently by her mother who was peeling an apple for her with Mr Whitman's penknife. I ate them as they were, peel and all, so did Mummy Grace, in spite of her false teeth. The only fruit she couldn't eat were raspberries because the pips got stuck between her palate and the false teeth. We didn't own a penknife anyway. Only men had penknives.

I wandered off alone, towards the Punch and Judy stand. I knew I couldn't stay too long because I didn't have any money to put in the hat that was passed through the crowd. The raucous voice of Punch carried on the wind. 'That's the way to do it.' I didn't understand why everyone laughed when he hit Judy with his stick. Perhaps I'd missed the bit that explained why they laughed when he hit Judy. Anyway, I could see the red and white tent bulging at the back when the man moved from puppet to puppet. That was more interesting than standing in the front like everyone else. The canvas stretched with his shape as he moved from side to side, and Judy and Punch became lifeless flabby things as he dropped one on the shingle to pick up the other. I didn't understand why the string of sausages was funny either—Mummy Grace put them into Yorkshire pudding and called them toad-in-the-hole.

'Mrs Chisnall says you've got to come back now.' Margaret appeared beside me as I stood sucking my thumb, standing at the edge of the crowd no longer caring why the silly man with the ruff round his neck and the big nose was still so cross with the silly woman who had the same voice as him, only higher. I heard that voice each Christmas in the carpet department of Footmans store when Mummy Grace gave me threepence to watch the marionettes in *Sinbad the Sailor* while she shopped for pork cheese in the food department on the ground floor. It must be the same man. He was bald with a red perspiring face and a big stomach. The magic vanished.

'Mrs Chisnall says you've got to come back now.' Odd that Margaret never called her Mummy Grace, but it didn't bother me.

'Oh, shut up, I heard you the first time. Race you back,' I said, giving myself a head start. I was way in front of her before she'd even realised I'd said it. I ran, churning up the soft wet sand near the water, leaving a spray of sand behind me, just like the speedway bikes, feeling it catch the backs of my knees and trickle into my socks. 'Brrmmm Brrmmm', I was a speedway bike careering round the kids and their lumpy castles, threatened by the incoming tide, 'Brrmmm Brrmmm'. I was huge and strong and bigger than the sea. 'Brrmmm Brrmmm.' The spittle flew out from my lips and stuck to my face. I stumbled as I ran on to the shingle; it slowed me down, wrenching the buckle off my strap and sending the sandal flying ahead of me. I picked it up and carried on running, one shoe off, one shoe on. 'Diddle diddle dumpling, my son John.' The stones hurt my foot, but I didn't care. Tar stuck to my sock, and dried-up bits of cuttlefish, like the Haywards put between the bars of their budgerigar's cage, crunched underfoot and stuck to my sock too. I caught my toe on a piece of glass hidden amongst the pebbles. I slowed down. A faint trickle of blood reddened my grey sock. I stared at it, mesmerised by the vividness of its colour; veered to the sea again, limping, to wash it in the salt water, not so much for first aid, as to remove the evidence. The coldness of the water made me gasp and shudder and the salt stung as it penetrated the tiny cut. The tar wouldn't budge but although the sock was wet, it was now, at least, cleaner than it had been before. I put my sandal back on and walked as sedately as I could to where Mrs Whitman was pouring a cup of tea for Mummy Grace from her vacuum flask.

'Lor-luva-duck, look at the state of the child,' said Mrs Whitman disapprovingly. 'She's a right little tearaway and no mistake, in't she?'

'Oh, Jane, what have you been up to now?' said Mummy Grace, turning towards me, pushing away the strand of grey hair that had blown out of the roll along the back of her head. It caught in the wind between her glasses and her eyes; I knew she couldn't see me properly.

'Oh, it's all right! I'm going in swimming now anyway. The socks'll dry in the wind, won't they?' I pulled off my navy-blue jumper with CLS on the pocket and hid the offending articles underneath.

' 'Ere, 'ere, just a minute, young lady, you can't go stripping off just like that. Wrap the towel round you properly, and sit down and do it. What will people think?'

Stupid business that. It made getting into my swimsuit so much more difficult, wriggling on the cold stones to get out of my knickers, keeping my dress held down over my knees while I tried to get a leg into the shirred elastic swimming costume.

'Where's my Margaret anyway?' said Mrs Whitman. 'I sent her off to find you, what have you done with her?'

'I haven't done anything with her,' I retorted.

'That's enough of that now,' said Mummy

Grace. 'Keep a civil tongue in your head.'

'Look, there she is,' I said quickly, pointing some distance behind me. Margaret was walking slowly along the beach, well away from the water, hardly a hair out of place, still clutching her bag of crisps. She was easy prey really; I always won because she never joined in. Not like Carol Jones who took up my challenges in the playground and frightened me by fighting back. And her father was a policeman.

I felt bad about having answered rudely; it felt like a betrayal of Mummy Grace somehow, and I didn't like that. I stuck out my tongue.

'Ja-ane!' She cracked out my name like a whip. 'What *do* you think you're doing?'

I kept my tongue out and held on to it with my fingers, aping pushing it back into my mouth.

'Jane!'

'I'm keeping a civil tongue in my head,' I mumbled with some difficulty through my fingers. Mummy Grace looked surprised, then chortled, and, taking off her glasses to wipe them on the hem of her dress, laughed out loud. Everything was all right again.

I stood up, letting the towel drop around my ankles, tied the strings of my costume behind my neck, let out a whoop which made Mrs Whitman flinch, and made a dash for the grey water before the biting wind on my shivering body could make me change my mind. I hesitated for a moment as the water lapped my knees. It was very cold. Big waves curled menacingly ahead of me, breaking into froth a few feet away. I couldn't see anyone else swimming. This wasn't as easy as Pipers Vale pool where the school took us, where I'd learned to swim not so long ago. There you could just jump in, if you had the courage, and the only waves were the ones a belly-flop made; the only water that got up your nose was from the splashes of the other kids as they flailed about. The sea was unpredictable though. Just when I thought I'd got the measure of a wave and was planning to head right through it as it broke, it would shift sideways, disappear into flatness, then sneak up beside me, and creep up my thighs making me withdraw.

I jumped. Or tried to. The sea dragged itself away from me just at that moment and I ended up sitting in shallow gravelly water, small pebbles draining away underneath me, spits of foam splattering like needlepricks on my shoulders. I looked behind me to see if they'd noticed. Margaret stood sniggering a few yards up the beach. I'd make her pay for that when she came in. I waved my arms about in the water as if my sitting down had been intentional, making great curves of foam beside me, and then crawled along with my heels on my bottom until the water was deep enough to engulf me.

The world was silent and very cold, my ears and nose filled with water and made me gasp for breath. I managed a few feeble breast-strokes against the strong current, came up for air again, my fringe dripping stinging water into my eyes, and shouted through the blur in their direction.

'It's warmer in than out! C'mon in, scaredy cat.' I jumped up and down, my teeth chattering, while Margaret hovered beside her mother who was washing her face with a flannel that she'd brought in her wash bag. How silly, I thought, the sea could've washed her clean, not that she's ever dirty, that one.

I bore it as long as I could. The skin on my fingers had gone all wrinkly, like it did when I stayed in the bath too long, all the ragged bits round my chewed nails showed up more than usual, and some fingers stung where the nail was almost bitten to the quick. I splashed and showed off a bit more, screaming, as waves, that didn't frighten me at all, came towards me. Then spotting Margaret, hovering at the edge in her swimming costume, the water barely lapping her ankles, I leapt out of the water and splashed through the shallows as fast as the undertow would let me, making great waves with my feet, and, showering her with as much water as I could, ran past her up the beach, hobbling on the stones towards the warmth of the towel that Mummy Grace was holding out towards me.

I was irritable and uncomfortable on the way home. I dragged behind them as we walked up the road to the station. My sock hadn't dried thoroughly, and sand had got trapped inside it. It felt gritty between my toes as I walked. My broken sandal strap flapped with each sulking step I took.

I had to clench my toes to keep it on at all, which rubbed them, and a blister was beginning to make itself felt on my heel. My pigtails had worked free of their elastic bands, and damp salty hair hung in sticky spines about my neck, making me feel itchy. My face felt tight and caked with salt and I wanted an ice-cream with brightly coloured hundreds and thousands all over it.

'I Want Never Gets,' said Mrs Whitman primly and she tightened her grip on Margaret's hand as I caught up with them in a limping fashion.

I slipped my arm through Mummy Grace's.

'Cupboard love,' she said.

'You can always tell when they're after something,' Mrs Whitman continued.

Murderous thoughts about her went through my head. My requests didn't need any signalling, that gave Mummy Grace the time to see them coming, which she normally didn't have.

'Oh, git along with you, then. Only a threepenny one, mind, I'm not made of money.'

The sun came out as I ran across the road, not bothering to wait for Margaret. The sun always shone when we were on our way home. It crept through my chilled body as I licked the creamy coolness, munched the hard bright slivers, licking them off where they fell, leaving coloured saliva trails across my fist. I felt warm for the first time that day, and lifting my head up and squeezing my eyes almost shut against the light I ate my ice-cream and smiled into the sun.

CHAPTER 4

She came back again, the woman with red nails, who smelled so good, only this time she wasn't alone. 'This is your sister, Lolo.' I'd never heard a name like that before, except in a song on the wireless: 'Whatever Lola wants, Lola gets . . .' She was pretty and brown. She had curly hair and wore pretty clothes, prettier than I'd ever seen. She didn't talk much, and what she did say, I couldn't understand. She sounded like Margaret Hayward's doll that clicked its eyes shut when she put her down. 'Mama' she said, not 'Mummy'. The beautiful lady picked her up and hugged her a lot. I hated that; she hardly touched me. They slept together in the front bedroom and took ages getting up every morning because they did something the lady called their 'toilet', but they didn't go anywhere near the outside lavatory. Mummy Grace would carry steaming kettles of hot water up the stairs and the lady would wash in the big china bowl, pouring clean water into the matching jug that had stood on the old wash-stand and had never been anything but ornaments before. Then the baby would be brought downstairs in another outfit I hadn't seen, and the front bedroom would smell for a long time afterwards of that special smell. It was heady and strong and different. It was nothing like Mummy Grace's 'Devon Violets' or '4711 Lavender Water' or even the tin of Avon talcum powder that Pat would leave when she came to bring Mummy Grace a new vest that she'd brought from Footmans or the Co-op in the town. The lady would sing to the little girl in a language I didn't understand and the little girl would smile until her brown eyes almost disappeared and she'd gurgle and chuckle with delight, while I stood and watched, feeling stupid and ugly. Five years younger than me the lady said this baby was; why could she understand things that I couldn't? I felt even more stupid. I hummed one of the tunes intermittently under my breath as I became familiar with it, but the words just wouldn't come.

'What does it mean?'

The lady carried on fastening a fine gold bracelet that the baby wore round her chubby wrist. Why didn't I have one? She explained.

'Do you know how to plant cabbages?'

'No,' I said stupidly, interrupting.
She went on.

> 'In the way
> In the way
> Do you know how to plant cabbages
> In the way that we do in our house?'

I thought it a silly song, but I was too frightened to say so. I wanted the lady to think me clever, so I tried to learn it.

'Um, um, voo plantay'—I couldn't get the first two words but the last bit was all right, that sounded like plant.

'Lay, shoe'—shoe didn't sound like cabbage at all.

'A la moder, A la moder'—that bit was easier because it was said twice.

> 'Um, um, voo plantay lay shoe
> A la moder
> Derchay noo.'

I wouldn't let on how difficult it was to remember the order these funny sounds came in. I tried harder and harder and boiled with rage inside at myself. There was another song that began 'sewer ler pon davvy non', and in the bit where the notes got slower and longer the baby would wriggle her arms in time to the lady's singing:

> 'da da da da da da *come sa*

da da da da da da *come sa'*

I could join in that all right. I was pleased and ran into the kitchen. 'Mummy Grace, Mummy Grace, I can speak French: da da da da da da *come sa . . .'*

''At sound like come suck to me,' she said, pushing her tongue under her bottom teeth making her lip bulge with displeasure, and carried on peeling potatoes under the cold water. She thought it was rude, I could tell from the look on her face.

I was allowed to push the baby in the park with the lady. I felt grand and important. I'd never pushed a baby in a tripper before.

Holywells Park looked and felt different with them there. The lady spoke to a man who was walking in the park while the baby sat on the grass and pulled the heads off daisies. Mummy Grace said I was never to talk to men in the park but the lady didn't seem bothered. She laughed and chatted to the man while I stood by, feeling gawky and uncomfortable, wishing I were small and brown with pretty curly hair, hating my large white feet in the Cliff Lane sandals that were now stained green from the grass.

A huge alsatian dog bounded up, and jumped around the man. It frightened me, it was so unruly. I went towards the baby to pick her up.

'No, leave her alone, Janie darling, leave her alone.'

She didn't call me darling in Mummy Grace's house, but I felt hot and shy, hovering uselessly between the pushchair and the baby with nothing to hang on to.

The dog leaned towards the baby, she put her

hand out fearlessly towards his pointed nose and he licked her and she laughed.

'The dog licked Lulu, the dog licked Lulu,' I gasped, unable to contain my amazement.

'It's *Lolo*, darling, *Lolo* not Lulu, and of course she's not frightened, we have lots of dogs at home.'

Now the man must really think I'm an idiot, I thought. I can't even get my own sister's name right, and he must think I'm really odd, not remembering that we have lots of dogs at home which of course I don't, but *they* do . . . I couldn't work it out at all. I just wanted to get back to *my* home and to Mummy Grace.

I sat disconsolately on the wooden step between the kitchen and the living-room watching Mummy Grace cut the lard into the margarine for the pastry for a steak and kidney pie. She wiped her hands on her pinafore irritably and showered the red tiles under the rickety old table with flour.

'And she wasn't frightened, Nana, she likes dogs.' So the lady hadn't seen how frightened I was. I'd got away with it after all.

'Animals give her asthma,' Mummy Grace mumbled.

'She gets asthma because she sleeps in your bed, Nana.'

'Animal hairs get on her chest,' Mummy Grace went on, 'they give her asthma. She don't ought to go near them.'

We'd had a tortoise a long time ago. He hadn't made it difficult for me to breathe, but he hadn't lasted long. 'Eat up by ants,' said Mummy Grace. We'd had a cat once, a mangy grey old thing called Smokey. I don't know where he'd come from, but Mummy Grace hadn't liked him, especially when

46

he'd been fighting and his fur was tangled with dried pus.

'Get that cat off the settee,' she'd say. 'I'm not having it in here on the furniture, getting hairs everywhere; look at my new cushion covers from the Co-op, they were clean on last week. Go on, put it out the back door.' Her dislike of Smokey must have eventually communicated itself to me. I'd capture him in the back yard, until he learned to avoid me. I'd make sure I didn't touch the scabby bits, then I'd drop him in the lavatory and pull the chain. He was nearly always quicker than I was, and was out and away, long before the flushing water could catch him. She knew what I'd been up to if she saw him wet and I would be scolded.

'Well you don't like him anyway, *so*!'

'Don't you answer me back, my girl.'

I wasn't her girl now, though she seemed so irritable with me. No wonder too that the lady had left me and she didn't even know what I'd done to Smokey. No one knew what I did to the spiders in the lavatory. Lots of them there were, great daddy-long-legs sleeping in the musty corners between the flaking whitewashed ceiling and the wall. They didn't frighten me once I'd found out I could be quicker than they were. I'd hold a leg in one hand between a thumb and finger, and pull a leg off with the other. Sometimes I'd be brave enough to pull several legs off and watch the lopsided body hobble back into the safety of a webbed corner behind a withered leaf.

No wonder the lady liked the baby better. If she liked dogs so much, she'd certainly like cats. This smiling pretty baby would never have put Smokey down the toilet bowl and, I bet silently to myself, she probably hated spiders too, wouldn't go near them or even touch them, like most little girls, and like most little girls she didn't have great scabs of dried-out blood on her knees from falling in the playground, but I did. I looked down at my knees as I sat there on the step. I used often to double myself up as I sat there watching Mummy Grace cooking and get comfort from the smell of them mixed with the smell of starch from my school summer dress. They didn't comfort me now.

'No, *Lolo*, I mean Nana dear, *Lolo* wasn't frightened of the dog,' said the lady laughing, edging her way past me on the step, holding the baby. She said something that sounded like 'Fate la bee zoo' and the baby puckered its lips and gave my Mummy Grace a kiss. Inside me war broke out.

'There now, fancy her understanding that,' said Mummy Grace.

Well, of course she can understand it, stupid, I thought, it's French, she speaks French. The baby wrinkled her nose under the impact of Mummy Grace's moustache.

'Come on now, all you lot, get out of my kitchen so I can get this pie in the oven or we'll have the dinner still on the table at tea-time.' She meant me too. 'Go on, get out of the way so your mother can get past. Sitting there, cluttering up the step.'

I always sat there. Why was it wrong now? My chest tightened.

'Now don't you start wheezin',' Mummy Grace said. 'Course it's hot in here with the oven on. I'm gettin' flustered, there's not room to swing a cat. Go out, out you get, the lot of you.'

She pushed her glasses back on to the bridge of her nose, scattering a light dusting of flour on her red cheeks. Why couldn't I stay? I'd wanted to come back from the park to be with her. She'd never called me 'you lot' before. I didn't understand. But I hated her too now. And the baby. And the lady, but most of all I hated myself. And that was the only thing I was sure about.

They went away. But it wasn't the same. Letters came. Letters in envelopes with red and blue stripes round the edges that smelled of that special scent too. I sniffed them when Mummy Grace wasn't looking and ached inside, but I didn't quite know what I was aching for. Letters had to be answered and that was a bore, but I learned very quickly that somehow my unwillingness pleased Mummy Grace and it became a game between us, a different kind of arguing game from all the others that we had now.

'That letter from your mother's sat on that there sideboard for two weeks now. You'll have to answer it or I'll get into trouble.'

'I don't want to write to her—why should I? I'll do it when I come in from the rec.'

''At's no good keep puttin' it off; she'll think thass me keeping you from writing.'

'Oh, I don't know what to say to her.'

'Oh, just tell her what you did at school, dear.'

Tell her that I pulled Carol Jones's button off her coat and scratched her in a fight in playtime and how she'd said her mother would get on to Mrs Chisnall about it. How Susan Gower had invited me to her birthday party and when I'd got to Avondale Road I'd heard laughter from the front room and I'd rung and rung the bell, but no one had answered the door and I'd given up eventually, and, cross and bewildered, had slouched all the way back to Levington Road. Perhaps she'd seen that I hadn't got a present for her, even though I'd told her I had.

'No, you can't have any more money this week,' Mummy Grace had said. 'You're always worryguttin' about money. That's all I've got till pension day, and the rent man comes on Tuesday', but I'd kept telling Susan in the playground for days after the party that I'd got her present. Every morning was a torment, inventing a new lie as to why I'd forgotten to bring it with me again that day.

Mother wouldn't like that. And would she understand why Miss Howell called me Scatty? Miss Howell taught sums and didn't call me Jane for the whole year that I was in her class.

'Out you come, Scatty, and tell us what nine sevens are.'

She always chose the really nasty ones. I knew what seven sevens were, and even six eights. My face burned as I stared down at her feet with their lumpy toes and bunions, just like Mummy Grace's, poking through the gaps in her sandals, and wished I were dead.

'Come on, Scatty. You can talk enough in the back row when I'm talking. What's the matter, cat got your tongue?'

The class sniggered, as I would have done had I been sitting safely in my seat watching someone else go through this torment. I hated them and I hated her, but most of all I hated the rows of numbers on the blackboard that meant nothing to my dazed eyes. My heart thumped loudly in my tightening chest. Surely they could hear it? That made me feel even more ashamed. She cleaned the blackboard with an impatient swipe, catching her fingernails against it. The thin screech made me wince and turned my teeth to chalk.

'Nine eights then, Scatty?' Her floury fingers pointed at the meaningless shapes.

I licked my lips, hoping that would enable me to speak. My legs felt like wavy tubes of water and I was frightened that thinking of water would make me wet myself like Raymond Gilbert had done on the Assembly Hall floor one morning after we'd had prayers. I'd had a good laugh about that. I felt far from laughing now. My throat hurt and tears stung the back of my nose. I fought to keep them back, heaved for breath which wouldn't come, lifted my chest to gasp for air, till it felt as if my ribs would burst through my skin. I dug my fingers into the palms of my hands till my knuckles ached, wishing for once that I had nails so that I could hurt myself some more, managed to mumble in staccato gasps, 'I—don't—know' and then the tears came uncontrollably, and with them a loud ugly sound. Now it was only a fight for breath. Now it was worse than when the easterly winds hit me, worse than the cold water of the sea against my skinny chest. I forgot Miss Howell, and the giggling class, my whole being concentrated on lifting my chest to get air in, forgetting in my panic to breathe out. Sobs in my throat getting in the way of my trying to fill my lungs.

'Course you never had that trouble till *she* came,' said Mummy Grace, rubbing my back later to ease the ache in my shoulders. '*She* thinks it's 'cause I take you into my bed in the front room at night. Course what Louie don't know is that you wouldn't breathe at all if I didn't rub your back. It take so long for those Ephedrine tablets to start to work.'

51

She'd prop herself up on her pillows, with me beside her, and slowly rub my back for hours it seemed. It made her arm ache and I knew that it was bad for her heart, she told me so. The struggle for breath made me cry sometimes.

' 'At's no point in cryin', dear. You got to be patient and wait for the tablets to work.' Her words would come out slurred sometimes because she'd taken hers. 'Feeno barbitone' she said they were; she was cross with the doctor for prescribing them as they made her feel dopey in the morning and I found it difficult to wake her in the night when I had an attack.

'If you ask me, 'at's 'cause she tried to get rid of you, she did. That's what I reckon caused it. She was always pig-headed, your mother. I used to make her go round the rec on walks, but she didn't look after herself properly. Course she went out to pubs and suchlike, she didn't care. It didn't matter to her what people thought about the way I'd brought her up. I worn't ashamed to be seen with her, even though I knew they talked about her behind my back. My back is broad, the Lord be praised, but she didn't look after herself properly, all the same, when she was carrying you. That's why you're like this now, and no mistake.'

I couldn't tell my mother that. I stared into space, my mind a blank.

'And git your elbows off the table; you'll be goin' through another of those Cliff Lane jumpers afore we know where we are and Pat won't knit you no more, not now she's got a husband to look after and is goin' to live on the Chantry Estate. She's got her work cut out for her now.'

I'd been bridesmaid. Mummy Grace had given

52

me a whole half-crown one Friday night. I gripped it tightly in my hand as I ran up to the hairdressers on the Felixstowe Road.

'Tell 'em I can't afford a perm, it's a Marcel wave you want; two and six I hope should be enough,' she'd shouted at me as I slammed the back gate, making the tin fence between us and the Kerridges shudder. 'And mind the tins.'

The pale blue taffeta dress had hung ready in the front bedroom wardrobe for days now. I crept along from my bedroom most mornings just to feel it and make it rustle to assure myself it was real. It smelled faintly of the moth-balls that Mummy Grace put in the drawer underneath where she kept her hats. I didn't know why. Moths didn't eat felt hats with net I was sure.

The shop bell rang as I opened the door. A couple of men turned their heads to look, and the barber paused with his clippers in his hand. I headed for the ladies' section on the left divided from the men's by a glass and wood partition. 'Which twin has the Toni?' screamed a brightly coloured advertisement on a table. I couldn't tell. The blonde girls in the picture looked like the Beverley Sisters, except that there were only two of them. I was going to look like that soon. I hummed, 'And Lord help the sister, who comes between me and my man,' over the distant chatter of *Mrs Dale's Diary* on the wireless.

The air in the shop smelt bitter. Like the smell from Mummy Grace after Pat had done her hair with those papers that looked like the green Rizla that Doug used to roll his cigarettes in.

'Oh, someone's happy . . .'

'Mrs Chisnall made me an appointment—'

53

'Yes, I know all about it, dear,' said a lady in a bright pink nylon overall, smiling as she came towards me. 'Sit down here and wrap this round you while I heat up the tongs.' She struck a match and lit a flame underneath an iron contraption that stuck out from the wall. 'So your sister's getting married tomorrow, is she?'

My mind whirled. 'Well, she's not really—' Where could I begin to explain?

'Oh, isn't it tomorrow, then?'

'Yes, yes, it is, Alan Road Methodist Church, one o'clock and—'

'You're going to be bridesmaid . . .'

'Yes, yes, I am and—'

'It's the first time, is it?'

'Yes, yes, it is . . .' I said, lapsing into my posh polite voice that I felt a visit to the hairdressers required.

The tongs made a hissing sound when they came into contact with my hair and a thin feather of smoke rose from my head. It had the same smell as when Mummy Grace cleaned her comb and threw what she pulled from it on the living-room fire. That made a sizzling noise too, just like my hair was making now, but I didn't mind. My hair was going to be full of curls tomorrow just like Lolo's and the girl on *Children's Hour* in Noel Streatfeild's *White Boots* who could ice-skate so well. Now I could be like her, even though I'd never seen a rink. I wasn't sure what that was. There wasn't one in Ipswich. I daydreamed and then flinched as the tongs caught my ear.

'Don't move, dear, or I'll burn you.'

You just have, I thought, wincing at the smart. Bridesmaids didn't have such thoughts I was sure.

54

Then I heard Mummy Grace's voice saying, 'Pride must bear a pinch.'

I ran all the way back down Levington Road, avoiding cracks in the pavement, in case stepping on one of them would make being a bridesmaid not come true. Past the only cars in the street. The Revetts' Mayflower and the Wilkinsons' Morris shooting-brake, all cream paintwork and shiny varnished wood, up the posh end of the street as Mummy Grace called it, and past an old sit-up-and-beg bike with a plastic dress shield on the back wheel that belonged to someone in the street I didn't know. Hoping, hoping that Margaret Whitman or Margaret Hayward would come out so that I could show off my new wavy hair. Only Holdy was standing at the front gate of number 87 puffing on his pipe.

'All poshed up for tomorrow then, are you?'

'I'm going to be bridesmaid—'

'I know you are, daft,' he said. 'That's all we've heard about for weeks. I expect Mrs Chisnall'll be glad when it's all over.'

'They're having the reception at the Conservative Club on the Felixstowe Road.'

'And Mrs Chisnall's been Labour all her life,' he said, putting his pipe back in his mouth, and between clenched teeth went on, 'I don't know what the world's coming to, I'm sure.'

'Do you like my hair then, Holdy?'

'Don't swank now, pride comes before a fall.'

That's what Mummy Grace said.

'Well, do you?'

''At'll be twopence to talk to you soon,' he said, turning to walk up the path. 'I can't stand jawin' here to you all day, I've got to get my lettuce under glass.'

' 'At look very nice, dear,' said Mummy Grace as I opened the back door. I pulled the old kitchen chair out from in front of the old black lead stove which wasn't used any more except for keeping shoe polish and brushes in and screwed-up bits of newspaper that Mummy Grace used for cleaning the windows. Mice lived in there, I knew. Sometimes the newspapers were chewed up into small bits and I'd shut the heavy door with a bang. Difficult to believe that food used to be cooked in there when the fire was lit in the grate beside it. I stood on the chair and perched precariously, leaning on the draining-board, to peer into the small blistered mirror that hung by twisted fuse wire from the flaking kitchen wall. I didn't look quite like the Beverley Sisters but my hair was wavy and different. I was pleased.

'I shall have to sleep sitting up,' I said.

'Don't be so daft,' retorted Mummy Grace. 'You'll need a proper night's sleep or you'll be good for nothing in the morning.'

I woke up stiff and irritable, having slept at an uncomfortable angle. My hair stuck out like twisted straw all over my head. There was barely a wave to be seen. Even Mummy Grace was hard put to find a word of consolation.

' 'At look all right, dear. Now don't get yourself worked up into a state or I'll get blood pressure.'

I cried. Along with my skinny legs that stuck out ridiculously from underneath the blue taffeta, my feet huge in their new white sandals, my head at the opposite end of my miserable body looked as if someone had stuck an unruly hair hat on to it, that simply didn't belong to the rest of me. Two puffy

56

swollen eyes stared out from underneath the fringe.

My sorrows were forgotten in the delight of tables laden with blancmange and jelly, sausage rolls and chocolate finger biscuits. I ate so much the taffeta bulged across my middle. Doug gave me a cuddle as he talked to his mother and father. I felt very important. I hadn't seen him cuddle the other bridesmaid who had naturally curly hair. She was called Pat too. Doug's niece, someone said, whatever that was. Mummy Grace and I didn't have a niece.

'Come on then, sparrows' kneecaps, let's have a dance or you'll crease up me suit and then what'll I say to the missus?' he said, loosening my grip from around his waist. I didn't know whether the gramophone in the corner was playing a Victor Sylvester foxtrot or a quickstep, but it didn't matter because I couldn't do either of them. I could stand on his feet like I did sometimes in the kitchen and he'd lift me around on them in time to the music.

'Course she'll miss him,' I heard Mrs Andrews say. 'He's been like a father to her, poor little mite.'

I liked being called a poor little mite although I wasn't sure what a mite was. The widow in the Bible had one inside her purse. It made me feel even more important.

'She'll miss all the things he used to get her too.' I thought of the new doll that he and Pat had bought me.

She had thick wavy blonde hair under the pink lacy bonnet that Pat had knitted for her, that matched her dress and bolero jacket. It tied under her neck with two pink ribbons. When I laid her down she closed her thick fringed eyes with a click and bleated out 'Mamaaa'. Like Margaret

Hayward's doll. Like that silly Lolo's voice. That noise came from a round metal disc with holes in her stomach. I'd undressed her to find out. Her body was solid plastic. Her arms and legs could move, because they were slotted into her body and were held there by elastic bands. I'd found that out by pulling them and twisting them the wrong way round so that it looked like she was going backwards. Her hands were stiff, with sharp pointed fingers that wouldn't move. They dug into my shoulders when I tried to hug her. I liked undressing her; her hard pink body looked so ridiculous with no clothes on. She didn't have a doodleeum, as Mummy Grace and I called it, and that made me laugh. I'd stick my finger into her eye as I laid her down to try and stop her eyes from closing but she was nearly always faster than I was, though I could pull them open again by holding on to the eyelashes and tugging them upwards. I combed her hair a lot and washed her face, dripping enough water on to her for it to dribble out by her arm and leg joints when I shook her. I did her hair with Mummy Grace's big comb that was kept in the sideboard drawer next to the rent book; it had ridges of dirt along each of its teeth except on the ones that were missing.

'That poor doll'll go bald afore you know where you are, then what'll you say to Pat and Doug?'

'Sophie likes it.'

'Sophie? Now where did you get hold of a name like that?'

I didn't know anyone at Cliff Lane called Sophie. I must have heard it on *Children's Hour*. It sounded posh and different. So Sophie she was. Until she became Mary or Susan. Until I poked her metal middle with one of Mummy Grace's hair-grips one day and then she didn't say 'Mamaaa' any more, just 'maaa' and I got frightened that they would find out. So I hid her in the drawer at the bottom of the wardrobe in the front bedroom amongst the half-used boxes of Christmas crackers and Mummy Grace's felt hats.

'Mr and Mrs Andrews will now cut the wedding cake.'

The music was switched off and the hall went quiet.

'What are Doug's Mum and Dad going to do?' I pulled at Mummy Grace's new two-piece bought with Mutuality coupons from the Co-op.

'’Ere, don't do that, you'll have it off me.'

'But why are Doug's mum and dad—?'

'It's Pat and Doug, silly. Ssshhh now.'

'But why's Pat called Mrs Andrews?' I knew her real name was Willy. I sniggered every time I saw it written down. But I avoided saying it. 'Why did Mr Stebbings "give her away"?'

I wasn't sure what that meant except there'd been a lot of talk about who was going to 'give Pat away' for weeks before the wedding. When the organ had played 'Here Comes the Bride', and I'd thought 'short, fat and very very wide', Mr Stebbings had walked up the aisle in front of me at Fat Pat's side, and when the minister asked, 'Who giveth this woman?' or something like that he had said, 'I do.' Doug's brother Putt was best man; he'd read out the telegrams and made us all laugh. His wife was called Ray. It was all very confusing. I'd eaten a crunchy afters at their house once. It was like a tart filled with hard sweet stuff. I'd never eaten anything like it before. I loved it, but didn't

59

like to ask what it was called in case everyone knew and I was the only one who didn't. Ray wore lots of orange make-up, bright pink lipstick and very high heels. I thought she was very glamorous. I wondered if Doug minded Pat being so fat. She didn't look at all like Ray even with her new girdle on under her wedding dress. She'd bought it specially for the wedding. I'd heard Mummy Grace say so.

'But why . . . ?'

'She's married to Doug now, dear, that's why she's called Mrs Andrews.'

'But there's two Mrs Andrews now. How will they know which . . . ?'

'Well she'll be Mrs Andrews Junior. Now hold your tongue.'

It was all very complicated.

I could understand Pat not wanting to be called Miss Willy any more.

'Why did Mr Stebbings give her away?'

The Stebbings had a house on the other side of Levington Road that was full of yappy pekinese dogs and smelled. I was frightened of the dogs and so was Mummy Grace but Mrs Stebby was her best friend so she went to see her just the same. Why had Pat wanted Stebby to give her away?

'Why is the other bridesmaid Doug's niece?'

'She's Sonny's daughter, Doug's other brother who lives in Hull.'

I felt very muddled in my head. Families seemed so complicated. I was glad I didn't have one.

Everyone applauded as they held the big knife and cut through the cake together. I wondered who was going to eat the little dolls that had stood on the top tier.

'Go on, dear, look, Doug want you to go up there with them.'

'C'mon, sparrows' kneecaps, give us a hand to cut the next slice,' said Doug, and everyone laughed. I felt very hot and red and proud. Sonny's daughter was 'family' and she wasn't asked to cut the cake. Perhaps what I had was better than a family . . . anyway, I wasn't worried.

Mummy Grace had wiped her eyes several times during the reception, and I cried and clung to Pat's ridged middle when she'd changed into her going-away suit because Mummy Grace had seemed so sad and had said she was losing a daughter and that made me sad too, because she still had me. But she was called Chisnall, and my name was Jane Burgess and I couldn't make any sense of it at all.

It seemed odd going back to 85 alone. Just Mummy Grace and me. I knew Pat and Doug would be living in the front room after they came back from their honeymoon, but I sensed that something big had happened, that things had changed somehow. I didn't like change.

CHAPTER 5

'Pop up to the post office and get my pension, dear, I'm feeling bad this morning.'

It was bright and sunny and the birds were singing above the long grass in the back garden. A trickle of fear wound its way through the cornflakes in my stomach. I hadn't noticed till then how listlessly Mummy Grace was sitting in the utility chair next to the wireless.

61

'It's this hot weather I 'spect. It don't agree with me. I'll be all right in a minute.'

Instantly willing to make reparation for all the bad things I'd ever done to her, I lurched from the chair, abandoning the *Girl Friend* comic. I'd pleaded with Pat for ages that *Sunny Stories* was too babyish, and finally she'd given in. I ran cold water over her face flannel and carried it, dripping up my arm, to her.

'Put that thing back on the draining-board. No, it's not one of my heads.'

'Well, shall I rub your back then, make it easier for you to breathe?'

'No, I can breathe all right, it's not that, I'm just worried I'll have one of my blackouts. I feel a bit faint.'

'Shall I get Joan Holden, or Mrs Kerridge?'

'No!' she said spikily, 'I don't want *them* in here. Don't fuss me, now. Just go up the road and get me pension, 'cause it's rent day today and I've got to put another one pound seventeen and six into the envelope before the rent man calls round for it tonight.'

I cleared the table of my cereal bowl and the milk jug; she would never allow the milk bottle on the table, she said it looked common, let the cold water run over the bowl leaving several flakes of cereal under the rim and grains of white sugar at the bottom. Put the milk into the pantry, the only place where it was cold enough to stop it going sour, next to a jug of home-made lemon barley water covered with a little muslin cap edged in sea shells, and charged upstairs to get my shoes. Or rather Janet Murphy's. I hated Janet Murphy. Or rather, I hated her shoes. They were thick, crêpe-soled ones with a strap, and a buckle. They had been red, once. The toes were all scuffed and cardboard-coloured but the crêpe soles were intact, their caterpillar-like ridges unworn. They may have looked all right on Janet Murphy's stocky, well-rounded legs, but on my skinny spindles they were ridiculous. I felt as if I were walking on spongy stilts.

It was all Mummy Grace's fault for dawdling in the front garden when she cleaned the doorstep. I felt guilty for entertaining such thoughts about her when she was downstairs feeling ill. But I couldn't see the point in doing the step anyway. It was worn away and the stone flaked off in patches, but regularly she'd kneel down on the hard hall mat which made those nasty grey patches of skin on her knees, and with a lot of huffing and puffing she'd spread the thick Cardinal Red Polish on to the stone. It was like wax and smelled strongly. It never polished up to much of a shine, and her face would glow red with the effort. She'd stand up and lean on the old garden broom to survey her efforts, her arm on her hip, catching her breath. Then of course she'd chat to whoever was passing, going up to the shops in Felixstowe Road. That must have been how these dreadful shoes came my way.

She always complained about how much work there was to do, but she never seemed to mind about wasting time in the front garden chatting. Or she could have been hanging out the front door curtain, to protect it from the sun. I couldn't see the point of that either. The light wood varnish that stained the door was peeling off in places. But she'd take the stool that Doug had made for her, its seat woven in thick green and beige twine which didn't quite meet in the middle of its star-shaped pattern. I liked putting my fingers down the gap and making it bigger, if she wasn't looking. He'd made it when he was 'convalescing in the San', she'd said. I wasn't sure what that was, but I knew he'd had to wear an iron corset for a while and Mummy Grace's white cotton one with the bones made her feel bad, so perhaps that was why Doug hadn't managed to make the pattern come out right.

She'd place the stool carefully on the uneven black and red tiles whose diamond pattern made up the front path, stand on it, and holding on to the door frame with great difficulty, she would balance the bamboo pole that held the faded bold striped curtain into the two hooks on either side at the top of the door. Everybody else had a curtain in the same sort of material, perhaps that was why she did it, but theirs protected freshly painted doors. Holdy kept his in good repair, and even Mr Whitman was bullied into touching up the paint on number 81 occasionally, a cigarette hanging from his lips, the ridge where his conductor's hat sat more evident than ever, his face red with exertion. But we didn't have a man to do jobs like that, and however much Mummy Grace complained about the landlord I'd never seen him, and he never came to do all the jobs she wanted to be done. Perhaps she put the curtain up to hide the door.

I lay on my stomach on the bedroom floor, looking for the shoes under the bed. I could hear Mrs Kerridge singing in the garden. A high trilling sound. She sang in the choir at Tackett Street Congregational Church so Mummy Grace said, so she must have a good voice. It seemed wobbly to me. The lino was dotted with balls of fluff that danced away from my breath and got caught up in some of the feathers that had dropped from my second pillow. I wasn't allowed to sleep on it any more as Mummy Grace said it made me wheezy. I had to sleep on a Terylene one that wasn't so comfortable. My bridesmaid's white sandals were there, and for a moment I was tempted. No, they were for best. I was only allowed to wear them for Sunday School, and I didn't want a row this morning. I was going to be a good girl, then Mummy Grace would get better. If I wore Janet Murphy's shoes she'd get better even quicker. Anyway I wasn't likely to bump into Janet Murphy. She lived in Cliff Lane, and so far, even in the playground, she hadn't noticed the shoes, although I lived in dread that she would. I grabbed the shoes, pushing aside several abandoned *Girl Friend* comics that must have fallen off my bed as I slept (I wasn't really allowed to read in bed: 'Don't you keep that light a-burning all night. I'm not made of money'), caught my hair in the bulge of the iron springs that hung lower than the rest where the bed sagged in the middle, rubbed my head where the scalp felt snagged, pushed my feet into the hated shoes and hurled myself downstairs, the buckles undone, jingling as I ran.

'You sound like a herd of elephants, the way you thump down those stairs. You'll have the plaster off the ceiling one of these days—and do up those straps, you'll be falling over and there's no Pat here now to take the gravel out of your knees.'

Thank goodness, I thought. Pat and Doug lived in a posh new house on the Chantry Estate now.

'Chantry Two,' she'd said proudly when she'd

65

called round with a new nightdress bought with the Divi from the Co-op for Mummy Grace. I didn't even know there was a Chantry One, but Chantry Two was obviously even posher just from the way she said it. I was glad she'd gone. I had Mummy Grace all to myself now, and I liked it. Except on days like this when she didn't feel well.

'Jane, did you hear what I said?'

Stupid, should have done the shoes up upstairs, wasting time, Mummy Grace was ill. Had to hurry. The latest scabs on both knees had almost healed. I'd been terrified of Pat when I fell and grazed my knees.

'Well, *I* can't get the muck out. It make me feel bad. You'll have to wait till Pat gets home from the laundry, she'll sort you out. You always moan that I tie the knots right over the sore place, so you better wait till she can do it.'

Pat, being considerably bigger than me, could somehow manage to hold down one of my legs in the plastic washing-up bowl of hot water, placed on the kitchen floor so that she could trickle a piece of cotton wool drenched in Dettol and stinging hot water into the wound, and with the other arm keep my protesting self well and truly held back in the chair. She always tied the bandage so tight that hurt too, but it was better than when Mummy Grace did it, when it became a loose, frayed, uneven lump that slipped down to my ankle in no time at all.

I shot the sideboard drawer open so fast it came out, and the tin that contained the pension book fell with a clatter on to the floor.

'Oh, patience,' said Mummy Grace, lifting her head from her hand. 'You always want to do

66

everything in such a blinkin' hurry.'

Another black mark.

'Sorry, sorry. I'm trying to be as quick as I can.'

'More haste, less speed. And don't go up the road waving my pension book in your hand, I don't want everyone to know my business. Take my shopping bag, and put it in that.'

I hated the shopping bag. It was an ugly plastic rectangular thing with frayed handles that were sharp and made it difficult to carry comfortably. But I wasn't going to complain. Not today.

'Fetch me a pen. I'll have to fill in that form on the back so they'll give it to you.'

'But they know me up there.'

'Don't argue, there's a dear, when I'm not feeling up to much at all today.'

Her spidery old-fashioned writing was even more shaky than usual. I felt worse.

'And don't slam that gate.'

I shut the gate very carefully indeed, and then I ran, as fast as those hated shoes would let me. I ran till my heart thumped in my chest so hard that it almost hurt. My ears were filled with the sound of my heart thumping. Blood rushed into my face and made it throb. Somewhere a race had been set up, and I had to beat the unseen competitor or Mummy Grace would get worse and it would be my fault.

The street was empty. Privet hedges and lace curtains whizzed by at the side of my vision, but I just kept my concentration on the cracks in the pavement under my charging feet. I noticed the Revetts' big grey Mayflower parked outside their house. They had taken Mummy Grace and me out in it twice. He owned a bicycle shop in the centre of town. I thought them very rich. The Wilkinsons' cream and wood shooting-brake was further down. She was a teacher. That was how they could afford a car.

The post office was small and dark and busy. I fished the pension book out of the depths of the plastic bag and waited impatiently for my turn. There were a few shelves stacked with birthday cards, the kind that Mummy Grace liked with roses.

On this your special day,
These greetings come to say,
That love and joy and cheer
Be yours throughout the coming year.

They had a picture of kittens on the front with ribbons round their necks, or Labrador dogs standing beside vintage cars. Those were for boys, though. I liked the man who worked behind the counter, who looked at me over the top of his glasses as they perched on the end of his pointed nose. His wife seemed much older, or maybe it was his mother; she was so slow and asked so many questions. I was in the wrong queue. I could see her grey head with its tightly coiled bun, bobbing around behind the wire grille, through the gaps in the crowd ahead of me. I stood irritably with one foot on top of the other trying unconsciously to wrench one of the straps free of its buckle, then they'd really have to be thrown out, the hated red shoes. I caught myself doing it, and stopped. Mummy Grace wasn't well and anyway it wouldn't work. I'd often abandoned Margaret Whitman on our way home from school, and made a forbidden detour through Holywells Park, scrabbling through the mud in the undergrowth by the rhododendron bushes, in an attempt to destroy them completely, but Mummy Grace simply scolded me, cleaned them up, sewed the buckles back on, and they appeared, polished to an eye-catching brightness, ready for me to wear at school next morning.

'Hallo, Louise.'

I thought she was talking to someone behind me. I turned and saw a man in a trilby hat holding a postal order and his football coupon.

'How are you, Louise dear?' she said, looking straight at me.

'I'm not Louise, I'm Jane.'

'Oh, you look so like your mother. How is she?'

I was confused for a moment. 'Oh, she's not feeling too good today.'

'Oh, is she over again then?'

Why did grown-ups talk in riddles? I'd heard Mummy Grace say she wasn't up to it, but over? Was that another phrase for being ill? People from the north said 'proper poorly', because that's what Mrs Young said at number 79 because she came from Bradford. Wilfred Pickles said it too.

'No, she's not over it. She's had to sit down because she's got hearttroubleandbloodpressure.'

'Oh, dear, that won't do, will it.'

The man behind me chuckled. I felt uncomfortable and wished she would ink the wooden stamp lying on the velvety black pad within tempting reach, just the other side of the wire grille. I was going to ask for a post office set for Christmas, I decided there and then. I liked the sound the stamp made on the pension book as she brought it down with a thud. Perhaps post office sets came complete with one of those lovely red tin pillarboxes, with a slit for the money in the place where you posted letters in the real ones. Margaret Whitman had two, and they were both full. They stood on the best sideboard in their front room. When we were allowed in there for her birthday parties, the room darkened by the many loops of paper trimmings that hung from the corners across the room like stretched-out concertinas, I would pick up the money boxes enviously and rattle them.

'Why doesn't Margaret open it now it's full?'

'Lor-luva-duck,' Mrs Whitman would say. 'You're a right little spendthrift you are, and no mistake. She's saving it for a rainy day. It'd burn a hole in your pocket I reckon.'

Grown-ups didn't make sense most of the time.

'Well, will you be wanting an airmail letter for your mother, then? She's not in Le Tookay any more now, is she? Cassablanka I believe Mrs Chisnall said. She gets about your mother, don't she?'

I didn't know, and that made me feel foolish too. Everyone knew where their mothers were.

'Yes, yes,' I said quickly, hoping she couldn't see I didn't know.

She pushed an airmail letter across the counter at me. 'I'll take it out of the pension, shall I?'

Four one pound notes and a few threepenny bits and sixpences were pushed towards me before I could answer. I felt myself flush red and hot. Mummy Grace would be cross, but I would make her laugh by saying that if I wrote big, I could fill it up in only four or five sentences.

It was hot outside. I wished I hadn't run so fast. I felt sticky. The smell from the fish and chip shop

70

wafted across the Felixstowe Road. I wished I'd asked for some money to buy three penn'orth of scraps, lovely little bits of fried batter that had fallen off the fish, that were scooped up with a deep wire net from the vat of sizzling oil. I tried to form a lie in my head about having to go in there because . . . no, it wouldn't work. Not today. Anyway they weren't open yet. I could see that the door was shut, and the 'Closed' notice hung inside it. Above the tall metal counters that warmed me through my Cliff Lane mac on cold days, if I leaned against them while I waited, I could see the fish shop lady, with grey hair tinged the colour of cigarette smoke, cutting up the newspaper squares to wrap the fish in. I crossed to that side of the road, narrowly missing a cyclist who muttered something under his breath as he swerved to avoid me.

I couldn't spend any more money anyway, not after the airmail letter. Stupid thing. Stupid woman. Why did everyone know things about me that I didn't? That frightened me. I dawdled outside the chemist. Through the window I could see its large glass vials with their twisted stoppers, like big teardrops, catching the light. I was in awe of the green and red and blue liquid they contained. I wondered what illnesses they were for, although I'd never seen the chemist take any of the liquid out. My socks had worked their way down under my heels in an uncomfortable lump. I bent to pull them up and a half-a-crown rolled out of the bag towards the door. Panic. I rescued it before it completed its circle, put it back in the bag, breathed a sigh of relief, and thought of Horlicks Tablets. I loved crunching their powdery milkiness . . . No. No, I

71

mustn't. Ginger nuts came in a blinding flash of inspiration. I'd get Mummy Grace some ginger nuts. Even she liked crunching those or dipping them in her tea. I tightened my grip on the shopping bag and tore round the corner to the Co-op.

It was dark inside after the brightness of the morning, and for a few seconds I could see nothing except whirling shapes in front of my eyes.

The darkness stretched right to the back of the shop from where I could hear the clicking of the brass cylinders as the cashier, in her tall narrow room that overlooked the shop, unhooked them from the overhead wires, removed the money and the yellow 'Divi' receipt, placed the correct change in them, and sent them, with a sharp tug on a wooden handle, swinging and clanking back. Along the wires they went, above the heads of the girls in their pale green headscarves tied turban fashion who stood serving behind the counters. It always surprised me how the cylinders knew which track to travel on. Often they would slow down at a junction, where many wires joined in a complicated fretwork, then would continue their way over to the bacon counter where the bacon slicer stood, its huge Catherine-wheel of silver metal polished to a mirror-like brightness. Or they'd stop short above the yellow bars of washing soap stacked neatly beside the blue and white packets of washing soda.

I stood by a mahogany counter near the door of the shop, breathing deeply that special spicy smell that only the Co-op had. On the floor, near my feet, were huge packs of sugar and dried fruit, the hessian rolled neatly back, revealing the glistening white grains and the dark sticky jumble of raisins

72

and currants with the occasional strip of candied peel which was my favourite. I would pick those bits out and eat them if Mummy Grace was unwise enough to leave me alone in the kitchen while she was preparing steamed mincemeat pudding. Feet in peep-toed shoes came into my line of vision, a shop assistant in a matching pale green overall, which I thought very smart, dug deep in the 'gran' sugar, as Mummy Grace called it, with a metal scoop and I watched as with a quiet whooshing sound it was poured expertly, not a grain falling to the floor, into the dark blue paper bag. With one movement the bag was swung into the scale, a few grains removed and deftly with a quick flutter of her fingers the top was folded over in a neat envelope-shaped flap, doubled under once again, and placed beside a box of suet on the counter.

'A penny for 'em.'

'What?'

'You were miles away. Give me your order book and I'll get what your mother wants.'

'Oh, I haven't got the order book today.'

'Well what is it you want, dear?'

I felt her patience beginning to run short. What was it I had come in for?

'Oh, yes, a packet of ginger nuts, please.'

'You don't want the loose ones? They're a bit cheaper, you know. Only sevenpence halfpenny a half.'

Mummy Grace didn't like those because some of them were broken.

'No, a proper packet, please.'

'That'll be ninepence. You *are* being extravagant today.'

Yes, I was. More than she knew.

'Anything else?'

I cast my eyes longingly at the bars of Cadbury's nut milk chocolate. I could buy one of those, I didn't need to bring the ration book any more. They always used to know then how many you'd had, because they cut a square out of the ration book each time you bought one. But now, for some reason that nobody had explained to me, you could buy as many as you liked and nobody would know, that is if you had the money. 'No, no, thank you,' I said quickly, frightened by how near I had come to giving in to temptation. I was in for trouble anyway because of the stupid airmail letter which probably cost more than a bar of chocolate.

'So that's all for today, thank you,' I said, mimicking what I heard Mummy Grace say when she was being extra posh and polite.

'And what's your Divi number?'

'5743,' I said before she'd hardly finished the question. I hoped she'd be impressed by my remembering it so well, but she made no comment, wrote the number with a stub of pencil that she took from behind her ear and licked, pressing hard on to the pad that had a sheet of shiny dark blue paper sticking out from underneath it. That blue paper was magic. It made the writing show up on the piece of paper underneath it. I was going to ask for some of that with my post office set.

I pushed a two shilling piece that I found loose in the bottom of the bag across the counter.

'Haven't you got anything smaller?'

I fished into the bag again, ruffling the pages of the pension book as I did so.

'Oh, thass all right. 'At don't matter. But you want to be careful, though. All that money loose in the bag. You could lose that running home. Have you got far to go?'

Without looking what she was doing she clicked the cylinder shut, tugged on the handle and sent it on its way. That was clever. I'd like to be able to do that. But I wouldn't like to have to wear a turban, even though you could hide your hair curlers underneath it. Still, the Co-op girls looked smarter than the ones who cycled down Bishop's Hill on their way to work at the Burton Son and Saunders factories by the docks; they didn't have matching overalls and hardly any of them wore stockings. Most of them came from the Nacton Estate and Mummy Grace said they were common.

'Oh, I live at the bottom of Levington Road, number 85.'

'Oh, that's Mrs Chisnall, in't it?'

'Yes, yes, it is.'

'And what's your name?'

'My name's Jane.'

I was pleased to be able to answer so many questions and get them all right. I felt it was like some sort of test, and I was doing very well. Not a familiar feeling.

She tucked a stray curl of hair back into her turban then pressed her lips together as Pat did when she'd put her lipstick on, ran her tongue over her teeth to check the lipstick wasn't smeared on them, unhooked the cylinder, handed me the change and smiled.

'Now you run along home, Jane Chisnall. Mind how you cross the Felixstowe Road and be very careful with your mum's money.'

The sun had gone in when I got outside. I pulled my cardigan tight with one hand, wishing I'd got my

Cliff Lane blazer on, and held even tighter to the bag with the other.

I walked slowly down Levington Road. There was a hopscotch game chalked in brick on the pavement outside Rex Roberts's house in the middle of the street. I hadn't noticed it before. I couldn't imagine Rex Roberts playing hopscotch on his own. He was fat and bull-like, he'd find it difficult to jump. And David Wilkinson wouldn't have played it, not on this side of the street. Anyway, David went to Northgate Grammar School, and Rex went to Nacton Road Secondary Modern, so they never played together. I jumped on to the square marked with a one with both feet, then jumped on to two and three with a foot in each square. The numbers were further away from each other than I thought and I landed with both feet on the cracks in the pavement. It must be a big boys' game. We didn't put our numbers so far apart down our end of the street, Margaret Whitman, Margaret Hayward and I. The money jumped and rattled in the bag. I stopped guiltily. I mustn't lose any. That would be even more terrible. It was a silly game anyway. I wasn't out, because nobody had seen me step on the cracks.

Mummy Grace was propping up the washing on the line as I pushed open the back gate; the long wooden pole that forked into two prongs at the end was heavy and difficult to manage, but she must be feeling better if she'd done the washing. Even though she was grumbling to Mrs Kerridge as the line with its looped sheets, my ankle socks, and her long bloomers kept dancing away from her as she failed to catch it between the prongs.

'Oh, this b— thing, 'at drive me mad. And

course, now I've got the washing out, the sun's gone in. Thass always the way, in't it? Still there's a nice wind gettin' up. They might be dry by tea-time if it don't rain, though I s'pect it will.'

She was better. Although the sky was grey and filled with scudding clouds my day brightened.

'Oh, and where have you been, you little tinker, you've been gone ages. I was getting worried you'd been knocked down.'

'There was a big queue in the post office and the lady—'

'Of course, it's pension day, 'at's like a mad-house up there on Tuesdays.'

The gate slammed shut behind me in a gust of wind.

'You'll have Mrs Kerridge after you if you let the gate slam like that. You'll have her tins down.'

Mrs Kerridge never 'got after me' which was only fair because I never heard Mummy Grace 'get after' Vivien or Hazel. They were much younger than I was so I never played with them. Mr and Mrs Kerridge wouldn't let them come and play 'Please Mr Farmer may I cross your golden river?' because they thought it dangerous. One person had to stand in the middle of the road and be the farmer, and ask for something the rest of us couldn't possibly have in our pockets, so we'd have to dodge the farmer and get to the pavement on the other side of the street as best we could. They weren't allowed to play outside their very well-kept garden, along with the rest of us down our end of the street. Anyway, I hardly knew they were there. They never made a noise like I did, or argued, like I did with Margaret Whitman.

'Hallo, dear,' shouted Mrs Kerridge from

77

somewhere behind the high corrugated iron fence. I wasn't going to climb up on it to see her, because Mummy Grace was there. Anyway the last time I'd done that, Doug's stool had slipped from under my feet and I'd fallen, cutting the palm of my hand on the jagged edge at the top. There was still a blue mark under the scar where the skin had healed over the rust, but it didn't hurt any more. But I liked Mrs Kerridge, and found it difficult to talk without seeing her.

'Have you been a good girl then, shopping for Mrs Chisnall?'

Grown-ups had such an uncanny way of making you feel bad without knowing they were doing it.

'Come on, Mummy Grace, it's getting cold out here now, and you weren't feeling well this morning.'

'Oh, I'm all right now, dear. I feel a lot better now that mugginess has gone, but I'd better get in and get on with the dinner—'at'll be tea-time at this rate if I stand here jawin'. Go on, gee up, the wind whip round this corner somethin' awful.'

She wiped the draining-board down with an old piece of cloth that she called a dwile, singing under her breath, 'What a friend we have in Jesus' in a high voice even more wobbly than Mrs Kerridge's. She really was a lot better.

'I've brought you a present,' I said, emboldened by her singing.

'Oh, Jane,' she said in a voice that sounded perilously near a scold, 'where did you get the money? You din't steal it, did you?'

'Ginger nuts. From the Co-op because you weren't well. I thought they'd cheer you up.'

I gave her an energetic kiss, and with a flourish

placed them on the kitchen table. 'There!'

'Well, you shouldn't have spent the money, but 'at's the thought that counts. Thank you, dear.'

She lifted the oval metal bowl with the handles that she did the washing in and poured the soapy grey contents down the sink.

'If I get that bit of smoked haddock on in time we can listen to *Workers' Playtime*.'

I hated that bright yellow chewy fish that was so salty and hard to swallow but said nothing.

'Now don't go doing too much, now,' I said, quoting her own words back at her.

'Oh, you're a right worryguts, just like me,' she said smiling.

I gave her another kiss and I hopped up the step into the living-room and carefully put the pension book and the rest of the contents of the bag on to the highly polished living-room table, without another word.

'What's the matter with you this morning? Do you want to borrow something?'

'I'm just glad you're better.'

She followed me in, wiping her hands on her apron, scooped up the money, put some of it into the envelope that held the green rent book, put the rest in her purse that she took out of her apron pocket like a kangaroo pouch, not noticing the airmail letter, and sat down opposite me.

'Mummy Grace, why is my name Burgess?'

'Well, because that's your name, that's why, silly billy.'

'No, but why is it Burgess? Why can't it be Chisnall?' I knew very well why it couldn't be, but I knew it would please her.

'Oh, you don't half ask some questions

79

sometimes,' she said, taking off her glasses and wiping them on the hem of her summer frock. 'Well, you know I'm not your mother now, don't you?' Her voice trembled dangerously.

'Oh, but you are, really. Really, really you are,' I said, overdoing it. I jumped up from the settee and gave her a hug.

She smiled. Things were going well.

'Is Burgess my father's name?' I don't know where the question came from. It didn't even sound like my voice asking it.

Silence. She looked up at me without her glasses on and squinted. 'Now who on earth's been putting ideas like that into your head?'

'Well, is it?'

'No, don't be so daft, of course it in't. Burgess is your mother's name.'

'But Pat's called Mrs Andrews now and she was called Willy,' I suggested tentatively and she smiled, 'and your name was Davidson before you married Walter, so what was my mother's name before she married?'

'Well, she worn't married, was she?'

Why did grown-ups answer questions with more questions?

'So you've got her name, see? You didn't have a dad.'

'But everyone has a dad, that's just silly.'

'Now don't you go being rude—'

'Sorry, sorry, so, your name was Davidson before you married—you said.' I was going over safer ground hoping to prompt her.

'Yes, but I didn't have a dad either,' she said. 'Well, of course I *had* a dad, but my mum worn't married to him. I never knew who he was, either.

80

So I've got her name too you see, just like you.'

'Oh, I see,' I said, not understanding at all. 'So we're quits.'

She laughed as she put her glasses back on her nose. 'Well, I don't know about that, I'm sure.'

'So who was my dad? Where is he?'

'Well, I don't know. You'll have to ask your mother that. It's not up to me to tell you; anyway it's none of my business really—'

'Don't say that. I *am* your business. You're my mum.' The word almost stuck in my throat; it didn't sound right somehow now we were having this conversation. 'So old Nana's name was Davidson then, like yours.' I was beginning to grasp the facts slowly.

'Yes, dear. She was in service, you see. I've heard tell he was quite well-off so he couldn't marry Nana, could he? We lived with *my* Nana for a bit. My grandfather worked the mill at Needham Market.'

I knew that. I didn't want to talk about *that*. I wanted to talk about me.

'What, a real windmill with sails that went round?' I asked disinterestedly.

There was one near Thorpeness that I'd seen from the Revetts' car once when we'd gone to Aldeburgh for the day, but its sails never moved all the time I'd stared at it from Aldeburgh beach.

'Well, of course, he used to grind the flour for people . . . in those days you see . . .'

We were getting away from what I wanted to talk about. I'd have to be careful.

'So you were called Davidson because that was your mother's name?'

'Yes, I'm illegitimate too. Now do you see?'

81

'What?'

'Illegitimate. That's a word for people who haven't got fathers.'

It was difficult to say and even more difficult to remember, but it sounded important. I liked that.

'And if you catch anyone calling you a bastard you just let me know. I don't like that word and I won't have anyone calling you that, not for all the tea in China.'

I liked it when she stuck up for me; that made me feel good too. I'd listen very carefully from now on to see if anyone called me that funny word then I could tell tales on them with her permission.

But my mother was in that long word—Casablanca—wherever that was, and she was French.

Who'd told me that? Burgess didn't sound very French. But where was my father, then?

'My mother's French, isn't she, Mummy Grace?'

'Oh, I don't know. Louie tells so many stories.'

'People say I look like my mother. Do I look French?'

'Don't be silly, dear.'

'Well, do I look like my dad then?'

'No, of course you don't. You're as like your mother as two peas in a pod, but I just hope you'll turn out a bit better than she did.'

'Why?'

' 'Cause I've had you ever since you were a baby, that's why, and it'll be my fault if you go the way your mother did. I hope you'll be a credit to me. Don't you get into trouble like your mother.'

'Why, what did she do?'

'Well, she had you, didn't she? That was what she did.'

Somehow without my noticing, this had all gone terribly wrong. I could feel a sinking feeling in my stomach as if I'd done something frighteningly bad.

'I don't think I feel very well—' I stopped. I couldn't call her Mummy Grace now, I just couldn't. 'I think I feel sick.'

' 'At's all this talk, thass what's upset you. We should never have started it. Best to let sleeping dogs lie. We'd better have our dinner early. 'At's probably 'cause you in't had nothin' to eat since breakfast. I'll put the fish on and you get yourself a glass of lemon barley water from the pantry. That'll help settle your stomach. 'At always make me feel better when I have to take those new tablets the doctor give me. Then you can go down to Fowlers when we've had our dinner, and get us both a cornet each.'

That was a real treat. Something really serious must have happened for her to offer, without my even asking.

'I'll be all right soon, don't you worry about me . . .' I couldn't call her anything. Tears came.

'Oh, we are a pair. I worrygut about you and you worrygut about me.'

She brushed my fringe off my forehead as I drank the barley water. I didn't like it much, but at least it was Robinsons from a bottle, and not the stuff she made herself. That had nasty soggy bits of barley floating at the top that tasted like the soup she made in winter, and spoiled the nice lemony flavour of the drink.

'There now, do you feel better?'

I nodded silently, knowing I could make the most of the moment now. I gasped for my breath a bit, to show how brave I was.

'Now you're not getting an asthma attack I hope—'

'No, no. So did you ever meet my dad?' I asked in a quiet sad voice, hoping she would feel even sorrier for me. It worked.

'Well, I s'pose I must have done, dear.'

'What was he like? What was his name? Where is he now?'

'Oh, I don't know what he was like, do I?'

'Why not?'

'Well, of course I don't, and, if the truth be told, I don't think *she* did either. There were so many.'

Silence.

I didn't know what to say, it had all got out of hand, and now I was more muddled than ever. My head began to throb. I put my hand up to my forehead as she began to take the grid out of the grill pan and fill it with water from the kettle ready for cooking the fish on the hot plate. The clattering jarred and I winced.

'Now you go and lie on the settee while I get this ready, there's a good girl, and if your head's not gone after dinner, you can have an Aspro or a glass of Andrews Liver Salts—'

'What, before I have my ice-cream?'

'Well, you won't want an ice-cream if you've got a headache, will you?'

'Oh, yes, my headache will have gone by then.'

That night I dreamed I was in a waiting-room waiting for something very important to happen; nobody else was in the room. A woman opened the waiting-room door that led into a dark lounge beyond.

'You can go in now,' she said. 'Your father's in there.'

84

I walked into the room and for a moment I could see nothing in the blackness. Then I began to distinguish a shape that was huddled by a wall on the far side of the room. It was a man dressed like a tramp, old and dirty in bedraggled clothes. My father. He turned towards me, his face unshaven, his eyes bleary and red, looking at me from underneath a shabby trilby hat. He was smelly and he frightened me. My father. I ran towards him. Stopped for a second as I reached him. Looked down at his crouching shabby figure.

Then I put my skinny arms around him and hugged him hard.

CHAPTER 6

The blue fairy disappeared. In her place I put Rusty Devon, my boyfriend. He had blue eyes and red hair, and a few freckles. Not the kind that made the kids in the playground laugh, but the nice attractive kind. He was as beautiful as all the film stars whose initials we tested each other with, Margaret Whitman, Margaret Hayward and I.

'R. H.'

'Rita Hayworth. Oh, that was easy . . .'

'I. L.'

'I. L. ? There isn't a film star with those initials, you've made it up.'

'Ida Lupino . . . ner, ner, ner.' A sneer of triumph.

'R. T.'

'Robert Taylor,' I screamed before Margaret Hayward had finished speaking.

'It's your turn now, Bugalugs,' said Margaret Whitman quietly, dipping her yellowed finger into her bag of lemonade crystals.

'You're not allowed to call me that,' I protested hotly. 'My . . . my . . . Mrs Chisnall said so.'

'It's only 'cause your name is Burgess,' she said timidly, losing ground. 'You call me Whitty.'

She sidled up to Margaret Hayward and stood sheepishly next to her. I'd make her pay for that, the next time we played alone. She'd be sorry.

'Well, your mum calls your dad Whitty, so there,' I retorted.

'Well my mum says your mum was called Bugalugs when she was nursing at Allington House.'

'Bugalugs doesn't sound like Chisnall,' said Margaret Hayward who, being two years older, was above it all.

'No, her real mum. The French one.' Margaret Whitman's voice trailed off under my glare. They were my words. She fished for her handkerchief under her dress. I could never find mine, but most girls kept theirs in between the elastic of the navy-blue pair and the white ones we were made to wear underneath them because we'd been told that wearing dark navy-blue next to the skin was bad for us. She wiped the corners of her mouth with it. The same gesture as her mother's.

'C. C.,' continued Margaret Hayward.

'Cyd Charisse,' I crowed.

'Is that a man or a woman?'

'I don't know but it still counts, it's a film star's name. Can I have one of your aniseed balls?'

Margaret Hayward handed me a much-thumbed paper bag. 'Swap you for some Black Jacks.'

'Haven't got none left, but I've got some Sherbet Fountain.'

I handed her the red and yellow tube, its paper torn away to reveal the soggy cardboard.

'There's hardly any in it. Where's the licorice straw?'

'I ate that first.'

'You're supposed to suck the sherbet through it,' Margaret Whitman tentatively suggested.

'Oh, shut up,' I said crossly. 'Let's play ball.'

Six, overs, five, unders, four, letting the ball drop on the ground before we caught it, three, the ball thrown behind the back first, two caught in one hand, and one on its own. I was good at that. I had plenty of time to practise alone when there wasn't anyone to play with.

'No point in playing here,' said Margaret Hayward. 'The balls go skew-whiff on the path outside your coal-house and that's the only bit of wall you've got to play on, under your bedroom window.'

'Let's go and play on the wall outside Fowlers' shop then.'

'My mum doesn't like me to,' started Margaret Whitman.

'Let's play stilts then,' I interrupted, not wanting her unwillingness to put paid to our being together. It was better with three. I made an effort when Margaret Hayward was there. Her mum sometimes made me a dress on her Singer treadle machine. Mr Hayward kept canaries. I liked to hear them chirping when their cages were put out in the garden in the sun. I didn't play with Margaret Hayward often, and rarely was invited into number 89, so I thought they didn't really know how nasty I could be, unless Joan Holden told them she could hear me shout at Mummy . . . Mrs Chisnall through her kitchen wall. Mrs Hayward wouldn't be so nice to me, though, if she knew that. It paid to keep in with the Haywards.

'Shall I get my wooden ones?'

'That's not fair. I haven't got wooden ones. Anyway, they're your brother's not yours and you can't walk on them then, so . . .'

Ray Whitman was a tall remote figure who rode a racing-bike with dropped handlebars.

'Get the Golden Syrup tins then,' said Margaret Hayward, ever placatory and practical.

My spirits sank. Why had I suggested stilts? It took me and Mummy Gr— . . . It took us ages to finish a tin of Lyle's Golden Syrup and there only ever seemed to be one empty one in our house. Never two. I got shouted at for asking for a meat skewer and trying to bang a hole through each side of the green and golden tin with a hammer. The holes, even if I did manage it, came out wonky and either their jagged edges wore through the string that was threaded across them, or I so bashed it with my hammering that the tin lost its shape and the lid wouldn't fit back on over the join in the string. There was never enough of that in our house either. 'String? Whatever next? You're always wanting something that I haven't got, sure as fate,' was the inevitable answer to my request. I often ended up with string loops of different lengths which made clattering along the pavement at a reasonable speed quite difficult.

'We could always steal some cherries from Bowles's back garden,' I suggested. Bowles was a silent man who sloped up and down Levington

88

Road with a hat pulled well down over his eyes. He practised ringing handbells in his garden shed and I'd heard it said in hushed tones that he wasn't really married to the pale woman who hardly ever ventured outside their house next to the Haywards.

'No, we can't do that,' said Margaret Hayward. 'My mum's doing her washing, she'd see us trying to get under the fence. Anyway it's not the time of year for cherries, they're all gone.' We bowed to her greater knowledge. Pity. I was beginning to enjoy stealing.

'I think I'm going to go indoors and do my cheese label collection,' said Margaret Hayward.

I knew the day would dissipate like this, I just knew it. We stuck the labels off the triangular portions of processed cheese into scrap-books, or at least they did. 'I'm not buying none o' that processed muck!' would be the reaction to my despair at the pathetically few labels stuck with Gloy into my scrap-book with its different coloured pages that I'd bought from the post office. I only had the blue and yellow Kraft Dairylea ones and they were the most common of all. Nobody wanted to play swaps with those. 'I like a nice bit of English Cheddar cut on the slab,' echoed in my head.

'I'd rather we did orange labels instead,' ventured Margaret Whitman, 'I've got more of those.'

You would have, I thought meanly, your mum can afford to shop at the Co-op van when it comes round. He puts money on the price of fruit and vegetables to pay for the petrol so my . . . so my . . . so Mrs Chisnall says.

'Let's go and play on the rec.' Desperate measures. The last time we'd all gone to the rec a gang of boys from Copplestone Road School with their unfamiliar maroon uniforms had terrorised us on the swings and had pulled Margaret Whitman's pigtails till she cried. An easy feat really; I had been frightened too, but had run faster and escaped. I'd jumped off the swing when I was going quite high, and although I enjoyed the lurch in my stomach as I descended towards the ground, in what I imagined to be a beautiful, curved, arc-like movement like the trapeze artists I'd seen once on the high wire when Bertram Mills Circus had visited Christchurch Park, that time, I panicked and left the swing in an uneven fashion, trailing one of my arms behind me, catching it in the metal chain from which the swing was suspended, and I landed in a messy lump that provoked jeers, and grazed my knee on the concrete. It hurt but I wasn't going to let anyone see how much, as we ran away, as fast as we could, towards the safety of Levington Road.

'G. K. G. K.'

'Gene Kelly,' said Margaret Hayward casually, as she went.

'Anyway, I'm going off to play with R. D.,' I added tantalisingly.

'R. D.?' A pause. 'Robert Donat?' Margaret Whitman asked.

'Oh, you are daft sometimes. Robert Donat doesn't live in Tomline Road, does he?'

'What, near the library?'

'Yes, of course near the library, dopey.'

I wished I hadn't used that word; it reminded me of the pictures of the Seven Dwarfs, faded as they now were, that were drawing-pinned to my bedroom wall. Mummy Gr— had told me a long time ago that my mother had sent them, but I

90

hadn't understood what she meant then. Now I did, and I didn't like it. I didn't like words much any more either. They didn't seem to mean the simple things I thought they'd meant before.

I loved the Tomline Road library though. I escaped there whenever I could and read indiscriminately, especially the books with the dirty bits in. I could recognise easily which ones they were, just by picking a book out and holding it loosely by its spine to see if it fell open at a certain page of its own accord. I had understood for a long time that there was something not quite nice about men and women 'going together', as Mummy Grace would say, on seeing Mr Kerridge viewing his prize dahlias with his arm around his wife. 'Well, I know what *he's* after . . .' I didn't, but it sounded mysterious, bad and rude.

'Oh, well, I give up.'

I had no idea what she was talking about. 'What?'

'R. D.,' she insisted. 'Who's R. D. ?'

'Oh, that's my boyfriend, Rusty Devon; he's got reddish hair and freckles. Not too many,' I added hastily. 'And he's my boyfriend, he likes me more than all the other girls he knows; he said so. He doesn't want to come down here and play with you lot, so that's why I go up there and play with him.' I stopped to draw breath and folded my arms across my chest daring her to disbelieve me. She stood silently staring. I didn't know whether she was impressed or dumbfounded.

'Does Mrs Chisnall know you go up there?'

'Well, of course she does, she signed the form for the library tickets, didn't she, daft?'

She hadn't known what to put in the space

where it said Parent or Guardian, so we'd decided to leave it blank. The woman at the library hadn't noticed our two different names, thankfully. I'd planned to say she was my grandmother if asked. 'She's the old lady that I live with,' I knew was nearer the truth, but it was such a mouthful and sounded off-hand.

'You couldn't have the smallpox vaccination. I couldn't sign the paper. I'm not your proper mother.' I hadn't got an ugly round circle of pin-pricks on my arm. Nobody in our street or even our school had caught what the round mark was supposed to prevent, so it didn't worry me. But Mummy Grace had cried for a moment or two after she'd read the form, shaking her head and rubbing the tears away from under her glasses with the corner of her apron. 'I can't sign this,' she'd said, sniffing. 'I haven't got the authority.' That worried me, I didn't like to see her cry, especially if I was the cause.

'No, I mean, does she know you go up there to see Rusty?' she sniggered behind her hand, too embarrassed to go on with the name.

'She likes him a lot. She thinks he's a very well-brought-up boy,' I said, braving it out. Somewhere above my head, unseen, the angel was filling the page furiously, but I was in too deep to stop. Funny that, I'd noticed recently how one lie seemed to spawn many many others. However much I promised myself just to tell the one, it was impossible to stop others tumbling out all around it.

'I could have sworn I had a half-a-crown in my purse yesterday after I'd paid the milkman. *You* in't taken it, have you, dear?'

92

'Oh, no! Didn't you give it to the Prudential man on Monday? No, I think I saw it on the living-room table near the rent book, or maybe Pat took it when she went into town with your Mutuality coupons when she bought you those new corsets.'

That sort of thing. It was easy. Especially if I confused her first. Pat was an easy target too. She'd stolen when she'd lived with Mummy Gr—.

'And he lives in a posh house too. His father's a pilot.' My invention left her in silent awe. 'Anyway, I'm going in now too, to get my library books. I'll change them on my way to Rusty's. I've just finished *Dimsie Goes It Alone* and they've got *Dimsie, Head of the Sixth* in now, the woman in the library said so. Rusty and I play real games, he doesn't think I'm a cissy girl,' I added for good measure. 'I'll just go and tell my grandmother where I'm going so she doesn't worry.' It was out, almost as if I hadn't said it. It didn't sound quite right, but it was a step.

Margaret Whitman, busy folding her handkerchief into a neat square, maybe hadn't heard.

The living-room was cool and dark. *Workers' Playtime* was on the wireless. Everyone was singing:

> There once was an ugly duckling
> With feathers all stubby and brown . . .

I joined in: 'And the other birds in so many words said . . .' (I made a squawking noise.)

I knew all the words. Elated, I added a 'shuffle-hop-down' for good measure that I'd learned in the only Co-op juniors' dance class I'd been to. It didn't matter that they all wore pale green tunics edged in red and had proper black tap shoes which made a lovely clicking clatter on the wooden floor because even in my Cliff Lane beetle-crushers the teacher had singled me out as a perfect example of 'shuffle-hop-down' and I'd had to go round the room doing it on my own for everyone to watch and admire. We'd done 'shuffle-ball-change' too but that was a bit more difficult. Irene Hayward went every week. She had a tunic too. Her mother had made it. She'd been in a show once at Derby Road School and we'd gone to watch. A woman had sung:

> Love is where you find it
> Where you find it . . .

and had gone around looking under all the furniture on the assembly hall stage and everyone had laughed. I hadn't understood why.

The classes cost ninepence so I expect that's why I didn't go again but it didn't matter because for once I'd been the best in the class.

Everyone on the radio applauded. I bowed and opened the living-room door.

> O what a foretaste of glory divine
> Watching and waiting
> Looking above . . .

I joined in with the reedy wobbly soprano coming from the front bedroom. I knew all the words to this too.

> Filled with his glory
> Washed in his love

This is my story
This is my song
Praising my Saviour all the day long . . .

'Is that you, Jane?'

'Ye-es,' I shouted in the direction of the banisters. 'Can I play before dinner-time?'

'I thought you were playing in the back yard with Margaret Whit and Margaret Hay?'

'No, they've gone in.'

'Well, who're you goin' to play with then, the blue fairy?'

'No, not *her*. I've grown out of *her*,' I said dismissively. 'I'm going to play with Rusty Devon.'

'And who's he when he's at home?'

'Oh, you *know*,' I said meaningfully.

Silence from upstairs.

'Or could I take my library books back, then?'

'No, you in't got time to go gallivanting all the way up to Tomline Road; I've got the potatoes on, they'll be ready shortly.'

'All right then, I'll go and play with Rusty.'

'Where does *he* live, then?'

'At the bottom of the garden,' I said scornfully, blaming her for not knowing.

'Oh, all right, dear.'

I could hear the sound of the stiff brush on the bedroom mat.

'Give me a shout when dinner's ready, will you, Gran?'

Silence.

'What did you say?'

I gulped. 'I said just give me a shout when dinner's ready, Gran.'

Silence.

'Blessed assurance Jesus is mine . . .' the hymn continued. It was all right. 'Oh what a foretaste . . .'

It was going to be all right. Things were in a terrible muddle but somehow in a very little way I'd begun clearing up the mess.

I hopped and skipped all the way into the garden. Rusty Devon was always there. He'd want to play with me. He never turned away. I felt good. Life was good.

'Hallo, Rusty,' I said, just loud enough for the Margarets to hear if they were in their gardens. 'I can't play with you for long. Just until the potatoes are done, but I'll have to go in when my Gran calls me. Will you tell me if you hear her, my Gran?'

CHAPTER 7

I came home from school to find Gran sitting downcast on the old upright wooden chair in the kitchen. I thought at first that her heart was playing her up, then I saw that she was holding a brown envelope.

'What's the matter? Are you feeling bad?'

She shook her head and rubbed a hand slowly under her breast, where the edge of her new corset often gave her trouble, and waved the envelope at me with the other.

'It's this,' she said. 'It's come at last.'

'Oh,' I stopped in my tracks. 'Oh, no, I've failed, haven't I? I've failed?'

'No, you've passed.'

I couldn't believe my ears or my luck.

'I've passed? I've passed to go to grammar

school? Aren't you pleased? Why aren't you pleased?'

'I don't know where I'm going to get the money to buy the uniform from, I really don't.' Her eyes filled with tears and she turned away and reached out a hand to support herself on the sink.

I had no time for considerations of that sort. Everything inside me sang; I couldn't believe I'd done it. There wasn't even time for me to think that maybe there had been a mistake, or even that I'd just scraped through, that I was one of those borderline cases that I'd heard Miss Jones and Mrs Cussins talk so much about at Cliff Lane lately. I was flying. I wanted to tell the world, I wanted to run down the garden and shout it out, so that everyone could hear I hadn't failed. Who could I tell? Margaret Whitman hadn't even passed the first part, the only girl in our class who hadn't. I couldn't tell her, and Margaret Hayward had already been at secondary school for over a year. I banged on the tin fence between us and number 83.

'Mrs Kerridge, Mrs Kerridge, I've passed to go to grammar school.'

I heard her come out through the glass conservatory porch that backed on to their kitchen door.

'Is Mrs Chisnall all right, dear?'

'Yes, she's all right. I've passed to go to grammar school and she's worried that she won't be able to afford the uniform.'

'Don't tell everyone your business,' Gran muttered, coming out to join us. 'You always tell everyone your business.'

'I've passed, Mrs Kerridge, I've passed.' As I couldn't see over the tins, as Gran called them, I shouted even louder. 'I've passed.'

'Shsh,' said Gran, 'you don't want the whole street to hear.'

I did, I wanted the whole world to hear.

'That's nice, dear,' said Mrs Kerridge from somewhere behind the fence. 'Shall I pay the rates for you when I'm in the town tomorrow, Mrs Chisnall?'

'I've passed. I've passed.'

'Don't get yourself so worked up,' chided Gran. 'Pop down to Fowlers and get us a quarter of Cheddar. I'll make you cheese on toast for your tea.'

How could they think of things like rates and tea? I ran and jumped all the way to the corner. It didn't seem so far today. I leaped off the pavement. I could easily clear the thick green privet hedge that bordered the Harts' garden and catch a glimpse of their dark house. He was something at sea, Gran said. He wore a navy-blue sailor's hat and was hardly ever there. I dodged the cracks as I ran just in case stepping on them would make it not true. Mr Fowler was a town councillor, portly and important and didn't often serve in the shop any more. His wife helped, but she got things wrong, or forgot where things were, and he'd have to repeat himself several times until she understood. The front of her hair was yellow from the cigarette she always seemed to have in her mouth. Bob wasn't there either. Pity. I was in love with Bob. He had blond hair and wasn't married. He must have been about thirty but I thought him very good-looking. I knew he liked me too because he often pulled my leg.

'Bottle of Vimto? You'll blow up with all this

pop you drink.'

The Fowlers sold provisions not groceries; Gran didn't have much time for them, because, she said, he added the odd halfpenny on to almost everything, but it was quicker to shop there when she needed something in a hurry and couldn't wait for me to dawdle to the Co-op and back.

Mrs Fowler shuffled out from somewhere behind the bacon slicing machine.

'Quarter of a pound of cheese and I've passed to go to grammar school.'

She took her cigarette out of her mouth briefly and the ash dropped off it on to the floor somewhere. She bent down, disappearing from sight, grunting as she did so; reappeared a few seconds later, panting, and put a packet of Kraft processed cheese slices on the polished wooden counter.

'No, *your* cheese, please,' I said in an untypical fervour of politeness in case forgetting to say please would make it not be true.

She picked up the wooden handle that lay on the marble slab and drew the wire across a corner of the huge yellow wax-like slab and put an uneven triangle on the scales.

'Six ounces all right?' she asked grumpily through yellowed teeth. Gran had said a quarter, but I couldn't make her cut that little bit off, not today.

'Northgate, eh?'

'Yes, I've passed to go to Northgate.'

'Not Amberfield then?' she said, somewhat disapproving. Amberfield was a private school, I knew, very posh. Out on the road to Felixstowe. They wore brown and orange uniforms. Northgate

Girls was green. Green was now my favourite colour.

'That'll be one and threepence.'

Gran had only given me a shilling. 'Ask them to put it on tick if you haven't got enough.' Bob understood; I didn't like asking Mrs Fowler though. She wrapped the cheese in a small sheet of greaseproof paper and as she was putting that in a white paper bag I said, handing her the shilling, 'I'll just go back and get the threepence. I won't be long.'

I jumped all the way back too. Mr Holden was standing at their front gate puffing at his pipe, staring nowhere in particular as he often did.

'Holdy, Holdy, I've passed to go to grammar school.'

'Oh, have you, you'll be too hoity-toity to speak to us now, then.'

'Don't be daft, course I won't.'

'Daft am I? What kind of talk is that for a Northgate girl?'

I was chastened. The Holdens knew better than anyone else in the street how often I raised my voice to Gran. Things would have to change now. I would be better. I'd promise the angel I'd be better.

'And where are you goin' to get the money from then? That'll cost a pretty penny, won't it?' Oh, why did grown-ups bother so much about boring things like money? I'd passed, hadn't I? Wasn't that all that mattered?

'Got to go now, Holdy. I owe Fowlers threepence.'

'Well, you're lucky if that's all you owe,' he said, putting his pipe back in his mouth. 'And that's

100

threepence more than I've got.'

I ran down the passage, kicking the gate open with my foot, too happy to open it properly. It slammed up against the Kerridges' fence.

'You'll have that fence down one of these days,' said Gran, still standing where I had left her, the envelope folded up in her hand. 'And don't slam that gate! It's rickety enough as it is and I can't afford no man to come in and nail it back together again.'

I ran towards her, the cheese rustling in its bag, and grabbed her round the middle and twirled her round, hugging her and pushing her at the same time.

'Here, you'll have my glasses off!' But underneath she was chuckling which was a signal for me to do it more. 'Here, here, you'll make me dizzy,' she said, supporting herself against the fence. 'Well, I'd better get in now, Mrs Kerridge,' she said, addressing the air above the fence, pushing my hands away from her waist. 'This won't buy the baby a new bonnet.'

Silly phrases. She was full of silly sayings. But today it didn't matter.

'Here, Gran, I'm starving.'

'You'll eat me out of house and home,' she said, getting a white pudding bowl with cold mashed potato in it from the pantry in the kitchen. She spread two thick slices of white bread with it, topped them with slices of cheese and put them under the grill.

'Well, I don't know how we'll manage I'm sure, still God is good . . .'

'Yes God is good

In earth and sky, from ocean depth to swelling
   flood
Ten thousand voices seem to cry
God made us all and God is good . . .'

I bellowed out with a mouthful of cheese that she'd
left on the table.

'Sshh,' she said, 'you'll have the Holdens banging
on the wall, they'll be wondering what on earth's
the matter. Calm down or you won't sleep tonight.'

I calmed down, just a bit, remembering the
promise I had made with myself about the angel.
The angel must have had something to do with my
passing to Northgate, so I owed the angel. I would
be better. I would.

*   *   *

God took a while showing us His goodness.
Another brown envelope came with a long list of
school uniform in it, that made Gran cry again.

'It says here, "Hockey stick"; where we're going
to get a hockey stick from, I *don't* know. Perhaps
Doris will still have one of her old ones.' Doris had
been good at hockey, she'd even played for Suffolk
once or twice but she'd been a mum for years now,
too busy bringing up her Gary and Clive to even
think about hockey. Besides, I didn't want a
second-hand hockey stick; I was going to grammar
school, I wanted a brand-new one.

'We'll get it from Sneezums in Fore Street of
course.'

'I don't know where you think I'll get the money
to go shopping in a place like Sneezums,' she said
grumpily. 'Money don't grow on trees,' she said.

'You said my mother used to go out with one of the Sneezum boys, didn't you?'

'I think she was engaged to him at one time; anyway that's what she said, although you never know *what* to believe with your mother.'

'Well, I could go in there and say good morning, Mr Sneezum, give us a hockey stick, I think I'm your granddaughter.'

She looked startled then chuckled in spite of herself.

'Oooh, you are a naughty girl. You'll wag that tongue of yours once too often—'

'—and I'll end up just like my mother,' I interrupted, finishing the sentence for her. 'Well, you're wrong; my mother went to Nacton Road, and I'm going to Northgate. So!'

*　　　*　　　*

God appeared to us first of all in the shape of a Mr Notcutt. I knew he must be important because Gran had invited him into the front room.

'You'd better come in here, there's a man from Notcutts.'

Notcutts were the nursery garden people out near Woodbridge. What they wanted to see me for I couldn't imagine, but, like all liars, I could never quite remember my last misdemeanour, I couldn't keep track of them all. I felt uneasy. What had I done?

He was well dressed and well spoken. He perched uneasily on the edge of one of Gran's best chairs, next to the fireplace, his hat resting on one of the curly bits of the brass fender. The fire was rarely lighted but even though it was late summer, the room felt chilly and smelt of Brasso. Gran was nervous too because she put on her posh voice.

'It won't take a minute to put the kettle on.'

'No, thank you, no.' He turned to me. 'So you want to go to Northgate?'

I thought it a dumb question; who would pass and not want to go? 'Yes, yes, please,' I said, my voice seeming to come from a long way away, not belonging to me at all.

He smiled. 'Well I think we'll be able to help with that.'

Relief flooded through me. I wanted to hug him, but he was posh and very polite. Better than hugging him, I thought, I wish you were my dad, or that my dad was like you; then I thought maybe he was.

'What's your favourite subject?'

It was like being questioned by our teacher, or worse, a policeman, not that I ever had been, but I probably would be soon if I went on stealing the odd threepence or sixpence out of Gran's purse. Someone would find me out soon. Someone more clever than Gran.

'English,' I blurted out. I didn't have a favourite subject, I didn't even like school but I liked Miss Jones in spite of her big teeth; there seemed too many for her mouth, though that was big too. She was our class teacher, in Class 9, and she taught English.

'Well, she's a credit to you, Mrs Chisnall,' he said, at the same time collecting his belongings.

I must have given the right answer, even though it was a lie, and he obviously hadn't seen the mud on my ankle socks that I collected coming home through Holywells Park, where I shouldn't have been. More importantly Gran hadn't seen it either. Yet.

She showed him out down the hall, and closed the front door with difficulty behind him. The wood always warped in the summer, even though it was protected by the curtain.

'Who was *that*?' I asked as Gran leaned her bulk against the door, forcing it shut.

'Notcutts the solicitors.' She had difficulty saying the word—like she always said 'cerstificate'. She offered no explanation as to how they had known about us and our problem. I never did know.

'He said they'd help us out with some extra money—and at Christmas there's the Poor Fund from the church.'

I wasn't interested in Christmas. 'But Northgate, are they going to help me get to Northgate?'

'Well, they can't do it *all*,' she said impatiently. I couldn't understand why she was cross. 'He said the child welfare people will have to be told.'

I didn't listen. 'So it's all right, then?'

'Well, it may be all right for you,' she said, lowering herself into the utility chair, taking off her glasses to rub her eyes wearily, 'but I don't like it, I don't like it at all.'

'Oh, you are daft—'

'Don't you talk to me like that—'

'Well you are, Gran. He's going to give us money—'

'It's not as simple as that, Jane. It's not just the money, that in't the half of it. It's charity, that's what it is, it's charity, and I don't like it. I've never taken charity before. I thought I'd never see the day . . .'

I was the only girl in the street who had passed.

105

Nobody seemed to want to play with me any more, but that didn't really bother me, I was full of my own importance and the happiest I'd ever been. Somewhere along the line I had got something right at last. I wasn't going to get married, have kids, live in Ipswich and be buried in the local cemetery where Walter was. I was going to have more. I didn't mind that some of the kids muttered 'Northgate bummer' under their breath as I passed. I was proud to be a Northgate bummer, whatever it was.

*   *   *

'You'd better come in, and meet Miss MacVean.' We'd never had so many visitors before. This must be part of the new life. I thought it all very exciting.

My spirits fell when I saw her. She had short grey hair, tightly permed, that framed a small pinched-up face with half-glasses, like a judge, and I disliked her instantly and I knew that she didn't like me. She wore a blouse buttoned up to the neck and sensible laced-up shoes. I felt that everything about her was tightly tied in. She worried me from the first moment she spoke, and everything she said worried me more.

'So, Jane, isn't it? We're going to look after you now.'

Panic. Was she going to take me away from Gran? Gran had often threatened I'd end up in a Home; was this it? I shot a glance at Gran. She was silent and subdued, like she always was when she was with people who were official. She was twirling one of her thumbs round and round the other, but she didn't look too upset. Perhaps she wanted me

106

to go away, then she wouldn't have to put up with all this extra worry.

'You'll get a list of the uniform that you'll need shortly from the school, and you will go to Edwards the outfitters who supply it.'

So you don't know everything, I thought. We've had the list already.

It was like a command, but at least it meant that she wasn't going to come with us. I didn't want to be with her any longer than I absolutely had to. But Gran, how could Gran manage on the trolley bus? She hardly ever went into the town any more. I wouldn't have to buy it on my own, would I?

'You will have free school dinners, and we'll look after that for you as well.'

Dinner at school? I wasn't prepared for that. I'd always run home up the hill like all the other kids, gobbled up Gran's cooking, then headed as fast as I could for the sweet shop for a gobstopper that changed colour or an everlasting strip that I'd chew and pull till it went wavy like old elastic.

'The school will provide the books.'

That was just as well, I thought. We didn't have any books. *Girl Friend* comics and my borrowed library books. The only other books in the house were Gran's copy of *The People's Friend* and her Methodist hymn book and an occasional copy of *The Methodist Recorder*. Gran didn't like me reading. She'd shout up the stairs, 'Ja-ane, Ja-ane, will you turn that light off. You'll be murder to get up in the morning,' but that was better than trying to read for any length of time downstairs in the living-room, where if I sat for long, she'd say 'What's the matter with you, then? Jane, answer me when I talk to you, will you! What's the matter?

107

Ja-ane!'

'Oh, nothing, Gran,' I'd answer irritably. 'Nothing's the matter for goodness' sake, I'm reading that's all!'

'It's like talking to a brick wall.'

'What?'

'Oh, talk to yourself, Grace,' she'd mutter as she padded off into the kitchen. 'Sitting there on the settee. Not sayin' anything for hours on end. You must be sickening for something and that's a fact.'

I felt sick now.

'I shall be calling in on you from time to time, just to see how we're progressing.'

Why did she say *we* when she meant *us*? I felt sicker, and lifted my chest to breathe easier. Supposing she walked in on one of Gran's and my rows? I was beginning to get the better of Gran each time we argued; I could shout louder than her now, and Joan Holden didn't frighten me so much any more, and would frighten me less. She hadn't gone to Northgate either.

Sometimes I could avoid a row by pouncing on her and squeezing her hard around the middle until she had to laugh and beg me to stop, but I could make her laugh more just by laughing myself, laughing and laughing until her eyes watered and she'd heave and gasp for breath, and she'd say, 'Oh, get along with you now, I've got work to do, I can't stand around here, fiddle farting the day away like this.'

'Oh, Gran! You said fart! What would the minister say, you naughty girl!' and she'd heave and laugh some more.

Miss MacVean wouldn't understand that. She didn't look as if she ever farted.

108

'Has she had all the usual vaccinations?' She turned to Gran as if I wasn't in the room.

'Well, they had them TB ones at school, but she never had the smallpox one.' Gran seemed apologetic.

'Well, why was that?'

'Well, they couldn't give it without permission, could they? And I didn't know where her mother was.' Gran's cheeks burned redder.

'Oh, so you're not the child's legal guardian, then?'

'Pardon?' said Gran.

'Did the mother never sign her over to you, then?'

'I've never seen no papers. There weren't no papers, not that I know of.' Gran was getting flustered now.

'I see,' said Miss MacVean, rather like a doctor without a trace of emotion in her voice at all. 'So you're the child's foster mother?'

'Well, I s'pose I must be, yes.'

As Miss MacVean rummaged in her briefcase amongst some papers, her glasses swung forwards from a chain round her neck, just like Mrs Cossin's who taught us history. At least they knew where their glasses were. Gran was always muttering, 'I wonder where I put my glasses? I know I had them here somewhere; oh, drat the darned things.' I was going to have my glasses on a chain when I grew up. It was the only thing I liked about this frightening woman.

'So would you sign this please now, Mrs Chisnall. It's simply your agreement to our care and control of Jane.'

The word control hit me like a brick. Control?

That didn't sound very nice at all. No one had ever controlled me, and I wasn't going to let them start now.

'I'll get your glasses, Gran dear,' I said in a phoney voice as she made a move. 'I know where you left them.'

I didn't. But it gave me a chance to escape into the living-room, where I could allow myself to hear the pounding of my heart as I threw open the sideboard doors and snagged my finger on the broken metal catch as I always did.

'Bugger,' I said, then wished I hadn't. Had she heard? If she had would Gran get into trouble? I rummaged about amongst the muddle; the tin with the rates book in it, odd gloves and the few bits of best china, scattering the crumbs from an open packet of biscuits as I did so. They weren't by the wireless either. I found them at last on the draining-board in the kitchen, next to a half-peeled onion, Gran's face flannel, and the remains of a cube of Oxo.

Gran had trouble getting Miss MacVean's Biro to work, but eventually in a very shaky hand she managed, 'G. E. Chisnall' and then wrote 'Gaurdian' in brackets after it. I would have to tell her about that.

'Oh, she did make me feel bad,' Gran said later. 'I'd better have one of those heart tablets, dear.'

I felt awful too. All this because of Northgate. I couldn't find it in me to wish I hadn't passed, however bad Gran felt. I was angry that Miss MacVean had somehow managed to dampen my delight too.

'Well, she can go and get her whiskers caught in her knitting somewhere else.' Silly schoolgirl jokes

110

nearly always won Gran round. This time she didn't smile.

'She'll be back,' she said. 'You'll see. Our lives won't be our own. They'll walk in here whenever they like, you mark my words.'

CHAPTER 8

The wind rushed past my ears blotting out all other sounds.

Shops and houses flew by, blurring into one long shape at either side of my vision. There was a group of Northgate boys ahead in their black and red uniforms. I had to overtake them. It was a race, though they didn't know it.

The wind threatened to lift my beret off my head. I held the handlebars with one hand and shoved it down lower over my fringe. My blue and green scarf streamed out behind me. I clicked the three-speed and pedalled faster. I was impressive. I was sure people on the pavement were watching me admiringly as I sped along.

I took one hand off the handlebars again and shifted the weight of my satchel from the middle of my back to my shoulders. I had homework to do. That was impressive too. It impressed me. We never had homework at Cliff Lane.

The street lights were coming on, piercing the dusk with pools of white. Past the bakery in Caudwellhall Road that emitted a band of warm yeast smell in the mornings that was a delight to cycle through. They bought our school doughnuts and cream buns from there for break. Doughnuts were sixpence and cream buns ninepence. Sometimes Gran packed me cream crackers with cheese inside, wrapped in greaseproof paper, but often I managed to wangle sixpence from her. A doughnut was something to look forward to.

I didn't mind school dinners, though. We had jam sponge with coconut on it that came with a treacly fruity sauce and cheese pudding, unlike anything Gran had ever made, served out of deep tin dishes by the monitor on our table. If we wanted more, we went up to the serving hatch where women in turbans and overalls served it directly on to our plates. The sixth form and prefects sat at tables raised on a dais at the far end of the room, grand and remote.

The windows of the long, low room were always steamed up, making it impossible to see the netball courts and hockey pitches outside—but it was always full of chatter and laughter. I liked it.

No one knew I had free school dinners except my form. My name went in a separate book each morning. But no one knew that, once I was in the canteen.

I overtook a Vespa that had slowed down at the traffic lights near Derby Road Station. Cissy, I thought, the light was still yellow.

An icy rain had begun to fall, pricking my face and misting up my shiny handlebars. My bike would go rusty if it got wet. I rubbed the rain away with my woollen-gloved hand, clicked the gear once more as I approached the Derby Road Station hill—only a small bump in the road but I could freewheel down the other side.

I felt unassailable. There were a couple of older Northgate girls ahead of me who lived in Hatfield

Road, chatting as they cycled together.

So I must have been one of the first ones out. I overtook them easily—applied both my brakes and came to a squeaking halt at Felixstowe Road. I didn't glance long to the right in spite of Gran's warning voice in my ear. 'Now you mind that Felixstowe Road; cars tear along there.' That was where the bicycle shop was. We hadn't paid for my brand-new bicycle yet. It had been a struggle to convince her that I needed one. For weeks I'd gone to school on the bus. Two buses in fact; it took ages and made me late home for the *Children's Hour* serial, and I wasn't going to Northgate on that stupid bike with the curved crossbar and sit-up-and-beg handlebars, that someone, I couldn't remember who, had given us, and Gran, intimidated by visits from Miss MacVean, Notcutts, and the Reverend John Blamey who donated a portion of the Poor Fund from Alan Road Church towards our upkeep, refused point blank to ask for any more charity.

'It's not charity, Gran, we're paying for the bike; it's only half-a-crown a week.'

'Well, I'm not going.' That was silly; she hardly went out at all any more.

'Nobody asked you to.'

So I braved it out and went myself. I wasn't too embarrassed to talk terms with Mr Finch, the bike shop man. I wanted it too badly. Ten pounds and half-a-crown a week for a year and a half.

'I don't know what they'd say if they knew ten pounds of their money went on a bike. It weren't meant for bikes.'

'Well, they don't have to know, do they? Anyway, none of them will see it. They don't go out and look in the shed, do they?'

'You've got the cheek of the devil. I s'pose you get that from your mother—'

'Oh, Gran—'

'Well, I don't like it—we've never had anything on tick before—'

'It's called hire purchase.'

'I don't care what it's called—it's on tick. You haven't paid for it yet.'

I didn't want to think about what she'd say if she knew that last week the half-crown hadn't found its way to the bicycle shop, but had stayed in the pocket of my school blazer in ever-diminishing quantities.

I loosened the scarf and undid the button at the neck of my cream shirt, and pulled at my green and blue striped tie.

I was hot, but I'd beaten everyone. I didn't know how long it'd taken me as I didn't have a watch, but I must have beaten my own record.

I was glad it wasn't Wednesday. Wednesday was Girls Life Brigade night at Alan Road, and I was getting bored with it. I'd got my embroidery badge sewn proudly on to the sleeve of my uniform, and I'd put my name down for the astronomy badge group. We'd learned about the Plough, Orion and Cassiopeiae but I was getting bored with that too.

The only good thing about belonging to the GLB was being allowed to wear the uniform at school on special days like St George's Day. We stood out amongst the sea of green on those days—those of us who belonged to the GLB and the Girl Guides. The Girl Guides were in a huge majority, though. Most people, I was embarrassed to find out, had never even heard of the GLB. But Audrey

Ward and her sister Daphne who ran it, who were officers, were proud of it. They had sleeves with hardly any space at all on them for any more badges. We'd gone to camp in the summer holidays for a whole week. I'd shouted at Gran because she wouldn't let me wear my brand-new Northgate mac. I wanted everyone at Alan Road to know I'd passed, but she'd won that round and I'd stormed off on to the bus that was to take us to camp in Kessingland without even saying goodbye to her.

Camp was an embarrassment too. We didn't sleep in tents like the Girl Guides did. We slept on palliasses in the church hall.

It took too long to explain that no, the GLB wasn't the Girl Guides, and no, we didn't march round the streets playing in a band like the Boys Life Brigade . . . how I envied them, especially the boy who banged the big drum that almost hid him it was so huge. He wore a piece of real tiger skin too. Initially it had been fun to get out of the house one night a week. It had been a natural progression from Sunday School; all the boys and girls joined up like we all signed the teetotaller's pledge—I'd signed it, then asked Gran what it meant after. I'd laughed when she told me. It was so easy. Why had they made such a fuss about it? There wasn't any alcohol at number 85. Except for the quarter bottle of brandy that Gran kept in the sideboard cupboard that she took in a minute quantity with some warm water when she felt bad, on bitingly cold days in winter.

I readjusted my satchel on my shoulders again and turned round to check that no books had fallen out of my saddle-bag behind me in my race to get home. I nearly always brought more than I needed.

I wanted people to see how weighed down I was with homework, and be impressed. Looking guiltily around I checked there were no prefects or sixth formers about, snatched my beret off and stuffed it in a gap in the saddle-bag.

'They used to wear velour at Northgate in the old days, and straw hats in summer, before Northgate went common. All those girls from council estates never used to pass the scholarship then; Lilian had to wear a velour, a berry's not the same,' said Gran's voice in my head.

A car honked somewhere behind me and I realised the lights were green. Cobbold's horses stood outside the Royal Oak breathing great jets of steam-like breath into the cold air, stamping their hooves on the cold tarmac.

The Revetts' Christmas tree was already lit up in their front window, so was the Cunninghams' further down on the other side of the street and of course the Whitmans' had been in their front window for weeks. Doug would bring ours soon, I hoped. We'd put it in the living-room. I'd decorate it with little metal holders that snapped on to the branches and then we'd begin the yearly hunt for stubs of candles to put into them. Nearly everyone had electric lights on their trees but we still had candles. I liked that best. Gran didn't seem to mind the wax that dripped on to the doilies that she'd put on the table—but she did mind the tree.

'That dratted thing dropping its needles everywhere. 'At make the room a beggar to clean and those needles get into my slippers and scratch my feet.' She had brown slippers with turned-down sides and pom-poms on the front. I had tartan ones like bootees that zipped up.

116

'Laurel Villas' it said across the border between number 85 and the Holdens. Laurel was what Roman emperors were crowned with. There was not a leaf of it in sight.

I cycled up the dip in the pavement outside the Kerridges' house, hoping Gran wasn't looking for me through the front room window, and, with what I thought was a flourish, got down between the two brick posts that bordered the entrance to the passage, carefully avoiding brushing the handlebars into the wet privet hedge, and pushed the bike through the open gate, slamming it noisily behind me. I scooted along on one pedal till I reached the shed, leaned the bike carefully against it and moved the sheets of corrugated iron that acted as doors from the entrance.

It was difficult to believe that I'd played in this dark musty space for months on end. I didn't go in here any more except to protect my beloved bike in a piece of sacking that Holdy had given me. I didn't play in sheds any more now that I went to Northgate.

I didn't play with Margaret Whitman and Margaret Hayward any more either. I was a grammar school girl.

'I could hear you coming a mile off,' said Gran, 'the way you thump those tins back.'

I dumped my satchel and my pile of books on the kitchen table and gave her a kiss, pressing my face up against hers.

'You little beggar,' she said, moving away sharply. 'Your face is like ice! That cold'll strike right through me, and shut the kitchen door. Were you born in a barn?'

'What's for tea, what's for tea?'

'You'll eat me—'

'—out of house and home,' I joined in.

She laughed. 'You can have crumpets now but I've got kippers for later—'

'Yippee,' I shouted.

'You noisy little tyke. Have you got much of that homework tonight?'

'I've got chemistry,' I said.

'Oh, yes.'

'Chemistry, Gran, chemistry.'

'What's that, then, when it's at home?'

'I've got to learn some formulae . . .'

'Oh, yes.'

'You know—H_2O for water, Na/Ct for sodium chloride; that's salt, you know.'

'Well, I've always called it Saxo,' she said.

'Ca—calcium. That's what we have in our bones and teeth; you get it from cheese.'

'We've run out of cheese.'

'Acetic acid—that's vinegar.'

'Sceptic acid,' she repeated.

'No, *acetic* acid.'

'Just think,' she said, 'I souse herrings in aseptic acid—'

'Acetic—'

'Get out of my way now,' she said, 'or those crumpets'll be burnt to a cinder under the grill—and you won't have anything for tea. Have you wiped that bike down properly?'

'Yes, Gran,' I said, hoping she wouldn't ask me what I'd wiped it with.

'That mac must be damp. Put it on the back of this chair. The oven's on; that'll dry it out in no time.'

'Better have the scarf too,' I added. 'What's the

118

time?'

'Oh, I don't know,' she said. 'All the clocks in this house say different times.'

They always had. She didn't have a watch either.

The Westclox alarm on the living-room mantelpiece said ten to five.

'Yippee,' I said again.

'Don't go in there with those shoes on, I've just polished the lino. Here, here are your slippers; they've been warming by the oven. And strikes me, my girl, you'd better take a towel to that hair—'at look wet to me. Those berries don't keep the worst off and that's a fact.'

'Give me a towel, then. Quick! I've only got ten minutes before *Cruise of the Ceol Mara* starts . . .'

'And then it'll be like a Quakers' meeting in here. Nobody allowed to speak . . .'

'Give me the scuttle. I'll put some more coal on the fire.'

'Thass roaring halfway up the chimney—or at least 'at was quarter an hour ago when I banked it up. I hope the blasted fire in't gone out. It was a beggar to light this morning. I said to the coalman when he came round on Thursday, don't you shoot me a lot of slate like the last lot. 'At take ages to get a hold and when 'at do 'at spit out bits at you. I've got several brown marks on that mat and that's been down no time at all.'

I grabbed the coal-scuttle and made a dash outside.

'You've got your slippers on,' she shouted after me. 'You always do everything back to front.'

'There,' I said, wiping my slippers carefully on the doormat. 'We won't have to go outside again tonight.'

'Oh, thank you, dear. Now, are you going to do your homework now? Just so's I know when to put the kippers on—'

'*No*, no, *after*, *after*—ouch. This water's freezing,' I said, making a gesture towards washing my hands under the cold tap.

'Well, of course it's cold—'at came from a cold place. You should've let me boil a kettle up—you'll get chilblains, you know, 'cos you will go and stick 'em up right in front of the fire. I know you . . .'

'No, I won't.'

'So when 'as it got to be done, this 'ere homework, then?'

'I don't have to hand it in till Monday. Page twenty-two and page twenty-three must be learned by Wednesday,' I said, sucking in air with every phrase as Miss Greenham did. She had this extraordinary habit, our IIID form mistress and science teacher, of opening her mouth as if she were going to smile and instead a great wheezing noise would be emitted through her bared teeth. Through my indoctrination Gran was familiar with this foible.

'Oh, you little tinker,' she said, laughing. 'You'll get what for, one of these days.'

I'd met Gran on my first day back from Northgate making her way slowly down Levington Road, having managed a bit of shopping.

'I'm in IIID,' I'd said proudly.

'Oh, dear,' said Gran, deflating me utterly and going straight to the truth.

'What do you mean, oh, dear,' I retorted defensively. 'They do it backwards at Northgate: the A form is for the girls who just scraped through.'

120

'Oh,' she said, but I knew she knew I was lying. Barbara Fox, who to everyone's surprise hadn't passed, had said, 'I'd rather be in the top class at the secondary modern than the bottom one at grammar school,' and that rankled.

I'd never mentioned it again and wisely neither had Gran, and any disappointment she may have felt and my resultant annoyance had been deflected by my stories of Miss Greenham's odd quirks—she dressed from head to toe in blue right down to her handbags and shoes. We'd bought her a form present of a blue chiffon scarf; and could hardly contain ourselves when, after opening it, she'd exclaimed through a sentence punctuated with great gulps of air: 'Oh, how delightful: a blue scarf. How did you know it was my favourite colour?'

'So,' gulp, I continued, 'I shall just go, and,' wheeze, 'press my ear to the,' gulp, 'wireless for an hour, then I shall complete,' gulp, 'my chemistry homework.'

Gran laughed some more, wiped the steam from her glasses and bent down to retrieve the crumpets from under the grill. I settled into the old utility chair by the wireless, switched it on and waited for the magic words, 'It's five o'clock. Time for *Children's Hour.*'

'Here, you'd better put this cloth down over you if you're goin' to eat them on your lap—we don't want butter all over that new gym slip.'

'Ssh! ssh! Gran.'

'Bar reety bar-ro,' sang the lilting Caribbean voice. 'In my heart I keep your love . . .'

I joined in.

Gran handed me crumpets dripping with butter and signalled me to unfold the tea-cloth.

121

'Ssh! Ssh!'
'I in't said nothing,' said Gran.
'Sssssh! . . .'

*   *   *

A piece of coal fell on to the hearth—disturbing the silence of the room. Gran jumped.

'What's 'at?' Her knitting and the *Methodist Recorder* slid to the floor.

'Oh, it's nothing,' I said crossly.

'Oh, that wind must be getting up—look at that,' she said as a cloud of black smoke billowed back down the chimney and curled into the room. She rubbed her eyes tiredly, searching for her glasses in the folds of dress on her lap. 'Doug only painted this last year. Strikes me I'll have to have it done agin if this go on—I've never known such a winter.'

'You always say that. Every winter.'

'I'd better go out the back and see if the paraffin lamp's still alight. We don't want them lavatory pipes freezin' up—that'd be a right lookout.'

'Oh, leave it—it's dark. You don't need to go out there any more. You've got your pail in. Stop fussing.'

She slept in the front room downstairs now, not being able to manage the stairs. If she wanted to go to the toilet in the night she went in a brown plastic bucket that she kept by the bed. During the day the bucket was kept in the lavatory in case the minister or the doctor or the insurance man called. It was liberally doused with Dettol that made the whole front room smell like the school dentist at The Clinic. He put a black mask over my face that had a sweet sickly smell that I liked. It sent me into the deepest sleep. When I woke there'd be a gap where a tooth had been. I could probe the blood clot in the gum gently with my tongue.

'You don't care, do you? If them lavatory pipes freeze—'

'Oh, ssh, Gran, ssh. I'm trying to do my homework.'

'You'll go through them sleeves on that Northgate jumper if you keep leaning on your elbows like that.'

'Gra-an—it's maths I'm trying to do—'

'Well, they won't give you another grant for another jumper yet. You can be sure of that—this lot o' uniform's got to last you a good while, my girl.'

'You've woken up grumpy—why don't you make yourself a cup of tea and take a tablet?'

'I can't take one of them yet 'at make me dopey. I'd be walkin' around bangin' into things.'

'Ssh, Gran, it's equations. I can't do equations.' I began to whine. I couldn't do them and I couldn't see the point of them either. What did x and y stand for? x apples? y houses? It didn't make sense. My mind couldn't grasp it at all. Or the problems that had two men filling baths with water at different speeds. Why? Who, in adult life, would need to find out the difference in arrival times between a train to York travelling at fifty miles per hour with seventy-three miles less to travel than a train to Edinburgh travelling at eighty miles an hour?

If you wanted to go to Edinburgh why would you worry about what time a train arrived in York? It simply didn't make sense: logarithms were the same. I'd never seen a grown-up use logarithms.

Mr Fowler used an old stub of pencil on a piece of greaseproof paper.

And Gran counted up things on her fingers. I'd seen her do it.

'Well, how much more've you got to do, then? I'd like to listen to *Friday Night is Music Night* and *Semprini Serenade*.'

'You said you don't like me leaving it all till the last thing Sunday night, then doing it in a rush.'

'All right, all right,' said Gran. 'Sorry I spoke.'

'Anyway, I can't do it tomorrow morning. I've got to go into town and pay the rates, haven't I?'

That had been a shock. Gran admitting that she couldn't get the tram into town any more on Saturday mornings. I'd felt very grown-up at first taking the shiny green book in its well-worn paper bag down to the rates office in Berners Street. They'd turn the book sideways and stick a strip of paper into it, having pressed one end into a sponge in a dish like they had in the post office.

I'd felt proud at first. I was always the youngest in the queue. I felt scared too, being so responsible for something so important. From the moment the rates were paid Gran worried about how she was going to pay the next lot. They were obviously important. But the novelty of my new status had quickly dwindled. Now it was just a chore. I couldn't lie in bed late any more. 'Jay-ern— Jay-ern,' Gran would shout from the bottom of the stairs. 'If you don't get up soon that rates office'll be closed, and that'll be a right lookout.'

'Jesus wept,' said Gran, 'I don't ask you to do much—'

There was a loud knock at the door.

'Now who on earth can that be at this time o'

124

night? I'm not answering the door this late,' she said, getting alarmed. 'I hope it's not the child welfare people. Fancy knockin' up someone at this time o' night.'

'Oh, Gran, don't be silly. She doesn't work this late—'

'Who's *she*, the cat's mother?'

'Miss MacVean.'

'You never know with *that* lot,' she said scornfully.

'Let's go in the front room and see who it is.'

'Don't put the light on,' she said hurriedly as she followed me into the icy hall. 'We can look through the curtains.' A favourite pastime of hers.

The front room was not as cold. A bar of the electric fire glowed in the dark of the hearth.

We giggled like naughty children. I snorted out loud and dug my fingers into her ribs as she edged past the table to the side of the bay window nearest the front door.

'Oh, don't, Jane,' she said, giggling, 'they'll hear us.'

We heard them first.

> How silently how silently
> The wondrous gift is given

A group of fifteen or so stood under the street lamp just up the street from the Kerridges' house.

Young people smiling as they sang, muffled in scarves and woolly hats. Some of the boys had their arms round girls' shoulders. They all looked so happy. Another knock at the door.

'I'll go, I'll go,' I said, bumping into the foot of Gran's bed as I turned. 'Ouch,' I said, rubbing my knee.

'Mind where you're going,' said Gran.

I fumbled with the knitted sausage that lay across the bottom of the door to block the draught from the gap where the door didn't meet the stone step.

'Stupid thing.'

The door was stiff and difficult to open.

A young man rattled a tin at me and smiled.

'We're from Alan Road Youth Club and we're singing carols on behalf of Dr Barnardo's Homes,' he said and rattled the tin again.

'Quick, Gran, quick, he wants some money,' I shouted.

'Who is it, dear?' She always talked posh in front of strangers.

'Alan Road Youth Club—I'll get the money, I'll get it,' I said impatiently. 'Where is it?'

'There's some change in the ornament on the mantelpiece in the living-room.'

I was embarrassed that he should hear we kept money in such odd places.

I tipped the tall vase with its fluted edges upside down. On to the mantelpiece fell several hair-grips, one of Gran's brooches with several of the blue glass petals of a flower missing, two pennies, a threepenny bit and a sixpence. The grips scattered on to the hearth, I scooped up the money and ran back.

'I've had girls from Dr Barnardo's—' Gran was saying.

'I go to Alan Road,' I interrupted eagerly, 'to Sunday School.'

An elderly man amongst the group waved at us as he continued singing.

'And Girls Life Brigade,' I said, reclaiming my allegiance with more passion than was honest.

'Well, you should come to Youth Club,' he said, smiling again.

'Oh, can I, Gran, can I?'

'I don't know, I'm sure,' she said hesitantly, drawing her cardigan round her throat as a cold wind blew into the hall.

The group had finished 'O Little Town of Bethlehem' and were moving away from under the lamp in a straggly line, laughing and talking.

'Come on, Tony—Dingaling's tin is full already.'

Several of them cheered as a boy with glasses shut the Harts' front gate opposite and caught up with the group. Suddenly I wanted to be part of that group more than anything else.

'Can I?' I repeated anxiously, dropping all the money into his tin.

'I'll have a word with Bert and Doris,' he said, backing down the path.

'Here, Bert, we've got a new recruit.'

Cheers from amongst the crowd. Someone with a long scarf was being pulled along the street by two or three of them.

The old man who'd waved came towards us. He was wearing a long mac which made him look slight and trim, his sharp-featured face topped by a smart grey Homburg hat. The steam from his nose reached us before he did.

'It's a perishing night, isn't it? God bless you both.'

'Can I join, can I?'

'You haven't finished your homework yet.'

'Oh that doesn't matter,' I said crossly—and then checked myself.

'I'm nearly twelve; my birthday's on Boxing Day so I'll be thirteen next year.'

He smiled. 'I've seen you at chapel, haven't I?'

'Yes, I go to—'

'I've been a member of the congregation for nigh on forty years,' Gran interrupted. 'I used to sing in the choir at Tacket Street Congregational when I was younger,' she added, which I thought a gross exaggeration—I couldn't remember her having gone to chapel for years. Not since I'd worn my grey bolero jacket and lemon blouse for the Sunday School's anniversary when I was six.

'Well, we start at fourteen,' he said, dashing my spirits. 'I'll have a word with our Doris. Doris, dear,' he shouted.

A woman with sandy curly hair peeping out from under a woolly scarf and a kindly wrinkled face shouted, 'What's up, Bertie?'

'This little one wants to join the Youth Club,' he said, tickling me under the chin. I flushed pink with embarrassment and pleasure. 'And she's only twelve.'

'Thirteen next December,' I added.

He laughed and said to Gran, 'I bet you've got your hands full with this one, haven't you?'

'Oh, you don't know the half of it,' said Gran almost seriously. I felt chastened.

'Well, perhaps we can make an exception in her case,' said the lady, lisping slightly on the 's's. 'We meet Friday and Saturday evenings. The boys play snooker and we have dancing and table tennis and we meet for fellowship on Sunday evenings after church. Now we must get on, Bertie. This lot are starving and I've got to heat up the mince pies when we get back—and we've still got Cliff Lane and Elmhurst Drive to do. They're like a horde of locusts, this lot,' she said and laughed again, a wheezing chuckle, her eyes disappearing amongst the creases of flesh.

'Now don't you worry about her getting back— Patrick here lives up the road; a whole gang of them walk back together. We've got our Christmas party the middle of January; why don't you come to that? Lots of goodies to eat and they play all that rock 'n' roll—terrible din,' she said, and chuckled louder.

'You'll look after her, won't you, Dingaling?'

The tall boy with glasses looked quizzically in my direction and several of them thumped him on the back and cheered.

'Can we have a volunteer?' the young man who'd come to our house with the tin said, and pointing towards Dingaling continued, 'You and you and you.' Several of them collapsed with laughter and cheered again.

'They're a caution, aren't they?' the old man said.

'Yes,' I said smiling, not understanding.

'Now don't you catch cold standing here, dear. Go on in by the fire. Now what's your name?' he said, lifting his hat to Gran like the man from Notcutts did.

'Jane,' I said meekly.

'Calamity Jane or plain Jane and no nonsense?' he asked chuckling.

'Oh, I don't know about *that*,' said Gran. I could've kicked her.

'Jane Burgess.'

'Well, Jane Burgess, we'll see you in January. Now you can go in or your mother will catch cold.'

129

I half drew in a breath to explain.

Gran nudged me sharply in the ribs. 'Don't tell people *all* your business,' she hissed.

'G'bye,' I said, topping her whisper.

'G'bye,' several of them shouted back and waved.

'Goodbye,' I called again. I had somewhere to go now. Fridays and Saturdays.

'I hope you din't give him all the money in the vase,' said Gran. 'Charity begins at home.'

CHAPTER 9

I slammed the bike into the shed catching the bell against the wall. It tinkled feebly.

I didn't bother to cover it up and I didn't bother to put the tins up against the gaping hole. It could rain for all I cared.

I hated Deirdre Thirkettle, Rita Nelson and Annette Macro.

And they hated me.

They had it in for me. They knew I was a liar and I knew they knew.

My father had been an RAF pilot. Then an American Air Force officer. Then he was killed on a boat that he was captain of for the Royal Navy. And now I couldn't remember any more what the last thing was I'd said he'd been.

And they knew I couldn't remember. They'd cornered me in the playground. I'd taken my doughnut out the side entrance by the Needlework Room and gone to eat it near the bicycle sheds but somehow they'd found me. Miss Freeman had seen

130

me pass the Needlework Room. She had a long neck and a face pitted with old acne scars and an abundance of thick wiry hair that was always arranged in immaculate waves.

'Don't pluck your eyebrows, Jane,' she'd said to me quietly one day while I was struggling with tacking a facing into the collar of my much thumbed grubby seersucker blouse. I had more facing than collar and was bunching up the extra material trying to make it fit. I hated the blouse anyway; I'd been sewing it all term, and was sick of it. I couldn't imagine myself ever wearing it. I was bored with the garish pattern of its yellow and red check.

I was startled by the quietness of her voice. As if I'd let her in on a secret.

How did she know I'd found a pair of slightly rusty eyebrow tweezers in a drawer in the front bedroom? Doris's I supposed they must've been.

'Don't pluck your eyebrows, Jane,' she'd said again in a sad, pitying voice. I looked at her thick well-defined black ones. 'Princess Margaret doesn't pluck her eyebrows,' she'd concluded as she moved away in her lofty gliding manner.

My knee was sore from hockey; when I'd finally had a chance to get the ball I'd fallen on the frozen ground and grazed it badly.

I hated playing a back. I stood about for most of the game talking to the goalkeeper. I wanted to be a forward, that was where all the action was. But Miss Jenkins thought I was the sound responsible dependable type so I had to be a back. I hated Miss Jenkins for that, and I hated the way she walked through the shower room and flicked the backs of our legs with a towel as we stood naked under the gushing hot water.

I played centre-forward in netball; that was more fun. I felt as if my legs had wings sometimes, I could run so fast and jump so high. I hadn't been chosen for the team, though. They were a select band who met at school on Saturday mornings and went by bus to Framlingham or Beccles to play girls' schools there. I hadn't been chosen as form captain either.

It was Gillian Gilbert.

I had been sure I would be chosen. I saw myself as very popular apart from the Rita Nelson gang. I was sure everyone in IIID would vote for me and I'd been proved wrong.

I hadn't bothered to shut the back gate and it slammed against the Kerridges' fence as I walked towards the back door.

I pushed open the back door and it stuck against the doormat that Gran put up against the door to cut down the draught.

'Oh, for goodness' sake,' I said irritably. 'You can't open the door with that stupid mat in the way.'

I kicked it and banged the door behind me. The key fell out, jumping on the stone slabs that weren't covered with lino. Gran put the key down my back sometimes between my shoulder blades when I had a nose-bleed, and made me lie flat on the cold kitchen floor until it stopped. I hated that because I could see all the greasy bits of fluff under the oven that she couldn't reach when she cleaned, but I hated it even more when she folded up her flannel and put that on my forehead. It smelled unclean and musty even when she sprinkled it with 'Devon Violets'. It still smelled like it needed a good boil.

132

The kitchen was empty and the door to the living-room shut. The oven wasn't on, and there was nothing cooking under the grill.

'I'm starving,' I shouted crossly. 'We had horrible gristly mince for school dinner and I'm starving.' I threw my satchel on to the kitchen floor and topped it with a jumble of beret, scarf and mac.

'Jane, dear, is that you?' came Gran's voice from the living-room.

'Well, of course it's me. Who d'you think it is, old Nick?' I said, echoing one of her favourite phrases.

For a second I felt guilty; maybe she was feeling bad and that's why she was sitting down. I dismissed the thought as quickly as it had come. She sounded all right. I peered at my irritable face in the mirror over the draining-board. I didn't have to stand on Doug's stool any more to be able to see myself.

I squeezed a spot that had appeared between my eyebrows, probably from using those old eyebrow tweezers. It was difficult to squeeze it out properly. I didn't have any nails. My fingers were covered in ink. Stupid school making us use pens that had to be dipped in inkwells. Why couldn't we use fountain pens or Biros? We even had a handwriting lesson on Friday afternoons with Miss Sinclair. She had cropped hair, wore no make-up and was very strict. I thought the lesson a waste of time, and spent most of it writing silly jokes on pieces of paper and getting the girl in front to pass them to Annette or Rita to try to get them to laugh and like me. Maybe the spot was a sign I was getting my period. All the girls in IIID who had theirs already always complained that they got spots at the same

133

time too. I did so hope so. I didn't think I'd ever get my period just as I wasn't ever going to get any breasts. 'Tits' we called them. 'Breasts' was such an embarrassing word. Annette Macro had huge ones. She'd started Northgate wearing a bra. I envied her even though she frightened me and guiltily I thought her common.

I had thought mine were going to grow further down my chest where my top ribs stuck out more than my nipples. I was embarrassed now that I'd ever had such a stupid thought, but that was before these funny lumps had appeared behind my nipples which made them stick out just a little bit and hurt.

Now I had a sore red mess between my eyebrows.

I stuck my tongue out at myself and felt worse.

I pushed open the living-room door.

'I really am hungry—I'm not kidding, you know,' I said threateningly.

A blonde woman sat in the chair on the other side of the fireplace opposite Gran. The lids of her eyes were silvery and her lips were shiny rosy pink.

'This is Mrs Brady, dear,' said Gran in her posh voice.

'Hallo, Mrs Brady,' I said, turning scarlet, not knowing how much she'd heard of my disagreeable mood. She can't be really important, I thought, or Gran would have taken her into the front room, and I felt better.

'Mrs Brady wouldn't sit in the front,' said Gran as if she'd heard my thought. 'She said it was more comfortable in here. I don't know what she must think; I haven't cleaned it properly since Wednesday and the window-cleaner didn't come on Tuesday like he said he would. I don't know,' she continued flustered, 'you can't rely on anyone these days, can you? I say to myself, "If you want a job well done, Grace, do it yourself."'

Gran was twisting a crumpled handkerchief backwards and forwards between her fingers as she did when she was worried. She caught my glance and let it fall and started twiddling her thumbs.

'Hallo, Jane,' said Mrs Brady. She had a warm kind voice and held out her hand to me.

I took it clumsily and gripped it very hard. I'd read somewhere, in the *Girl Annual* I think, in an article by Alice Hooper-Beck called 'How to Make the Most of Yourself', that flaccid handshakes were an indication of a weak character.

She wore a pretty pale blue blouse that matched her eyelids with a softly tied bow at the neck. I'd seen pictures of the Queen in Gran's *Woman's Realm* wearing blouses like that. I could smell her perfume as I got near to her. It was flowery and sweet. She reminded me of my mother, although she wasn't at all like her really, but anyone who wore perfume did.

'Mrs Brady's from the child welfare people.'

I swallowed hard. How much had she heard? And how much would she tell Miss MacVean?

'How are you liking Northgate, Jane?'

'Oh, I love it.'

Could she hear the insincerity in my voice?

'And you've all the school uniform you need?'

Should I tell her how I wanted the expensive version of the V-neck pullover from Edwards like Lorna Mayon-White had and not the cheap one that Gran had made us buy?

'Oh, yes. Thank you.' Should I tell her I wanted my own hockey stick? Nearly everyone had their

135

own. It was galling to have to borrow one of the school's old battered ones and they were old-fashioned too. The new ones were a different design with a shorter thicker curve which made it easier to hit the ball.

'And how are school dinners?'

'Oh, delicious,' I said, warming to her, and to my story.

'And there's no problem about you paying, Mrs Chisnall, is there?'

'Oh, no, she has free school dinners,' said Gran.

Stupid, I thought, she knows, Gran, *she* arranged it—or Miss MacVean did.

'And what's your favourite lesson?'

'Oh, English,' I said quickly. 'I love it.'

'Who teaches you English?'

'Miss Taylor,' I said, lying. She taught the sixth-form girls A-level. I'd seen her walking round the quadrangle. She was small with short grey hair and blue eyes and wore soft grey tweed jackets with Viyella shirts in pale mauve. She reminded me of a moorland shrouded in mist. She always smiled at me which made me think she liked me. They said she was Miss Short's, the biology teacher's, girlfriend and although I thought that mysterious and intriguing, it was silly—Miss Short lived with Miss Carter. Everyone saw them leave school together each day in Miss Short's car.

'And what do you like most about English, dear?'

'Poetry,' I said, lying again. Delia Nicholas, who had buck teeth and lived in a big house on Rushmere Heath in a posh part of Ipswich near Lorna Mayon-White, was best at verse-speaking. So all the teachers thought. She always won verse-speaking prizes. But I thought them wrong.

136

Here was my chance to prove it.

'We've learnt "Crocus" by Coventry Patmore and "The Donkey" by G. K. Chesterton.'

I launched into them before anyone could stop me, my hands clasped behind my back.

'The crocus while the days are dark
Unfolds its saffron sheen
At April's touch the crudest bark
Discovers germs of green.

The sleep the seasons full of might
While rounds the peach and swells the sod
And in the night
The mushroom bursts the sod.'

My voice quavered on the last line for fear of giving it IIID's alternative reading.

I plunged into 'The Donkey' while Gran surreptitiously rubbed the dust from the ledges in between the slats of her chair with her fingers. Mrs Brady didn't shift her respectful gaze. I continued reciting to the flames that licked round the coal.

'With monstrous head and sickening cry
And ears like errant wings'

I had never been sure exactly what kind of animal an errant was.

'The devil's walking parody
Of all four-footed things.

The tattered outlaw of the earth
Of ancient crooked hill

137

Starve scourge deride me I am dumb
I keep my secret still.'

I had always identified very strongly with the donkey during this verse.

My voice rose in a passionate crescendo. Gran was now smoothing her handkerchief very carefully over one knee, and beginning, with great attentiveness, to fold it up into a neat square.

'Fools!'

I said pointedly in her direction.

'I also had my hour
One far fierce hour and sweet
There was a shout about my ears
And palms before my feet.'

'Well done,' said Mrs Brady, clapping. She seemed genuinely enthusiastic but the sound of one person clapping in that small room had a mocking air to it. 'She speaks beautifully, doesn't she, Mrs Chisnall?'

I wished fervently that Delia Nicholas could hear.

'Oh, yes,' said Gran. 'She's never been broad Suffolk. Would you like a top-up?'

'No, I really must be going. I only called in on my way home. I mustn't be long or my husband will be waiting for his tea.'

I thought Mrs Brady's husband very lucky, and wondered if she had any children.

'She's a real credit to you, Mrs Chisnall,' said Mrs Brady as I bent down to retrieve her teacup from the hearth. 'And she's writing regularly to her mother?'

'Oh, yes,' I said quickly.

'Oh, yes,' echoed Gran. 'Here, give that cup to me, it's one of my best.' The spoon rattled in the saucer as she disappeared into the kitchen.

'She's very proud of you, you know,' said Mrs Brady. 'You're the only one of her girls who passed to go to Northgate.'

I had to think hard about what she meant. Girls: there was only me. Well, of course there had been Pat and Doris but they'd gone now; they didn't count. Gladys and Edna were talked about sometimes but I couldn't remember either of them. I was the most important one. I always had been.

'Course you're different,' Gran often said. 'You're like my own. I've had you since a baby.'

'Well, there was Lillian,' Gran said, returning. 'Lillian went to Northgate.'

I'd forgotten Lillian.

I was surprised that Gran hadn't.

'And what happened to Lillian? Was she returned to her proper parents?'

I didn't like it that somehow the conversation had switched from me.

'Oh, I don't know, I'm sure,' said Gran. 'The Barnardo's people took her back. She wasn't with me long. Jane had mumps and Lillian kept kissing her so she wouldn't have to do her exams.'

Mrs Brady doesn't need to know *that*, Gran, I thought poisonously.

'She was a right handful too,' she said, pulling her cardigan down over her portly frame. 'I think her mother wanted her back or something, they never said. It suddenly suited her, I suppose.' Her voice trailed away.

'Well, goodbye, dear.' She smoothed the top of my head. I liked that and didn't want her to stop. 'Don't come to the front door. I'll let myself out.'

'Will you come again?' I ventured carefully, hoping her visits would exclude Miss MacVean's.

'Oh, yes, oh, yes,' said Mrs Brady, smiling. I smiled back.

'Jane, see Mrs Brady out the front.'

'Of course I will,' I said between bared teeth as I followed the wave of flowery perfume down the hall.

'Goodbye, Mrs Brady,' I said, offering my hand—she didn't notice it.

'You're a real credit to her, dear.'

With a wave and a click of the gate she was gone.

I slammed the front door and hopped and skipped all the way down the hall.

'Oh, isn't she nice. Isn't she *nice*, Gran.'

'Oh, well, I don't know about that.'

'Oh, come on, Gran, don't be so mean. She's better than Miss MacVean.'

'Well that's as maybe,' said Gran. 'But she says your mother wants you back.'

CHAPTER 10

'Well, if you want it back, you'll just have to sit there till you *do* eat it,' said Pat, straightening the cushion on the settee and disappearing into the kitchen. I stuck my tongue out at her retreating back. I stared at the thick lump of Yorkshire pudding on my plate. The gravy around it had set with a greasy film across its surface.

The four mouthfuls of pudding that I had managed to swallow had made me gag. It was dense and thick, not full of fluffy crispy holes like Gran's. The Brussels sprouts were soggy and overcooked and lay stranded amongst the bits of gristly meat.

It was all right for her. She ate anything. That was why she was so fat.

I hated her. But I hated her Yorkshire pudding even more.

'It wasn't yours to take,' I shouted after her. 'You shouldn't have taken it. It's *mine*.'

'You can have it back when you've eaten what's on your plate.'

'I don't like it and I'm not going to eat it.'

'Don't you get cheeky with me, young lady,' she said. 'You might get away with it with Mum but you won't get away with it with me.'

'She's not your mum,' I mumbled. I thought it silly she called Gran Mum. Gran wasn't her Mum. Doris called her Mum too. I wished that Doris was here. I could bear Pat if Doris was around but she hardly came to Ipswich any more.

'What did you say?' she shouted from the kitchen through the clatter of saucepans and running water.

'I said I want my watch back and I want it back *now*.' I kicked the leg of the table for emphasis.

'You'll get a smack across the back of your legs, my girl.'

'I'm not your girl and you're not allowed to hit me *so*.'

'You raise your voice like that and you'll make Mum feel even worse.'

'You're not allowed to hit me,' I said quietly, feeling tears stinging the back of my throat.

'You've got too big for your boots since you went to Northgate.'

You're only jealous you didn't pass, I thought viciously, that's why you've taken my watch.

'Auntie Louie sent me that watch because I passed to Northgate,' I boasted.

'Yes, Mum said they'd all come out of the woodwork if you passed. They didn't want to know about you before, did they?'

'Auntie Louie sent me fur gloves for my Christmas and birthday every year.'

'Yes, but she didn't want to know about looking after you, did she?'

'She couldn't, she works for Doctor Guthrie and she's got Auntie Edith to look after too. That's why my mother had to go into Barnardo's because Auntie Louie couldn't look after her either.'

That much I'd pieced together. Auntie Louie was my grandfather's sister, which made her my mother's aunt and my great-aunt, so my mother had said. But my mother had said so many things.

She'd taken me to Tunbridge Wells once to visit them. Auntie Louie cooked the chicken with runner beans which was delicious and Auntie Edith, who was very old with skin like thin wrinkled paper, called me 'Janie bach' and spoke English with a Welsh accent. But we'd had to come back early just as I was almost enjoying being with my mother alone because Lolo had got measles and Gran panicked about looking after her alone.

I pulled a piece of gristly meat roughly about with my fork and splattered gravy on the table-cloth. I moved my plate to hide it, and chewed and chewed.

'Why can't I take this on a tray and eat it in Gran's bedroom?' I said with my mouth full of cold, tough meat.

'Because she's sleeping now. Leave her in peace.'

She bustled back into the living-room and opened the cupboard door to put the loaf of bread and the bread-board back in their places. The draught of air she made rustled the Christmas cards that I'd strung up on a loop of string across the room.

The tinsel on the Christmas tree caught the light from the fire and glinted as it moved. It was going to be a beastly Christmas, I just knew it.

I propped my head in my hands, elbows splayed on either side of the plate and stared at it. I chewed some more.

'Shall I heat up some more gravy? It's worse when it's cold.'

'No, thanks,' I said sulkily.

'You're spoilt rotten,' she said. 'You get away with murder. She's far more lenient with you than she was with any of *us* and that's a fact.'

Well, it's because I'm special, I thought.

'And you cause her more trouble than all of us put together.'

She bent her huge frame almost double to pick up the coalscuttle, her dress revealing almost all her thighs. There were dimples in the fat behind her knees.

I stared in disgust.

'Well, you won't finish it staring into space like that. I'm not rushing up here from Chantry to cook a meal and see good food wasted. You'd better

143

hurry up. I've got some more Christmas shopping to do in town before I go home. I haven't got all day.'

She patted her recently permed hair and wiped the sweat from her forehead, gave me a piercing glance and took the coal-scuttle into the back yard. How could she be hot? It was freezing in the room. She was mean with the coal, didn't stoke the fire up like Gran did.

I threw the mouthful of meat into the fire where it spurted fat and made a sizzling noise. I prayed for it to be burnt up before she returned with the coal. It shrivelled into a greasy mark on one of the ledges of the grate.

Encouraged, I sliced up half the Yorkshire pudding and carried it hastily, dripping gravy, and hurled it on to the cinders, raked a few coals over it, wiped my hands on the corner of the table-cloth and returned to my seat just in time to hear her shut the coal-house door. She was singing. How could she sing when I felt so beastly?

'*Que sera sera*, whatever will be will be . . .'

Her voice was thin and high. Such a small sound from someone so big.

'*You'll* wake Gran up,' I said to cover my guilt as she came into the room.

'Have you managed any more? There's a good girl,' she said, looking at the diminished amount on my plate. I pulled a face at her as she picked out a few pieces of coal with her hands and put them on the fire. ''At cost a fortune this stuff; it don't burn well, but it spits a lot, don't it?'

'I'll take Gran her tablets—I'll do it,' I said rather louder than was necessary, hoping to cover the noise that the Yorkshire pudding might make

144

as the flames caught it.

I was up out of my chair into the kitchen before she could stop me.

I took the little brown tumbler, a teaspoon with a monk-like figure at the end of the handle, the vile-looking liquid in its medicine bottle with the cork stopper, the two boxes of pills and made a dash past Pat for the front room.

'You little sod,' she said, making a grab for me which I ducked successfully.

I burst into the front room which was stiflingly warm and smelled even more strongly of Dettol than usual. Gran was propped up almost in an upright sitting position against several pillows. Her face was flushed red, and her breath rattled as she breathed in and out.

'She's taken my watch away from me and she won't give it back till I eat her shitty dinner and the Yorkshire's thick and it makes me feel sick when I swallow it—'

'Who's that?' said Gran, jumping as she came to.

'It's me and I'm fed up.' The tears came at last. I put the medicines on the mantelpiece and threw myself at her breast.

'Don't cry, dear, oh, please don't cry, you'll make me feel bad.'

She moved with difficulty to accommodate my extra weight. I clung on to her and buried my face in the bedjacket that Pat had knitted for her. She smelled of Vick and Friar's Balsam.

'She won't give me my watch back,' I moaned.

'Of course she will, dear—'

'She won't . . .'

'Now don't go on so, there's a dear.'

'Pat,' she shouted as best she could. 'Pa-at.'

145

'Who's been telling tales out of school?' said Pat, her eyes narrowing when she saw me crouching by Gran's bed. 'You cry-baby.'

'You're spiteful and mean,' I said, not daring to raise my head. The words came out muffled.

'Now, don't you start,' said Gran, tapping me lightly on the head. 'Give the watch back, dear.'

'When she's eaten her dinner.'

'Oh, she's fussy about other people's cooking. It's my fault I do know, but give her the watch back; you'll make me feel bad.'

I clung on even tighter, shifting my face so that I could see Pat with one of my half-open eyes. She glared at me and I smiled.

'Oo, I do hate it when you girls don't get on,' said Gran sighing. 'Now wipe your eyes; you look a right sight. What'd the Reverend Blamey say if he came in and see you with your eyes all red and puffy like that?'

I blew hard into the handkerchief she offered me. It didn't smell very nice and it didn't look very clean, but I tried not to notice it.

'Here you are,' Pat said, thrusting the watch at me. 'You'll ruin her, you know, Mum.'

I stuck my tongue out at her.

'Now that's enough o' that,' said Gran. 'It's Christmas, peace on earth, goodwill toward men. Go and wash your face, Jane, there's a good girl.'

I sang my favourite Christmas song pretending to be Petula Clark, as I waited for the kettle to boil:

'I can see his pipe and topper
As they lie there in the snow
Where did my snowman
Where did my snowman

146

Where did my snowman go?'

I managed a few shuffle-hop-downs in between the chorus and the verse, making a lovely clattering noise on the kitchen floor.

> 'Only yesterday I met Jack Frost
> Who knew there'd be a storm
> So I lit a little bonfire just
> To keep my snowman warm . . .'

I wiped my hands carefully on the towel and strapped the little square-faced watch with its shiny black leather strap back on to my wrist, admired it from a distance.

Pat had gone when I got back. I smoothed Gran's forehead.

'Oh, your hands arc lovely and cold,' said Gran.

'I've just washed them in warm water,' I said, but she was right, her forehead was blazing.

'You will be all right, won't you, Gran?'

'Oh, of course I will.'

'You'll be up in time for Christmas, won't you?'

'Well, I don't know about that, dear.'

'Pat said we'll have to go and spend Christmas with her and Doug and the children because you won't be well enough to cook.'

'Well, I can't see that happening unless Doug came over and pick me up in the car—all these people with cars now; Russell's the same. I don't git to go out and about in a car. I wouldn't mind an outing. I'm sick o' the sight o' these four walls and that's a fact.' She coughed and heaved and started to cry.

'Oh, don't cry, Gran, please don't cry,' I said,

fighting back my own tears. 'You'll get better, I know you'll get better. I promise I won't be a trouble to you any more.'

I carefully undid the laces on my shoes, and climbed on to the bed and lay down beside her.

'You're not a trouble to me, dear. Who on earth told you that?'

'Pat.'

'Oh, she's got a temper on her, that one. She used to fight something terrible with Doris when you were small.'

'I know, I remember.'

'But you shouldn't tease her, you know. You can be a right little tinker when you set your mind to it.'

'I know,' I said and giggled. 'I'm a little bugger—oh, I shouldn't say that,' I said and laughed some more. 'I'm as daft as a brush,' I said, mimicking Al Read on the radio. 'I'm a right monkey.'

Gran began to chuckle.

'I'm more trouble than a barrel-load of monkeys,' I said, approximating a Northern accent.

'You're as much trouble as your mother,' said Gran. 'I always said she'd want you back when it suited her.'

'Oh, don't let's talk about her. It's Christmas . . .

> Rudolf the red nose reindeer
> Had a very shiny nose . . .'

I sang into her shoulder.

> 'And if you ever saw it
> You would even say it glows
> All of the other reindeer'

148

Gran joined in.

> 'Used to laugh and call him names
> They wouldn't let poor Rudolf
> Join in any reindeer games.'

She ran out of breath and began to cough a bit.

'Don't let's sing any more. Let's have a doze,' I said. I snuggled into her shoulder and she moved her arm to put it around me. 'And don't let's talk any more about my bloody mother.' What did she mean she wanted me back?

'Oh, Jane,' she muttered.

I put my thumb in my mouth, played for a while twiddling her warm ear in a half-hearted fashion, kissed her on her bristly chin, and pretended to sleep.

CHAPTER 11

'Well, you're not going out looking like that, I hope.' Gran stood in front of the mirror threading her fat pearlised hat-pin with some difficulty through the brown felt of her shapeless hat. It was the one I particularly disliked but I said nothing.

I sat hunched up in my Northgate mac by the diminishing fire.

'I don't care what I look like,' I mumbled. I knew my eyes were swollen and red and I hadn't bothered to comb my hair. I picked up the poker and let it fall against the hearth in a series of ever-diminishing taps. Like a drum stick. Gran didn't complain.

'Oh, c'mon, dear, make an effort—for my sake,' she added as an afterthought.

I raked the poker through the ash in the bottom rung of the grate carefully and systematically. Coals shifted and ash fell on the hearth.

'Oh, drat the thing,' said Gran. 'It'll have to do.' I looked up at her. Her hat was on lopsidedly but I didn't care about that either.

'I s'ppose I look like Old Mother Riley,' she added, sighing. 'Now, where's my pension book?'

'What on earth do you want that for?'

'Well, we'll need money for the tram. I've got a few coppers in the pension book envelope.'

'*She* can pay for that, can't she? *She* can afford it. They've both got new outfits; she said so. She can bloody well pay.'

'Oh, dear. I don't like to see you upset like this. It upsets me. You never played with the doll any more, did you really, dear?'

'You'll be upset even more going into town on a Saturday morning; the trams'll be packed and you know you get blood pressure in crowds.'

'Well, it's got to be gone through. Now where's my chiffon scarf?'

'It's in the sideboard drawer where it always is.'

I stood up, dropping the poker with a clatter into the hearth; as I did so an Easter card fell off the mantelpiece on to the fireside mat.

'I s'pose I'd better put the fireguard up, we don't want the place burned to a cinder while we're out.'

'I'll get it,' I said as she bent wheezing to pick up the card. It had a silvery grey cross on the front and a bunch of primroses in the corner. 'Christ is Risen' it said across the top. Outside all was grey and bare and bleak. It didn't feel much like spring.

'Oh, shit. Shit. Shit,' I said.

'Oh, don't say those words, dear. She'll hear you.'

'It was *my* doll. Pat and Doug gave it to me. If you hadn't put them both in the front room she'd never have found it. She could have slept in the little back bedroom, couldn't she?'

'Don't talk daft, you'll get me riled. That room's damp 'at hasn't been slept in for donkey's years.'

There was a painting of Toad standing beside his brightly painted caravan in a country lane on the wall. I'd stuck it there thinking Lolo would sleep in that room, and that my mother would see it. Susan Inskip had painted it. I'd blanked her name out and put my own in its place.

'Anyway, she's got no right to go rummaging through other people's drawers being a nosey parker. You're not supposed to give away things that don't belong to you.'

I started to cry again as I reached for the domed fireguard from under the draining-board. I noticed the paint was beginning to peel off and bubble on the outside wall. I tapped it with the corner of the fireguard and great flakes of old paint fell on to the kitchen flagstones, revealing white plaster wall, stained and eaten up by damp. I wanted to kick the wall. But most of all I wanted to kick my mother.

I could hear them moving about upstairs still. They took ages 'doing their toilet' as my mother said. It must be a direct translation from the French as Miss Reid said in French lessons. It didn't make much sense in English but I knew what she meant.

'Now spruce yourself up, dear, or Miss MacVean'll think I've been ill-treating you.'

'I hate her too.'

She bent to kiss me in her rough way. Footsteps sounded on the stairs.

'Sssh now, here they come.'

Lolo pushed open the living-room door hugging my doll closely to her. The pink lacy cardigan, dress and hat that Pat had knitted for her all those years ago looked new. She'd spent a long time in the wardrobe drawer; she hadn't had a chance to get soiled. I hadn't liked cuddling her—her body was hard and plastic and her splayed fingers stuck into my bony chest—but all the same she was mine. Had been mine.

Lolo was cuddling her and the doll (I couldn't even remember the name I'd given her) looked as if she was cuddling Lolo back.

'Mommy says,' she said in her cute American accent which I hated because I envied it so much, 'Mommy says . . .' She paused seeing me glaring at her.

'You'd better get your coat on,' I said sharply. 'We're going soon and *you*'ve got to go round to the Haywards.' I tried to make it sound like a punishment. The Haywards loved her. She was different. Unlike anyone they'd ever seen. They called her Lulu too. Only my mother didn't correct them, I'd noticed.

'Go on, get out of here. Get your bloody coat,' I stamped my foot towards her. She took fright and disappeared.

'Oh, Jane, you'll get your mother on to you now.'

'Oh, shit,' I said again. 'I won't be a minute, Gran. Lock the back door and don't forget to check you've got the front door key and your other glasses in your bag. I won't be a minute.'

I followed Lolo up the stairs. She was dragging my doll by one hand so that her legs clunked and caught on every step. She closed her eyes as she fell into each stair and then opened them again as she was banged over the next one. She was looking at me disapprovingly, I thought. Lolo ran across the landing. I caught her by the shoulder and held her back till I could open the front bedroom door before her.

'I've come up to get Lolo's coat,' I said.

'That's kind of you, Janie darling. You are funny, it's hanging in the hall where I always put it.'

She spat into a little black box, rubbed a small brush across the contents and applied the brush to her eyelashes. I stood mesmerised.

'Well, you haven't made much of an effort, *chérie*, have you?' she said, glancing at me sideways through the mirror.

I unknotted the belt of my mac and threaded it through the buckle properly.

'Lolo, darling, *ton bébé, ton bébé*,' she said at Lolo. She was holding the doll by the edge of her lace dress; the rest of the doll swung slowly, just skimming the lino. 'You don't want her to get all dirty on the floor, *chérie*, do you? Janie's been so kind to give her to you. She loved her so much, that's why she cried—but she's a big girl now; she doesn't need dolls any more.'

I bent down and brushed the doll's dress free of dust, buttoned up her cardigan properly and handed her back to Lolo, forcing a smile.

'There you go,' I said. 'There's your dolly.' The words came out thin and tight so I smiled again— Lolo's eyes were rounder and larger than ever. She said nothing. I wanted to kick her too.

'Go and ask Nana to get your coat off the peg in the hall,' said my mother, putting a comb through her hair. '*Va, chérie, va tout de suite.*'

'*Maman, je ne—*'

'*Va quand je te le dis*—go on, sweetie, I want to talk to Janie for a minute.'

She went reluctantly, casting me a withering glance. My mother picked up a pretty glass bottle with a tube and a rubber bulb attached to it, squeezed the bulb several times holding the bottle near her neck.

'*Merde,*' she said, 'this stuff evaporates so fast in the heat. I filled it up before Papa and I went to Benghazi that weekend and now it's empty. *Mon dieu.*'

She took a tall bottle with a glass stopper from the leather vanity case, as she called it. It matched the two suitcases she and Lolo had brought. She unscrewed the tube from the smaller bottle and filled it up with the golden liquid. The room was filled with that special smell.

'Now, Janie darling, let's stop all this nonsense, shall we?'

I stared at my scuffed shoes and felt hot.

'I don't know what Papa would say if he knew about all this trouble.'

Half of me didn't care. The other half was terrified.

'You know I love you, don't you?'

'Yes,' I mumbled. It was easier to say to her back.

I prayed that she wouldn't ask if I loved her. I didn't. I never had. That must be wrong. The Bible said so.

She continued, screwing the top back on to the

154

tall bottle, and rearranging it amongst the others on the chest of drawers, 'And you'll love it, you know you will, won't you?'

'Yes,' even fainter.

'After all, I am your mother. Your place is with me. Isn't it?'

Why wouldn't the words come? Why couldn't I stop this?

'Yes,' I managed to squeeze out from a parched throat. Now I was wholly terrified.

'You were my first-born,' she said, turning to look at me. 'Don't stare at the floor, Janie bach, when I'm talking to you.'

I was embarrassed. First-born was such an odd word. All the first-born were killed in the Bible; somebody's curse, I couldn't remember whose . . .

'And you know I couldn't take you with me when you were born. I just couldn't. Nana wouldn't let me. I wanted to, Janie, I wanted to, believe me.'

I wanted to but couldn't.

'You'll have such a lovely time. Everyone's looking forward to meeting you, my big grown-up daughter,' she said smiling, stroking my uncombed hair. She licked her fingers and tried again. I knew the short hair stood up on my crown but I was shocked by the intimacy of her gesture. Gran licked her handkerchief and wiped my face when it was dirty but I could dodge that now. I didn't move.

'We've wanted you to come and live with us for such a long time but it just wasn't possible. Papa was badly wounded after the war; he only got the job because of his war record.

'The house in Le Touquet was so small it was hardly big enough for the three of us—we couldn't bring you over then.

155

'Then in Casablanca we both worked at the base. I had to work at the PX.' I didn't know what all these strange words meant but I kept my gaze resolutely on her face. 'We had nothing, nothing. It was my money that bought the furniture, the curtains . . .

'It's only since we've been in Tripoli that we've had a proper home. It's such a sweet little villa— we've had a room built specially for you; you'll love it, I just know you'll love it and swimming in the Mediterranean is so blue and warm. You *can* swim, can't you?'

'Yes. I learned at Pipers Vale.'

'Oh, Pipers Vale!' she said disparagingly.

I hated the open-air pool at Pipers Vale too. It had green scum on the bottom. Boys pushed girls in and the water was always freezing. But suddenly I felt protective about it, although I wondered what it would be like to swim in water that was blue and warm.

'You can walk to the beach, or go into town to the cinema or a café. Papa'll drop us off on his way to the bureau in his new car.' The Haywards had a bureau in their front room.

A car, I thought, and gulped.

'It'll be so good for you. You can learn French, and you won't get asthma in Tripoli, I'm sure. It's only damp here which gives you asthma, I'm sure; that, and sleepin' in Nana's bed. That's not good for you, Janie darling, d'you know that?'

'Yes,' I mumbled again, shocked that I could betray Gran so easily.

'So that's all settled then.'

She turned and squirted the perfume against her neck.

'Would you like some?'

'Yes, please,' I said.

The liquid felt cold against my neck, but I loved being enveloped by that musky, heady aura.

She bent to kiss me on both cheeks. I didn't move. There was a bright pink label on the bottle. I could read the label over her shoulder. 'Shocking by Schiaparelli' it said.

'I'm so happy that's all settled, darling—Nana understands, you know. Blood is much thicker than water.'

That sounded like one of Gran's phrases. Odd coming from her red lips.

'Now, you run along. I'll be down in a minute. Don't mention our little chat to Nana, we'll talk about it with Miss MacVean. If she's a mother she'll understand.'

Silly, I thought, how could she be a mother? She's a *Miss*. But then my mother had been a Miss . . . I went down the stairs slowly, my mind a whirl of blue seas and shiny cars, but my spirits as heavy as my legs.

I pushed open the living-room door. Gran was stooping to button up Lolo's coat, the doll dragging on the floor again.

'Nana's going to make me ootchi pudding and I'll go when Mommy goes,' she said defensively and rushed past me.

'Ootchi pudding?' I sneered.

I shut the door.

'Yorkshire. I said I'd make her a Yorkshire when we get back.'

I threw myself at Gran and hugged her tight, burying my face in her neck with that familiar smell and went on hugging her, till she stopped resisting and hugged me back.

'What's all this about, then?' she said after she'd kissed me. 'Do you want to borrow something?'

* * *

'I'll sit with Nana,' said my mother. 'You sit in that seat in front.'

I wanted to sit with Gran. I wanted my mother to feel the odd one out. She certainly looked it. Her face was tanned and made-up more than any other woman on the bus. Her eyelids were as black as her eyes, her lips red and gold jewellery dangled from both her wrists and round her neck. Her hair was silvery blue in the front where it lay in jagged wisps like a little cap fringing her forehead. Lolo had the same haircut. From the crown of her head to the nape, it grew darker. The same colour as mine. She looked far too glamorous to be on a tram. Most of the other women on the bus had headscarves on. The woman in front of me had metal curlers poking out of the bottom of hers. They all had shopping bags. My mother had a bag that looked like crocodile skin with a shiny gold clasp that matched her high-heeled shoes. Secretly I was proud she looked the best, and ashamed I didn't look good enough to be her daughter. That made me feel I'd betrayed Gran. I stared at the floor. My mother's legs were stretched out under my seat.

'I don't know how she manage to walk in them damn things,' Gran had said earlier. 'She'll come a cropper one of these days, especially on those paving stones at the top of the road. I don't know what we pay rates for. Some old dear'll go ass over head one of these days, then they'll wish they'd taken them up.'

I rolled my tram ticket up into a tight little tube and blew down it, making small misty patches against the window.

'Don't do that, Janie darling,' said my mother from behind. 'Sit up properly.'

I squeezed the ticket into a ball in the palm of my hand, digging my fingers into it, destroying it. Then hoped an inspector wouldn't get on to check the tickets.

'They've got rid of the old trolley buses, then,' said my mother.

If you'd been here more often you'd have known that, I thought murderously.

'Oh, trolley buses in't run for years,' said Gran.

'Oh, and there's Holywells Park. I used to get into such scrapes there, didn't I?' She laughed her throaty laugh. Gran said nothing.

'Oh, it's so green, so lovely and green. Look at all those beautiful trees. Tripoli's all sand, Janie. We could do with some of your English rain.'

Hardly anyone was talking on the bus. She could be heard quite clearly. I wished she'd lower her voice.

'My goodness, I'd forgotten how steep Bishop's Hill is,' she said as the bus began its descent. 'They're nice houses, aren't they?' she said, tapping me on the shoulder and pointing to the big houses that stood in their own grounds on the right of the hill. 'I wouldn't mind living in one of those.'

' 'At'd cost a pretty penny,' said Gran taciturnly.

'I keep telling Papa I'm sick of all this travelling and moving house. I'd love to settle somewhere green and cool.'

Please, God, don't, don't, don't let her come and

159

live in England. I prayed with all my might. Things are bad enough as they are. I'd done a lot of praying lately and so far not much of it had been answered, but I wasn't surprised. God didn't like liars.

'My goodness, there's the Fore Street swimming baths.'

How I wished she'd stop talking. We all knew what they were. We lived here.

'They've poshed this place up, haven't they?'

''At was for the Queen's visit last year,' said Gran.

'Oh, and Sneezums is still there. Do you remember the son, what *was* his name, Nana?'

I pricked up my ears.

'I nearly got engaged to him,' she laughed, 'but then I went out with old Whatsit's son in the Nacton Road.'

So what Gran had told me all along was true: she couldn't remember, there had been so many.

'Major's Corner,' said my mother even louder. I shrank inside my Northgate mac.

'I don't suppose old Sarony still runs that studio, does he?'

'Goodness gracious, no,' said Gran. 'He gave that up ages ago. It's a camera shop now, isn't it? Can you see?'

There was a photograph in the tin in the wardrobe drawer of me aged about four with my arm half-heartedly round a woman with long dark hair.

'Who's this?' I'd asked Gran.

'Well, it's you and your mother, daft,' she'd said only half-interested. 'That was when she came over the first time to see you, I think. I can't remember now.'

'Why does it say "Sarony" on the back?'

'Well, that was the man who took the picture, silly. Sarony, one of your mother's boyfriends, I 'spect,' she'd added dismissively.

It was odd looking at my face all those years ago. It seemed to me the little girl didn't know who the woman was.

'You were such a good girl that afternoon,' my mother said, interrupting my thoughts. 'You behaved like a perfect angel. Sarony really took to you.'

I could remember *that* name. He sounded like a foreign magician in a variety show with dark slicked-back hair. I'd seen men like him at the Hippodrome. We'd only been once or twice on a Saturday night, Gran and I. It cost one and threepence for her and ninepence for me. I loved the sound of the orchestra tuning up and the way the red velvet curtains were scooped up by their thick gold cords to the side as the lights dimmed.

'He thought you were a lovely little girl. You didn't cry even when the lights flashed.'

I was sure I hadn't liked him, and I didn't like having my picture taken even now.

'You sat on my knee so calmly . . .'

'They've turned the British Legion into a dance hall now,' said Gran behind me. 'There's a real rough crowd go there on a Saturday night now by all accounts. Russell say he don't like stopping at that garage opposite after dark, not when there's a crowd of them hanging about on the pavement. Ipswich in't what it used to be; 'at's gone right downhill. Old Nana'd turn in her grave if she saw it now.'

161

'Dear old Russell,' said my mother. 'I hope he pops in before I go back—he used to be such a naughty boy . . . tickling us girls.' She paused over the word tickling which somehow made it mean something else.

I was shocked. I couldn't imagine big, burly, red-faced Russell, Stebby's son, who worked in a garage on the Felixstowe Road and called in for dinner sometimes, as a naughty boy, but I could imagine my mother giggling as he tickled her.

'I'm so sorry I didn't see Stebby, his mama, before she died. Did she have those pekinese dogs till the end?'

'Yes, she did,' said Gran roughly. 'I miss her something dreadful. She were one of my oldest friends but I don't miss them damn dogs. Yapping all the time, leaving their fur everywhere. Her house always smelled of dogs.'

I sank even deeper into my mac and breathed deeply, burying my face into my clasped shoulders so I could smell the perfume better.

*   *   *

'Oh, do sit up, Jane,' said Gran sharply. The room was stuffy and hot. Her face was crimson.

I'd been staring at the door trying to make out the backwards lettering that was visible through mottled glass. Child Welfare Department Suffolk County Council, it said.

'You've been miles away. Miss MacVean just asked you a question.'

'What?' I said.

'Don't say "what", say "pardon".'

'Pardon?'

162

'I don't know what you must think about the way I've brought her up, I'm sure.'

'You've been a splendid foster mother, Mrs Chisnall. Please don't be upset, this is a difficult time for you all. But I'm sure Mrs Lapotaire . . .' She had difficulty saying the name. I was pleased to see her stumble over something. '. . . Mrs Lapotaire would be the first to acknowledge all you've done for Jane.'

Why was she talking about Gran in the past tense?

'It just wasn't possible,' said my mother, 'for us to have her before, you see.'

'No, quite,' said Miss MacVean. 'The situation is slightly more difficult now,' Miss MacVean went on.

'Oh, dear, oh, dear,' Gran sighed.

'No, it's nothing to worry about, Mrs Chisnall, but I have spoken to my colleagues and especially Mrs Brady, who's been visiting Jane lately,' she explained to my mother. Why did my mother need to know? She hadn't bothered before. 'And we all feel very strongly'—her voice was thin and pinched; she sounded like the Queen on the wireless on Christmas Day—'that considering Jane has begun her secondary education at Northgate Grammar School, it would be a pity to move her.'

I couldn't believe my ears. I sat up slightly in the chair.

'Oh,' said Gran, rubbing her nose with her handkerchief, looking surprised. Her cheeks had a worrying purple tinge to them just as they did before she had a blackout.

'Now what do you think, Jane?'

'Pardon?' I said.

'What do you want?'

I took a deep breath, as much as my tight chest would allow, and said as bravely as I could to the rubber stamp lying on the desk, 'I want to stay at Northgate.'

There was silence in the room.

'Well, that's a pity,' said my mother, tapping the ash from her cigarette carefully into an ashtray. Turning to look at me. 'But you want to come, Janie darling, you said so.'

I avoided her gaze. Inside I was screaming. You're not my mother. Why did you come here? We were all right before you came. You didn't want me then. Why do you want me now? But the voice in my head sounded like Gran's.

'Well, yes,' said Miss MacVean, breaking another moment of quiet, 'that's how it should be, all right and proper. You've put your education first—very sensible.'

Inside I shouted again. It's Gran. I want to stay with Gran. Images of blue seas and shiny cars became fainter.

'However,' said Miss MacVean, picking at her glasses from where they hung against her blouse on their chain, and putting them on her sharp powdery nose, 'we do have a policy in this department to return children to their rightful parents whenever possible.'

Gran picked at her tweed coat and rearranged one flap of it carefully over the other. I thought I saw a tear glint behind her glasses . . .

'So perhaps,' she continued, 'we could come to some sort of compromise?'

She peered over the top of her glasses first at my mother then at Gran. I could see Gran hadn't

164

understood what compromise meant.

'I only want what's best for Jane,' she muttered thickly.

'Well, of course, we *all* do,' said Miss MacVean. 'Jane's welfare is what matters.'

Somewhere amongst the jumble of raging feelings a trickle of my own importance began to grow. I wished I weren't feeling so wretched; on another occasion I might just have enjoyed all this attention.

'You did say, Mrs Lapotaire, that your husband is prepared to finance Jane now.'

'To a certain extent, we do have another daughter.'

'Yes, of course. So shall we say, Mrs Lapotaire, that a happy compromise would be for Jane to continue to be fostered by Mrs Chisnall but for her to go home to you during the school holidays?'

*   *   *

'She won't let you come back, you'll see; not *now*. Especially if he's sending you money; mind you, that'll be the day. I'll believe it when I see it—but they'll think they own you body and soul now.' She wiped her eyes, and sipped the tea that had spilled, from her saucer. We'd had this conversation so many times since my mother, Lolo and my doll had left.

'Gran, I keep telling you. I'm not going. I don't want to go,' I lied.

'Miss MacVean said you had to.'

'Oh, sod Miss MacVean. I'm staying with you. I said that I wanted to stay with you. You're my Mum. You've looked after me—'

'When she didn't want you,' Gran interrupted. 'No one seems to remember all these years that I brought you up on my pension—all that talk about cars and houseboys make me sick. Who does she think she is? All that muck on her face and all that jewellery. She were always like that were Louie. Always thought she were better than the rest of us and she's nobody, you know. She treat me like dirt—traipsin' in and out o' here like it's a hotel. I s'pose she think my house in't good enough for you now that you're at Northgate. She should 'a thought o' that before she went gallivantin' off to France or wherever she went with that there Lapotaire or whatever his name is—when you were born. She in't a Lapotaire—I bet he in't even married her. You mark my words. She was glad enough to have me *then*; if it hadn't been for me, you'd 'a been in a home. She forget that. She only remember what suits her, like the rest o' them . . .' and a fresh crop of tears ran down her flushed cheeks.

'Oh, don't cry any more, Gran. Please don't cry, you'll make me cry.'

'Oh, we're a right pair.' She blew her nose loudly.

'I'll make you another cup of tea, shall I? Shall I put a drop of brandy in it?'

'Brandy,' she said scornfully. 'I don't want any brandy in my tea at this time o' day. Just put milk in it. There's no need to go mad. If you say you in't a goin' I'll just have to take your word for it.'

CHAPTER 12

I awoke feeling dizzy, my thumb in my mouth; and removed it swiftly before anyone saw. My head felt unusually light, my thumb was wrinkled from hours of sucking and my hands were sticky from the peaches they'd given us in what they'd called the transit lounge at Malta airport. There had been four of them in a little cellophane wrapper with a twist of sweets—'candy' I'd heard a child call them—and some strange green-looking biscuits coated with sugar that tasted of almond. Gran said 'armond' but the girl from first class with the loud voice and the blue velour hat with the striped band pronounced the 'l'. She'd walked through the cabin of the plane earlier, just after take-off, when, still thrilled by my view of the propellers on the wings whirring increasingly faster till they blurred, and excited by the thrust of the plane as it had gathered speed along the tarmac, her curt, 'You may come and visit us in the first class' to some children nearby hadn't managed to dampen my spirits. I didn't know there was a first class. I was so pleased with being on a plane at all. Although I noticed that none of the children around me seemed excited. Most of them looked bored, or were hidden behind copies of *The Eagle* or *Girl*. Anyway, I didn't like her or her brother, who trailed behind her. They talked posh. They made me feel poor, and I hadn't even got used to the idea of being well-off.

The buzzing sound changed its pitch in time with the falling feeling in my stomach and I realised the plane was dipping lower.

I could see scattered lights way below me, and between them vast expanses of darkness. There couldn't be many towns down there. Perhaps we'd have a long way to go between the airport and 'home'. The word made my stomach dip too. I swallowed hard.

Lower we swooped, till I could see small square white buildings with flat tops and steps carved out of the walls leading up to the roofs. Small dancing areas of light confused me at first, till dipping lower I realised they were fires lit on the ground; dark figures in long robes moved about them amongst spiky silhouettes cast by the flames. Palm trees. I'd not seen a real one except in Dartmouth when we'd camped in a school with the Girls Life Brigade and it had been a shabby dusty thing windblown and battered by bad summers.

My stomach lurched once more. I swallowed hard again and the buzzing in my ears grew louder. The plane settled into a steady downward glide but my stomach danced more than ever.

What would 'they' be like? I couldn't really remember. What would she be like? She was seven now, not a baby any more, my half-sister. Funny how I hung on to the half. 'We don't have the same father,' I said mechanically to put paid to any further questioning if anyone asked. It stopped me asking questions too, for a while, and something deep in me was pleased about that.

After a long wait in a crocodile in the gangway while dark men with toothbrush moustaches checked the plane, and bags and tennis racquets were put down then picked up, catching the knees and the ribs of the people in front and behind, we moved slowly forward till it was my turn to say goodbye to the immaculate hostesses with their silvery blue eyeshadow and shiny pink lips—not a hair out of place. The pleats in my skirt were all crushed and there were splodges of orange squash on my white blouse. I thought the stewardesses' smartness was impressive but they made me feel uncomfortable. I'd doused myself liberally with the free eau de Cologne in the toilet and it had left stains on the cuffs of my blouse which stuck out from under my crumpled jacket. The girl in front of me had a smart navy-blue holdall which matched her school skirt. I moved the brown carrier bag, which contained tea and marmalade that my mother had requested in a letter to Gran, to the side of me, so that it was less obvious that it was mine. My hand was clammy, the string handles cut my palm. I put it down, wiped my hand on my skirt and moved towards the blackness that was framed by the doorway of the plane.

The air hit me in a blast of muskiness, sand and heat. I stopped, shocked by how difficult it was to breathe. It was like the kitchen in Levington Road after we'd had a bath, when the copper had been alight all day and Gran had been cooking. Only the kitchen cooled down. As I concentrated on not missing my footing on the metal stairs I realised that the heat was constant. My body didn't seem to do what I wanted it to do, my knees seemed to have no connection to my feet, I could only feel their twitching—I couldn't feel what I was standing on. The carrier bag banged against the metal sides of the steps that had been pushed up to the door of the plane. And while I tried not to worry about having broken the marmalade my eyes and ears

169

were assailed with so many strange sights and sounds that I stopped for a second and the boy behind walked into me.

My ears hadn't completely shed the droning of the plane but I could distinguish a constant chirp from somewhere in the blackness. There were trees in the distance edging the vast expanse of ground on which we'd landed. Small puffs of sand were pushed up along the ground by a breeze I could see but couldn't feel.

A constant stream of guttural shouts came from a group of men who were darting about near the underbody of the plane throwing suitcases and bags to each other. They wore long robes, striped like deck-chair material, and shoes with the backs broken flat by their cracked dried heels, which caught and puffed up the dust as they moved. The square red hats on their heads made them look like Tommy Trinder whose picture I'd seen once in the *Daily Mirror*.

The sand in the air made my face feel gritty, I was uncomfortably hot and itchy where my vest rubbed under my arms. How cross I'd been that Gran had made me wear it. I'd fought not to.

'Don't cast a clout till May is out.'

'But it's *July*—and it's hot over there.'

'I don't care. A change of climate and you'll go down with one of your bronchial attacks and then your mother'll say I don't look after you properly. You wear it, there's a dear.'

I'd given in, untypically. It seemed a small exchange for her letting me go away at all.

We'd only been away from Ipswich twice. Once to Beccles to stay with 'Auntie' Bibby and 'Uncle' Reg and their children Pauline and Peter. I hadn't

170

noticed Peter as he was only six or seven, but Pauline was older than I, and was at grammar school too. She was quiet and clever and frightened me rather. I didn't like her much after Auntie Bibby had given me one of Pauline's dresses: shocking pink with large white dots all over it. It had a square neck and a long flared skirt. I hated it. It was too noticeable.

Auntie Bibby's father 'Uncle' John, who had thick white hair and a matching moustache, and wore baggy brown tweed trousers and tortoiseshell glasses, took me to his allotment down by the river, 'The Broads' he called it, and on one never-to-be-forgotten occasion pushed me back to his house in a street called Northgate, like my school, in his wheelbarrow, which made me laugh till my eyes watered and my middle ached. Gran said they were Quakers. Like the picture on the porridge box, I thought. His wife, 'Auntie' Nell, cooked lemon curd and jam tarts in an oven built of brick, which were made of the most meltingly delicious pastry I had ever tasted.

When Uncle John wasn't caretaking the 'Friends Meeting House'—which was a bare room with wooden floorboards, a circle of plain wooden chairs and not much else. 'They wait for the spirit to move them,' Gran had whispered to me conspiratorially, confusing me utterly—he sat in his chair by the fire, sucking his empty pipe and reading a dictionary. I'd thought it odd that such an old man should be still bothering to learn, but he had twinkly eyes and Auntie Nell addressed every sentence to him starting with a 'John, dear'. I liked that. I liked them, but I didn't know why I had to call them Uncle and Aunt. They weren't Gran's brother or sister. She'd explained once, but it sounded far too complicated, something about second cousins once removed, so I hadn't bothered to listen.

We'd gone to Wolverhampton once, too, to some other 'cousins'. To visit 'Uncle Stan' and 'Auntie Muriel' who were caretakers of the Darlington Road Methodist Chapel. They had three grown-up children, Betty, Margaret and Keith. 'Betty's an SRN,' Gran said proudly. She was married to Brownie. 'Brownie was in the Navy, but before that he was at Barnardo's with your mother.' I couldn't make sense of it—perhaps Brownie didn't like my mother either, as he'd never mentioned her when we'd gone to tea at their house on a Sunday during the time they'd lived in Ipswich. Brownie had dark hair like Doug, and called me 'pet' and Betty made a fuss of me, but I never asked him how he knew my mother. I didn't like to mention her in front of Gran.

I saw Gran standing at the front door of 85, wiping her eyes on her apron as the taxi waited to take me and Bert and Doris past Fowlers' corner towards the Ipswich station. Her words echoed again in my head: 'You won't want to come back to an old woman like me once you've been with them. You mark my words—strikes me they won't let you come back. Now you're at Northgate, now that you'll be able to get a good job and earn good money—they won't let you come back, you'll see!'

It hadn't seemed fair to get cross with this silly logic so I'd hugged her goodbye with a degree more zeal in my grasp than could be deemed affectionate, and I'd slid my face down her sleeve as we'd loosened our embrace, turning my head away from her so she'd think I hadn't seen the water in her eyes.

I pushed Gran out of my mind, and scratched the back of my neck where my jacket collar had caught the dampness of my skin. Better get angry than sad. Fancy her making me wear a vest. For a holiday in Africa! I'd tell her I wouldn't wear one next time. Next time. Would they let me go? My stomach dipped another few feet and I dropped my Northgate mac into the dust. I burned at my clumsiness and felt hotter still. Maybe they'd seen? I dusted it down half-heartedly, and quickened my pace to catch up with the tired, straggly line from the plane that was heading into the low terminal building in front of me. There was a crowd of people behind some gates waving and calling names. Supposing they weren't there? What would I do then? Where would I go? PO Box 573, CTPL Tripoli, Libya, wasn't an address, was it? And that's what I'd scrawled on the crinkly thin airmail letters for a while now. Letters that I'd written in bad grace.

'Mummy, there's Mummy.' Shouts and yells came from behind me. The girl and her brother waved their tennis racquets in the air and charged ahead of me screaming and shouting. Only sixth formers played tennis at Northgate. Somewhere from behind the bars of the gate between the legs of the people a dog charged about barking its greeting. More children behind me waved. Should I wave too? I wasn't really sure what they looked like, now. How long ago was it that I'd received some photographs in a letter? I didn't want Gran to think I was interested so I'd shoved them into the sideboard drawer amongst her old chiffon scarves, odd knitting needles, and single gloves, without paying much attention to them. I was beginning to wish I had.

I looked away from the crowds. I felt shy that they might be watching me without my knowing. I redoubled my concentration on keeping my legs moving in a straight line with my feet.

The hall that was labelled '*Douane*' was ablaze with light and thronging with people pushing and shoving in every direction. I held on tightly to my brand-new passport—the man in the glass cubicle had looked through it backwards, but everything seemed to be in order; he took out the white card that I'd filled in with shaky writing after my meal on the plane, leaning on the little table that had pulled out neatly from the seat in front of me. 'Natty', Pat would have called it. 'Reasons for visit', it had asked at the bottom and after a moment of hesitation I'd put the unfamiliar words, 'Holiday with family'.

The guttural noises around me grew louder now, blond crewcuts punctuated the sea of red hats and black greased-back hair above me. When I looked down I could see sun-tanned legs in shorts, and long white knee-socks that surprised me. I smiled. No one wore long white knee-socks with shorts in Ipswich. Big bladed fans that hung in the ceiling above me moved slowly round, though I couldn't feel the air they were stirring up. Some of them seemed as if they would fall off their metal poles on to the mass of seething people below as they bumped round and round in their lazy uneven fashion.

There were posters stuck to the badly painted walls. Pictures of sandy beaches and palm trees

174

with undecipherable writing underneath that I supposed was Libyan. Underneath that was something that I recognised from IIID lessons to be French and under that was something I supposed to be Italian as it was all 'i's and 'ia's.

Under one picture of a building, its doorways edged in brightly coloured mosaic and topped with a huge gold dome, it said 'King Idris Palace Tripoli'. So they had a king called Idris; that was why it was Idris airport. The only Idris I knew was Idris ginger beer that the Corona man sold.

Behind the milling arms and legs I glimpsed a row of suitcases on the long benches that lined the room. They were being opened and inspected by more men in red hats. Their sweaty musty smells hung in the air tinged with a sharpness I couldn't recognise. What was it? Curry? I didn't know; we didn't have curry often enough for school dinners for me to recognise it. Customs men. They were trouble. It said so in books. I wondered what the French was for 'Have you anything to declare?' Would I have trouble with the marmalade? Would they open my suitcase, or rather Bert and Doris's? I'd never get it shut again. It was an old battered thing that I didn't like much, but Gran and I didn't have one and anyway where was it? I didn't know quite what I was supposed to do. I stood as still as I could, feeling panic rising and thumping against my ribs; unsteady on my feet as I was, the seething crowd elbowed me this way and that, as people pushed past me struggling with bags, shouting incomprehensible words in languages I didn't understand.

'BOAC children over here, over here,' came emphatic directions in English from somewhere in

175

front of me. I could see through a gap in the crowd most of the children lined up against a bench claiming their suitcases.

I elbowed my way through to the blessed oasis of faces I half-recognised protected by the sentinels in their smart navy-blue uniforms.

A man with his hands resting on my suitcase muttered something incomprehensible at me. I stared dumbly at his walnut-coloured face with its black moustache. Another phrase rattled out from between his yellow teeth. I caught the word *'valise'*. I wished I'd paid more attention to Miss Reid in IIID's French lessons.

'Yes, it's my case,' I answered, the words sticking in my dry mouth. I was thirsty and the neck of my blouse was now damp too . . .

With a piece of chalk he made a squiggle on the canvas and waved me away. I half-expected him to call me back to check the contents of my carrier bag but no. I heaved the suitcase off the bench, catching my legs as I did so, and stumbled uneasily through the crowd out of the only exit in the room.

'Janie, Janie darling,' came from somewhere amongst the babble of voices. Out of the mass of strangers stepped a woman whose close-cropped silver hair, bright red lips, deeply sun-tanned face, seemed familiar.

'Janie, *chérie*.' Arms went round me in such a way I found it difficult to hang on to my belongings. I was enveloped briefly in that heady musky smell once again. Only she called me 'darling'. I'd never heard the word before she used it, except when Clark Gable said it to Vivien Leigh in *Gone With the Wind*. It was the first grown-up film I'd seen. Gran had laughed incomprehensibly when the

176

black maid in the film suggested putting a light under the bed of a woman in childbirth. Why did my mind keep flicking back to Gran? I couldn't understand that either. Anyway 'darling' felt good and glamorous.

'Here's Lolo,' she said, standing back to reveal a not so small girl with cropped brown hair, the same vaguely familiar suntanned face and wearing a tartan pleated skirt with a white T-shirt edged in tartan that matched. I hated my green suit from the haberdashers in Felixstowe Road more than ever. She said something to the girl in French. She came forward unwillingly and gave me an indifferent kiss on one cheek. I moved to offer the tea and marmalade and our heads heavily collided as I realised she had planned to kiss me on the other cheek too.

'Both sides, Janie darling, like we do in France.'

I didn't think we'd ever done anything in France as I'd never been there. But I forced a smile as if I knew and offered up the tea and marmalade.

I'd moaned when Gran had asked me to shop for 'Louie'. 'It's stupid having to carry that all the way to Africa.' The word sounded strange and grand and rather frightening . . .

'Do what I tell you,' she'd insisted. 'That's what your mother said she wanted in that last letter. She said they couldn't get English tea and marmalade out there.'

'How silly!' The Co-op's shelves were full of jams and marmalades and teas of every kind. 'What on earth *do* shops sell in Libya? Anyway, you can't afford it out of your pension.' That made her feel good, when I took her side, and she hadn't felt good often lately. The arrival of the passport forms had sent her into a flutter.

'But you haven't got a birth cerstificate,' she said. 'How can we fill this bit in?'

'*Certificate*. Don't worry, Gran. Miss MacVean will sort it out—'

'You've changed your tune, my girl . . .'

'No, I haven't. It's her stupid idea that I should go . . .'

Supposing I hadn't got a birth certificate? Could I get a passport without one? If I couldn't, I wouldn't be able to go. A small snake-like curve of disappointment tinged with panic grew somewhere in my stomach. I wanted to see that birth certificate badly.

'Well, I'll be darned if I know what to put in a letter to Somerset House.'

*   *   *

I'd ripped open the envelope with shaking hands—carefully.

'If you tear it, we'll be back to where we started,' Gran had warned.

Not listening I spread the wide beige form on the living-room table. 'It says, "Mother: Louise—E-E-lise." ' I stumbled over the unfamiliar name. 'I suppose that's Eliza in French.'

'I don't know about all this French business, I'm sure,' Gran had muttered.

Louise Elise Burgess . . .

'Father . . .' I held my breath.

There was a dash diagonally across the oblong space for the father's name.

'It doesn't say anything . . .'

'Well, of course it don't, daft—what did you

178

expect? I keep tellin' yer—she don't know who it was.'

I felt flattened—I'd been so sure it would say . . . but I consoled myself knowing it was now only a question of time till I could ask my mother myself.

I'd scanned the front doormat every day when I came downstairs for my breakfast.

'Has the postman been yet?'

'No, he hasn't—you keep worryguttin' about that bloody ticket. Oh, I know I shouldn't swear but it's gettin' on my nerves and that's a fact.'

'Well, I expect it'll come by the second post. It'll be here when I get back from school.'

I did the journey from Northgate to Levington Road in record time every afternoon until it did.

*   *   *

'These are for you—English tea and marmalade.' My shaky English voice seemed to come from nowhere and sounded very out of place amongst the exotic babbling around me.

'Not now, darling, wait until we get home. Put that case down. Papa will carry it.'

'Papa, Papa, Daddee,' she called above the noise and babble of voices. Towards us came a short well-built man with stocky legs encased in white knee-socks too, his deeply lined and sun-tanned face fringed by a close-cropped haircut and a long moustache. His eyes were hidden behind sunglasses.

He looked nothing like the man who had made a surprising whirlwind visit with my mother last Christmas which had rather unsettled me. He had shouted at me, from the bottom of the stairs at

179

Levington Road when I'd got over-excited. I'd resented his interference and was angered by his judgement of my behaviour. I'd bullied Gran into letting me have a proper birthday party, and I'd invited Annette Macro, Deirdre Thirkettle and Rita Nelson. Deirdre had worn what she called a rock and roll skirt with pictures of boys and girls jiving picked out in pink felt from the black background, and black velvet slip-ons with no backs—Gran's eyes had bulged as much with disapproval as mine had stared with envy.

'Common,' she'd muttered as she passed me in the hall on her way to the oven for some warmed-up mince pies, 'from the Chantry Estate. Strikes me Northgate's gone right downhill lately—anyone can pass the scholarship these days.'

I couldn't tell her how much they frightened me and that's why I'd invited them. It didn't make sense, I knew, even to me, but I'd felt compelled somehow. We'd played hide-and-seek in the darkened rooms upstairs and on the landing until his 'Jane, if you don't stop that I stop you,' had halted me in my shrieking tracks.

I was, as he walked towards me, suddenly unnerved as I wondered if his visit to England had been to check up on Gran and me or, worse, to see whether I was worth being sent for.

''Allo.' His gravelly rasping voice sounded the same. His moustache brushed my cheek; his breath smelled of acid. I held my face still for him to kiss the other side.

'Cor blimey,' he said in his thick French accent which I thought made him sound like Maurice Chevalier—although the Englishness of the phrase hung oddly in it—''ow long 'ave you come for? You

180

got bricks in zis? I'll get the Taunus TTFN.'

He disappeared through the crowd, his broad shoulders bulging through the crisp white shirt with large pockets and epaulettes that gave him a military air except for the silly white socks. I wanted to laugh but didn't dare.

'Oh, there's Dick Templeton and Michael Drew. They must be going home to England on leave. Dick works for CPTL and Michael's a radio engineer who works down at the beach in Gargaresch. He calls in at the house a lot. You'll meet them all, Janie, and all the geologists,' said my mother.

'Oh, good,' I said and hoped it sounded more convincing than it felt. I didn't know what a geologist was.

'Let's go and wait for Daddy where there's a *courant d'air*—and, *chérie*, take your jacket off, it's stifling in here.'

I managed to extricate my arms from the jacket which seemed to stick to my body in the most annoying manner, swapping the carrier bag from hand to hand clumsily.

'Have you got a *vest* on under your shirt?' She sounded incredulous and I blushed with shame at not having fought Gran harder. 'You've spilled something down the front too ...'

'Yes,' I stammered, 'It's—'

'Don't travel in white, darling. Lolo and I never do ...'

Travel sounded awfully grand, but then I supposed that's what I'd been doing too today. Was it only this morning that I said goodbye to Gran? The child said something in rapid French and smiled behind her hand. I felt suddenly very tired.

The night was black outside the terminal building—a sky full of more stars than I'd ever seen. I couldn't spot Orion or the Plough that I'd learned about in Girls Life Brigade astronomy class but I felt better. There was a breeze like a warm draught from an open oven, but at least it made the world move. I could distinguish round shapes in the flower-bed opposite; they seemed like cartoon plants, one round oval stuck at an ungainly angle to the next.

'What are those?' I pointed through the darkness.

'*Figues de barbarie*—cactuses, darling!' Cact*i* I was tempted to say but didn't. 'You can eat the small ones. We'll buy some in the souk when we do the *marché* with Mohammed.'

A low calling sound came from beside me. 'Buckshee, buckshee.' In the darkness I could just see the outline of a crouching figure dressed in dirty white. A skinny brown arm appeared between the folds of the material and the robe, which had covered her head, hiding all but one eye and a triangle of her face, slipped out of her grasp, revealing the other eye which looked glutinous and watery. I realised it was blind. Within seconds flies were nestling in her nostrils and in the corners of both eyes. She waved them away with an unconcerned and ineffectual gesture. 'Buckshee, buckshee,' she repeated, straining a begging hand out towards us. Something stirred in her lap and I saw a thin brown sleeping baby unaware of the groups of flies that nestled on its nose and mouth.

'*Va t'en, va t'en,*' said my mother. I didn't know what it meant, but I knew the woman wasn't going to get any money from us. I thought of the pictures on the Christian Aid envelopes at Alan Road Church. Gran and I always put sixpence in them for the Methodist missionaries.

'Janie, don't *ever* give any piastres.' That wouldn't be difficult—I didn't know what they were and I hadn't got any, of that I was sure. 'Her husband probably sells peanuts on the Grand Boulevard and anyway, you never hear the end of it once you start. Papa says if he stops the Land-Rover in the middle of the desert, with only sand for miles, within seconds they're swarming over the dunes asking for bucksheesh—they're Berbers of course. Nicer Arabs than this lot. We liked the Moroccans best, although we lost everything in Casablanca. But it wasn't the Arabs, we lived in the Arab quarter of the town, it was the Foreign Legion who looted everything. They'd been called in after the unrest in '56. They took everything, our cooker and the television. The Egyptians are worse. Hotheaded Nasser *fanatiques*. The Libyans are just lazy.'

Cars drew up, one after the other, and people who had been standing in chattering groups near us, with much kissing and banging of doors, disappeared down the palm-lined road.

'There's Hansi—I expect he's picking up someone from Mobiloil. He and Papa's regiments fought each other during the war in Tunisia. Papa can't stand Germans. He was eighteen when the war broke out. Says the English didn't really know what the war was about, they never saw the swastika flying from the top of the Eiffel Tower, and his mother got pushed to the back of the queue in the *boulangerie* so the German *hausfraus* could get their *baguettes* first. But Papa and Hansi get on

183

like a house on fire.'

My brain recoiled, understanding barely half of what she said. Large palm leaves rustled overhead; underneath their spikes hung great clusters of what I supposed must be dates. The only dates we had came at Christmas in a long wooden box with a plastic trident like Neptune's in miniature for picking them out. The underneath ones stuck to the paper and I'd pick them out with my fingers which Gran said was bad mannered.

'Are those dates?'

'Yes, *chérie*—no more questions now. Wait until tomorrow when you can see everything in daylight.'

I felt chastened. Secretly I'd thought maybe they'd be impressed by my enquiring mind. All the really clever girls at Northgate asked questions.

'*Tiens, le voilà.*' A long, low, pale green car drew up. 'Papa loves the Taunus. He used to have a Beetle, *décapotable*, but that was the car of a *célibataire*; this is better for the family.'

I didn't dare ask what all those strange words meant but I arranged my face into what I hoped was an expression of calm understanding.

'*Allez, montez—non, Lolo, tu vas devant avec Papa.*'

The child rattled off another phrase in French and pulled a face. 'Papa' responded in a low firm tone and she clambered up into the seat in front, with him banging the door hard. '*Oh, ta fille, tu sais, Louise,*' he muttered under his breath.

'*A la maison,*' said my mother. 'Home, James, and don't spare the horses,' she added and giggled. I supposed they were using all these phrases to make me feel at home. I felt English and different and not entirely comfortable.

CHAPTER 13

The car sped away with a quiet swish of tyres through sand.

'*Ne conduis pas trop vite,*' said my mother. 'Oh, let's have some air. *On s'étouffe ici.* Open the window too, Janie darling.'

I fumbled across the door in the darkness feeling for a handle and pulled out what I supposed was an ashtray as my damp fingers dug into a fine powdery substance. In an effort to close it quickly it jumped out of my hands and clattered on to the floor, spraying ash around my ankle socks.

'When we go to Paris I make him drop me before we get to the Place de la Concorde and I take a taxi—it's like *le grand prix.*'

I scrabbled around with my feet, retrieved it, made several efforts to fit the sharp metal rectangle in a space in the door but it simply wouldn't fit.

'He's like all Frenchmen: they drive like crazy things. *I* won't drive in Paris, and when *he* drives I daren't look. I cover my eyes like this.' She laughed and put one beringed hand over her face, its fingers splayed enough for her to peep through. I was relieved that her laugh covered the noise of my scuffles. 'Now sit up straight, darling.' I flushed hot again, wiped my fringe out of my eyes and felt miserable as I placed the ashtray quietly on the carpeted floor of the car, promising myself that as soon as we stopped I'd open the door, throw out the cigarette ends and replace it before anyone had seen.

'The Parisians think we're from Marseilles because the car's *immatriculée* thirteen. Papa had it shipped over. The Marseillais are *fous* too—but the Parisians are worse.'

I found a handle at last, hoped that the door wouldn't swing open; as I tentatively moved it with sticky ash-covered fingers a blessed shaft of air trickled in and ruffled the top of my head. I turned the handle . . .

'Not too much or we'll all be *décoiffés,'* she said, patting her immaculate head.

'*Oh, Louise, tu sais, tu es trop nerveuse,'* he sighed and took a hand off the steering wheel and waved it in a dismissive way. I caught the glint of a thick silver bracelet on his sinewy wrist. I didn't know any men who wore bracelets. I couldn't imagine Holdy wearing one, or Doug or Russell Stebbings. I smiled at the thought and tried to settle back comfortably. This was our car. My family had a car! I was beginning to enjoy the added prestige this would give me at Northgate, when I felt my mother's hand searching out mine across the seat of the car. I let mine be taken, and sat rigid with discomfort, not daring to move as my palm against her palm grew even more clammy. I fought not to ease my fingers away from the hard ridges of her many rings. The tips of her long red nails dug into the back of my hand as the car sped over bumps in the road. My mother was holding my hand. I wanted to feel pleased but I just felt uneasy. The smell of her perfume became oppressive and a dull ache began over my eyes. I tried to concentrate on the flashes of intermittent light that sped past the car window but it was difficult to see without moving my body, and moving my body would mean moving my hand. She shifted her fingers and began to stroke the ends of mine. I sat very still.

'Janie, darling, you bite your nails!'

I flushed and felt hot and sticky. 'Well, it's maths,' I said feebly, relieved to have an excuse to withdraw my hand. 'I hate maths . . .' I wondered how far back to start to explain? Miss Howell Class 7? That was five years ago—and her severity had led to asthma. No, I couldn't mention that. Gran said it was my mother's fault I got asthma in the first place because—

'They are very important, *les mathématiques*,' came from the front seat, '*n'est-ce pas*, Lolo?'

'Oh, Papa.' She said the word so nicely, it didn't sound lame like it did when I practised saying it in my head. Again it was followed by a volume of French that passed right over me. I began to wonder what I'd been doing during my year of French classes with Miss Reid. I liked Miss Reid. She wore smart elegant clothes; often her scarf, which was caught in a stylish gold clip, matched the colour of her shoes and her handbag. Her white hair had a blue rinse to it and was always perfectly arranged. Her grey eyes twinkled behind her glasses. She called me 'Jeanne', and I'd played a game of pretending on several occasions that she was my mother.

'*Elle mange ses ongles, tu sais, Papa.*'

My mother's French sounded so English—not like Miss Reid's at all—I could almost understand it. I didn't understand why she should sound so English but it made me feel better. Released at last I turned my head and saw tall palms, rows of neatly ordered bushes, rows of scraggy trees that stretched out withered arms in all directions—like

187

the scary bits in Walt Disney films—fires with groups of people crouched around them, brightly lit doorways of modest shops which afforded quick glimpses of sparsely stacked shelves behind mounds of indistinguishable vegetables and fruit piled on the ground which cast long shadows towards the car. There was a moon low in the sky, bigger than the moon which rose over Ipswich, but no street lights, and as far as I could see no pavements either.

The child turned in her seat, kneeled up against the back of it and peered at us in the flickering dark. She made a gesture towards me as if she wanted to see my hands which, withdrawn from my mother's grasp, I screwed up as tightly as possible into clammy fists and hid under my despised skirt. A stream of rasping French ensued from the driving seat, out of which I could only pick the occasional '*le*' or '*la*'—the rest of it went completely over my head. What *had* I been doing during Miss Reid's lessons? Passing notes, and trying to make the girls who frightened me laugh, I suppose. The child replied equally fast and my spirits sank.

For my benefit, I supposed, he said, 'Don't be too cocky—you 'ave nothing to be proud of, my *fille*. You are terrible at your studies—you should get your sister to 'elp you. At least she work and—she *pass* her exams.' I felt pleased that he was proud that I'd got to Northgate. No one had mentioned it so far. It was the biggest thing that had ever happened in my life. Well, till this journey of course.

The child slumped back into her seat, muttering something in rapid French under her breath.

I said, louder than I intended, 'We had a terrible

teacher called Miss Howell in Class 7 at Cliff Lane . . .' hesitated and wondered whether I should stop to explain it. It all sounded so English, and out of place. 'Every morning she used to make us recite our times tables, out loud—every morning . . .' My voice trailed away. I knew I wasn't communicating the horror of Miss Howell's tyranny . . .

'What's that, Mommy?' the child said in perfect English with that burr of an American accent which always took me completely by surprise.

'Oh, *chérie*, it's *deux fois deux, trois fois trois.*' That sounded so nice and so unlike anything Miss Howell had made us say.

'Oh, I hate that; I can't do those stupid things.' She sounded like an American film—I wished passionately that I sounded American.

'It's maybe not the things that are so stupid, you know, *Laurence*, it's maybe you.' I wondered for an instant to whom he was talking—then it dawned on me that Laurence and Lolo were the same person. I thought Laurence was a boy's name. I'd thought her name was Lolo Lapotaire.

'*Alors, neuf fois neuf?* Clever clogs.'

The phrase sounded ludicrous coated with that Maurice Chevalier accent—I stifled a giggle. The child turned away from him in an irritated way, put her chin in her hand and concentrated sulkily on what was going past outside the window.

'So, what's nine *fois* nine?'

'Oh, Papa, you say nine nines *are*,' said my mother.

'So what, nine nines *are*?' came again from the front seat. I hadn't bargained for this—six nines I could do. I hoped against hope that he wouldn't ask me.

'Oh, papa, *je t'en prie*, not now, it's late and we're all tired. Look, Janie darling, we're nearly there; the lights of Gargaresch—see?'

The car began to slow down, its tyres making that swishing noise again on the sand-covered tarmac.

All was dark except for the outline of what looked like a castle way off into the darkness on the right side of the road.

'Is that it?' I said, peering through the window, pointing at the shape.

'No, no, *chérie*, that's some Arab settlement up there. We never go up there—they've got no arms or legs some of them. *Patienza*—we're almost home.'

The car swung left—off the road down a sandy track that felt full of stones as the car lurched from side to side.

'*La voilà, chez nous*,' said my mother, pointing across me at the darkness on my side of the car.

I could see a low square building covered with climbing plants. Patches of white wall glimmered dimly through dark leaves. Dogs barked. A light shone through windows hidden in the heart of the house. The car came to a stop inside a building round the back of the house. Heat blanketed us instantly. Heat that smelled of petrol and dust and that same bitter spice-like smell. The chirping noise started up again louder than ever, reverberating round the walls of what I supposed was a garage.

'Come along, darling, don't sit there dreaming—you'll melt,' said my mother's disembodied voice in the darkness. 'Papa will bring the *valise*. Oh, it's so humid!'

I found the catch, the door swung open. I scrambled out in an ungainly fashion almost scraping it on the garage walls.

'*Attention, la voiture.*' I didn't know what it meant, but I knew it was meant for me.

I dithered about trying to find the ashtray then abandoned it as my mother said, '*Tiens, donne-moi la main, chérie,*' and held out her hand for me to take.

I stood on shaky legs and breathed as deeply as I could, trying to get as much of the sticky air as possible into my lungs, to quieten the banging of my heart in my chest.

Countryside seemed to stretch away into the night as far as my eyes could pierce the darkness. The garage stood at the edge of what seemed to be a field of very ordered new bushes.

'What are those?'

'*Ceux sont des raisins.*'

'What?'

'Raisins,' said the girl sharply.

'Grapes, Lolo darling, they're grapes.'

She lit a cigarette which glared and made circular patterns in the dark like we did with sparklers on Guy Fawkes' Night as she searched for her cigarette-holder in her handbag and finally inserted the cigarette.

Grapes? The only grapes I'd seen growing were small, inedible bullet-like green ones on the vine on Mr Kerridge's greenhouse.

'Grapes,' I muttered to myself, idiotically.

The girl had gone ahead round the corner of the villa: and seconds later the shaft of light from the inside of the house grew and spread across the garden, and through it lurched along the ground towards us an enormous gyrating shape.

'Bebop, Bebop—*quel beau chien-chien.*' A huge brown and white dog charged at us, feathered tail waving wildly. '*Tiens, dis bonjour à Janie.*' He sniffed me in a desultory fashion then turned about, catching my legs a swipe with his tail and dashed off round the back of the house to find Papa—Yves—Daddy. What *was* I going to call him?

The villa had a small terrace which was almost covered with a thick growing creeper of some kind. The flower-beds were crammed with luscious-looking bushes and plants, none of which I recognised in the half-light.

'That's bougainvillaea,' said my mother close by, as if hearing my thoughts, 'and the garden here,' she said, waving her cigarette-holder in the direction of the flower-beds, 'is full of morning glory. Of course they've gone by *midi*— Mohammed and I have a terrible time trying to keep anything alive at all. The soil is all sand and it needs so much water—*c'est un travail.*'

This habit of chopping and changing from one language to another was very unsettling. But as long as the majority of the sentence was in English I could guess the unintelligible bits.

'Little Girl, Little Girl,' called my mother disconcertingly. After a few seconds I heard a scrabbling behind the wire door that led from the terrace into the house. The trim wooden frame jerked open and through it came a small sharp-nosed mongrel with long sandy hair.

'She's so cute,' said my mother, bending down to caress the waving body. 'She's a stray. Bebop brought her home. Some American family probably left her when they went back to the States. How can they do that to dumb animals?' You left me, a wicked voice in my head spoke. 'She hasn't had her shots yet—but she's so friendly. You'll love her, Janie darling.'

I could now hear Gran's voice in my head saying, 'No, you can't have animals, the fur gives you asthma.'

Anyway, I'd never insisted for long; I didn't have that much love to spare. I remembered guiltily what I'd done to Smokey the cat.

Bebop and Papa came round the corner together. Papa put my suitcase down and gave the dog several hearty pats. ' 'Allo, old fella—*quel beau chien-chien*.' The last words made a kind of comforting swishing noise and I resolved to practise them with the dog whenever I was alone. Even I knew what a *chien* was.

'Little Girl, 'allo Little Girl.'

I was surprised at the gentleness of the man as he stooped to stroke the mongrel. His huge rounded shoulders ended in large strong hands—I couldn't imagine Holdy talking to a dog like this. I'd only ever heard him shout, 'Get that bloody dog out of my front garden or I'll put my boot up its backside.' I didn't know anyone in Levington Road who had a dog now that Mrs Stebby was dead.

'If Bebop brings any more girlfriends home I'm going to shoot them full of formaldehyde and stand them on the terrace wall—*ça fera peur à ces cons*.' He guffawed in his deep throaty voice and coughed. 'Bebop, *où sont les vilains Arabes*?'

In a second the dog was alert, its nose and tail pointing in a line, then it charged round the flower-beds and in a swift practised jump landed with all four paws on the narrow wall that separated the low garden and steps from the terrace. He barked loudly with all his might into the darkness of the pine trees that were just discernible at the bottom of the steps that led to a sandy path.

'What a good guard dog you are, *mon fils. Tu feras courir ces cons d'Arabes.*' It was lost on me but my mother thought it shocking. 'Papa, *pas à cette heure-ci.*'

I thought it odd that she called him Papa all the time. So far I'd avoided calling him anything.

'Why are we standing like idiots in the garden?' he continued and entered the house, banging my suitcase and the battered carrier bag against the wall and letting the door swing shut in our faces as we followed him in. There was a glass jug of red-coloured liquid on the wooden table in the centre of the room. On the whitewashed walls were carved black wooden heads; black wrought-iron pot holders carrying red and green pots with vivid green trailing plants cascading from them; a row of miniature brass saucepans; a picture of the Eiffel Tower; a small black wrought-iron trolley with many bottles of amber and red liquid; a photograph of my mother, much younger with thick dark long hair, sitting on a bridge wearing some clumpy wedge-heeled thick-strapped shoes in white. Behind her sat a young man with thick dark hair and no moustache. Yves, I realised with a jolt. 'Paris 1946' it said at the bottom. I was two then, and living with Mummy Grace. I felt embarrassed that they looked so happy.

'This is the *salle à manger* . . . the *salon*'s through there . . . *l'autre côté de notre chambre* . . .' I recognised the words—my tired brain struggled to keep up and translate into English and failed.

'Go and put something cool on, Janie. Papa's put your suitcase in your room—it's been built specially for you, you know.' She grabbed the carrier bag off the table without opening it and led the way.

I gulped mentally at the enormity of what she'd said and followed her meekly through an opening on the other side of the table, past a bathroom, where, through the open door, I could see Lolo, looking at herself in the mirror.

'Don't use *all* my eau de toilette,' said my mother as she passed. The child pulled a face, at whom I wasn't sure, but my mother didn't see.

She clicked on a light and I saw a large square whitewashed room with speckled grey and white tiles, a small wooden bed made up with a single sheet; on the wooden bedside table there was a small photograph of my mother, Lolo and myself in Holywells Park some years ago—the day we'd met the man with the large dog—which made me uneasy.

'Now it's not finished, darling—there's no *grille* so you'll have to sleep with the *contrevents* shut just for the moment. Have you got a nice cool nightdress?'

'No,' I said, wishing I had.

'Well, I'll get you one of my cotton *chemises de nuit*. Now don't be put off by Lolo—she'll be a bit jealous of you at first. It's a big change for her too, you know, but underneath she's really proud of her grown-up sister.'

I wondered for a moment who she was talking about then realised I was the sister to whom she referred.

'Louise,' shouted Papa from the living-room.

195

'We forgot to put the bloody ice back in the Frigidaire before we left for the *aéroport*.'

'Oh, *merde*,' said my mother under her breath. 'I hope there's some in the ice-box; he won't drink warm whisky,' and disappeared. 'We' had a refrigerator too!

I wished she hadn't said that about Lolo—while I only imagined it, it didn't matter so much. Now she'd confirmed it my unease became much more real. I'd always bullied my way into winning fights with the Margarets, but I knew somehow this was going to be different.

I took my sandals off and threw my grubby ankle socks in the direction of Bert and Doris's suitcase.

I stretched my toes into the delicious coolness of the tiles and padded towards the shuttered window. Through the narrow slats in the wood I could see feathery branches, moving slightly, and far in the distance light glinting on water. Sea. The Mediterranean. It was hard to believe. All of it was hard to believe.

Dangerous-looking wires stuck out into the room underneath the window. I wondered if they were live. The walls were completely bare and white. My own room. Better than anything anyone had in Levington Road.

I stood wondering what to do. There wasn't anywhere to hang the contents of my suitcase. I didn't much want to get the clothes out anyway. I was ashamed of most of them except for the seersucker blouse I'd made in needlework class especially for my holiday in Africa. I was almost proud of that. It looked less mauled now that Gran had washed and ironed it.

I took off my soiled blouse and threw it at the

socks and stood in my vest, cotton bra and crumpled skirt—too shy to remove more. The chirping noises started up outside my bedroom window. It was that more than anything that reminded me I was not in England. Bebop padded in and flopped, breathing hard, on to the cool tiles next to my suitcase. He looked at me with mournful eyes, sniffing the edges of my suitcase guiltily. I wasn't sure whether he would growl or snap if I approached him—so we stared at each other across the space.

'*Tiens*,' said my mother, coming in with a cotton nightdress that reeked of her perfume even from the other side of the room. It seemed strangely over-intimate to offer me something that she had worn. I took it shyly—shy too that she had changed into shorts and a blue and white matching top that revealed most of her arms and all of her long thin brown legs. Her feet were encased in thin golden strap sandals, her toes varnished in a red that matched her long fingernails. I was shocked to see her feet: the shape of her toes; the way the three small ones were almost bent under—with a hint of a bunion on the big toe joint. They resembled mine exactly.

'Why on earth are you wearing a vest, *chérie*?'

'Well, Gran said—'

'Oh, and you have a *soutiens-gorge*. If you're anything like me you don't really need one—you've got nothing to put in it. But *tu es une jeune fille*, almost a woman . . .' So I wasn't going to have to fight her to keep it like I'd fought Gran.

'Josie gave it to me at Girls Life Brigade Camp in Totnes . . . Devon,' I added as if that explained everything. The words sounded so out of place

197

here in this warm white room with crickets chirping outside.

'But it's very English, Janie.' My face must have registered dismay, for she continued, 'We'll get you some Lou ones like mine—pretty, feminine ones. Lolo's going to be *very* well-developed. I can tell already—she's so *costaud* and so like Daddy. You're like me. Now come and have something to drink or you'll get dehydrated—you must take salt tablets too because you'll sweat so much. Oh, and mind those wires, they're for the air-conditioning. They're so slow the Arabs, it's always *domani*; they'll have it in by Christmas. Oh, and don't forget to make a fuss of Papa about the room—he had a big fight with the CPTL to get it built, so don't you ever say you're not wanted.' And with that she left the room, Bebop padding close behind, his claws making a light scratching sound on the tiles. I felt very quiet inside. Very unlike myself.

I took off the thick cotton bra whose empty cups had been squashed flat against the vest and hid it under my blouse. I was shocked to see the dirty brown rim across the collar of my blouse. I had washed my neck, was it this morning? I'd had a good 'stand-up' wash in the kitchen. Gran had said I couldn't have a bath; she wasn't feeling up to bucketing all that water into the copper—I knew my going away had made her hearttroubleandbloodpressure bad.

The nightdress smelled of the cigarette smoke that was now wafting into my room, from the *salle à manger* was it—or the *salon*? It reminded me of Yves's breath when he'd kissed me at the airport. It smelled so different from Doug's Woodbines, or Joan Holden's Players Weights.

I padded out of my room slowly and shyly. As I passed the bathroom, Lolo called, 'Janie, Janie, come in here. I pushed open the door. She was dressed in shorts and a matching shirt too. Her legs were the same lovely deep honey colour as her face. My white feet and stick-like legs stuck out from under the nightie. I sat on the edge of the bath and hid them under me. There was a low white thing with taps next to the lavatory: a baby bath, I thought.

'Look,' she said in a conspiratorial way, opening a small cabinet that hung on the wall over the basin. 'This is where Mommy keeps her make-up; she lets me use it when I play dressing-up.'

'Oh,' I said, not wanting to say anything that would spoil the tingle I felt from having been called 'Janie'.

'But you'll be able to use it all the time. You're older than me.'

'I'm only twelve,' I said lamely, not wanting to put a damper on such an encouraging beginning. She opened a small floral waterproof bag.

'Look, here's some *rouge à levres*.' She unwound several silver spirals. Cylinders of pink and orange and red popped up—shiny and greasy from the heat. They looked dangerously near melting. 'And the Rimmel—you do this.' She spat on the small wax-like block of black and rubbed a small brush over it. 'I'll make you up ...'

I backed away. 'No, perhaps we'd better not— it's late, I shall have to go to bed soon.' This didn't sound like me at all—careful and cautious. 'Let's go and have something to drink.'

'I'm not thirsty,' she said pouting. 'Anyway, I shall have to go to bed before you, I guess, 'cos I'm

199

the youngest and anyway Mommy only put the Kool-aid on the table because *you* were coming. We normally keep it in the Frigidaire. It'll be warm—it'll taste like *caca*—'

I giggled at the funny-sounding word.

'Do you know what *caca* is?' she said.

'Yes,' I said.

'Well, what is it?'

'I'd better go now and have a drink.' As I turned to go she pulled another face which I decided not to notice. It looked like war.

'Papa' was sitting at the table smoking cigarettes from a blue packet with a gypsy dancing on the front, a large tumbler of amber-coloured liquid beside him.

'*Oh, la voici la fantôme de l'opéra.*' He laughed. I didn't know what it meant but I smiled.

'*Oh, Louise, ta fille a l'air con comme ça.*' He inhaled deeply on his cigarette and followed it by a large gulp of what I guessed was whisky.

'Well, it's only to keep her cool,' said my mother defensively.

' 'Aven't you got anything of your own?'

'I beg your pardon?' A voice came from somewhere inside me that didn't belong.

'Clothes, clothes of your own—what do you do with all the money I send you?'

I thought of the fifteen pounds a month that came so irregularly that Gran and I had given up counting on it, because when it didn't come it only made her irritable—if she'd planned to pay bills with it—and it made me cross if I'd seen something in a shop and set my heart on having it.

'I suppose Nana spend it all on whisky?' He laughed again and I joined in, in spite of myself.

'Darling, would you like some Kool-aid?'

'Yes, please,' I said meekly.

'Oh, give the girl a glass of wine,' he said. 'You want a glass of wine?'

I thought of the teetotaller's pledge I'd signed at Alan Road. 'Oh, no, thank you, no, thanks.'

She poured a large glass of the red liquid and plopped ice-cubes in it from a black container with a lid. I'd never had a drink with ice in it before. The cool chunks bobbed against my lips and I gulped thirstily. It tasted like red lemonade crystals mixed with water. I tipped the glass too far and more of the liquid ran down the side of my mouth than into it, over my chin and on to the nightdress—I felt myself blush and tried to scrub the deepening red stain off the frill.

'*Oh, c'est bien ta fille, Louise—maladroite comme toi.*' I felt as scarlet as the drink.

'*Ne t'en fais pas*,' said my mother and disappeared into the kitchen.

'What's long and green and hangs on the wall and you blow it?'

'What?'

He repeated himself emphatically. My mind was blank. I couldn't think of anything that fitted that description. Now he'd *know* I was stupid.

'A long green wall whistle.'

It took me a second to register. It was a joke. He was telling me a joke. I laughed louder than it warranted, I was so relieved. It sounded false. But he seemed pleased. He took another gulp of whisky, inhaled again and blew a series of smoke rings in the air. I was amazed.

'Can you do this?' he asked.

'Oh, no,' I said in wonderment as several small

rings floated in succession through the air.

My mother returned carrying a sponge. She gestured me over to her side of the table, opened her legs and stood me between them. That made me feel good. Her gold bracelets jangled as she sponged the front vigorously. Instinctively my hands flew up to protect my breasts. The little lumps that had started to grow under my nipples lately were painful if someone caught me a blow there in netball or out on the hockey field. We all swapped stories in class IIID of how much they hurt except for girls like Anne Howard and Annette Macro and Gillian Gilbert whose breasts were fully formed and had even started Northgate wearing brassières.

'Ah ha, your titties are growing, yes? Let's have a look.'

'*Non, mais alors, non*,' said my mother firmly, brushing back the fringe from my sweaty forehead. I didn't know what to do with my hands. If I let them dangle they would be dangerously near her bare brown thighs. She tilted my chin up with her long brown fingers so that I had to look straight into her eyes. They were beautiful, huge and brown, their long lashes coated with the black stuff that Lolo had shown me in the bathroom.

'Now, *chérie*, are you hungry? Would you like some pâté, or some pasta?'

'No, no, thank you,' I said, not wanting her to stop touching me, and not wanting to spoil the moment by asking her to explain exactly what it was she was offering me.

'No, we had a lot to eat on the plane; we stopped in Rome—and then in Malta they gave us . . .' I was impressed I'd been to these places even for half an

202

hour: but no one else was.

'*Lolo, viens ici, chérie; qu'est-ce que tu fabriques dans la salle de bains?*'

She came out, her cheeks rouged with lipstick—large black circles round her eyes; a pair of sparkling earrings dangled from her ears—her short brown hair crammed in a bath cap.

'*Tu te crois Madame de Pompadour?*' said Papa.

She posed, with one hand on her hip and the other in the air above her head. My mother moved me aside, put her cigarette in its long black and gold holder into the ashtray and threw back her head and laughed a delighted husky laugh. I thought it was the most glamorous sound I had ever heard; it ended in a series of guffaws that shocked me with familiarity. It was my laugh.

'*Un oiseau rare,*' said Papa and, getting up, retrieved a small bamboo feather duster from the corner by the standard lamp and stuck it between Lolo's legs so that the red feathers protruded from behind like a pert red tail.

'Oh, Lolo darling, *viens, donne-moi un bisou,*' said my mother, laughing more.

The child came smiling towards her and offered up her face for a kiss, turning her back to me. I stood lamely by, not knowing what to do—trying to remember if '*oiseau*' meant 'bird' and whether '*bisou*' meant 'kiss'. I'd never seen kiss in a vocabulary book at school.

'If your daughter was as good at her studies as she is at *la comédie, Louise, tu sais . . .*' He waved his hand in that dismissive way again.

'Oh, Daddee, don't be such a spoil-sport,' she cried. '*Viens, chérie.*' The child clambered up on her knee and put her arms around my mother's neck; a flicker of a smirk crossed her face as she looked in my direction. She still had a gold bracelet, too, round her wrist; it caught the light as it slid up her arm.

'Now Janie is very good at her studies, Laurence,' he went on sternly. 'She pass to go this—what d'you call it?' he said in my direction.

'Grammar school,' I said, my pride stirred by his interest and walked back round the table to my seat next to him. Did he know I was in III*D*, I wondered anxiously.

'You see she concentrate, she work hard—she don't spend her time thinking about boys or *le cinéma*, or whether her socks are the same colour as her dress. *Lolo, écoute-moi quand je te parle!*'

The child jumped at the loudness of his voice and so did I. She took her arms away from my mother's neck, the gold bangle catching the edge of the table with a clunk as she did so.

'Oh, that's pretty,' I said, my eyes glued to it with envy.

'Oh, we'll get you one; they cost nothing in the souk. Daddee, it's late—they must go to bed. You can have a *douche* tomorrow, Janie. Say goodnight then, *alors, brossez les dents, et puis do-do . . .*'

Do-dos were asthma tablets Gran gave me when we'd run out of Ephedrine—they could be bought without a prescription.

> 'Do, do, l'enfant do,
> L'enfant dormira plus vite'

they all chanted and sang together. It reminded me of 'Rock-a-bye baby on the tree top'.

I went to kiss him, aware that the neck of the

nightdress would gape open as I bent down, but I was too frightened to clasp it to my chest.

'Whoops-a-daisee,' he said in his funny French accent peering down the front. My cheeks felt hot against his as I carefully kissed him on both sides of his face, trying hard to avoid his thick grey moustache. He caught my hands in his before I had time to snatch them away, turned them over and inspected the chewed nails.

'No more of this, huh?' he said. 'It's *dégoûtant* for a *jeune fille* to 'ave 'ands like this. What boy would want to 'old these? So don't bite them again, huh?'

I'd never thought of that. 'No,' I said, squirming inside, alarmed by a lump in my throat that made it difficult to speak.

'No, what?' he said.

'No, Papa.' The word flopped out of my mouth and sounded nothing like the word my mother had used.

'No, no,' he said. 'Listen carefully. "Papa, papa."' He stressed the second syllable emphatically. His lips were thick and pink between his moustache and I caught a glimpse of gold at the back of his mouth.

'Papa,' I said obediently.

'*Très bien, fais de jolis rêves.*'

'I'll come in and kiss you when I've finished my whisky,' said my mother.

'*Embrasse-la, Lolo, je t'en prie.*'

The child came towards me and offered me her face passively with her eyes closed, so I had to kiss her. She'd won the first round.

I padded gratefully and tiredly into the room, pulled back the sheet and flopped in the bed. The air in the room was thick and still. The repetitious rasping went on relentlessly outside. I wished it would stop. It was so strange, reminding me constantly that I wasn't in England, and that for some reason was beginning to make me feel sad.

My head was full of strangeness and words I didn't understand. My body felt weak and dry and hot. I longed to take the nightdress off but thought better of it, in case Mummy was offended. Did she like the tea and the marmalade?

I was tired of names too; again such simple things seemed to require such big decisions.

The maze of spots behind my closed eyelids formed themselves into an ordered pattern and moved in unison towards me then away from me. Blessed relief. That was always a sign of my being about to fall asleep.

Gran was calling me, trying to wake me up. Only it didn't sound like her usual shout from the bottom of the stairs. 'Jay-yern, Jay-yern.' It was gentler. I opened my gummed-up eyes, and saw by the light of the bedside lamp which I hadn't turned off, Lolo standing near the doorway.

I heard the distant gushing of a recently flushed lavatory.

'Janie—Janie,' she whispered, a smile playing about her lips.

'What? What is it?' I muttered thickly, my throat parched, my neck damp with sweat. I tried to sit up. I did like being called 'Janie'.

'Janie,' she repeated quietly. 'Why have you come here?' She smiled again. 'They're my Mommy and Daddee not yours. Why don't you go back home?'

Then she disappeared as silently as she'd come.

CHAPTER 14

Bert and Doris Jones, when they weren't running Alan Road Youth Club, or Doris wasn't at choir practice, and Bert wasn't lay preaching at Chelmondiston or Woodbridge, were 'at home' to us in their house in Lattice Avenue. It was always warm and bright and stood in large gardens front and back.

'Oh, it's detached!' Gran had said, impressed and not a little curious when I described it. 'Well, I s'pose it would be in that part o' town. It's been donkey's years since I've been up Rushmere Heath way—course Walter and I did some of our courting up there.'

Bert would often take my hands in his and looking straight into my eyes would say, 'Now, you do know I love you, don't you?' I did. He had said it so often, but I still shifted from foot to foot as he spoke in case his waylaying me in the hall would lose me my place on the sofa next to one of the boys.

It hadn't taken me long to settle in, though I was the youngest. I wasn't even supposed to be there. But I was getting used to feeling that too. Doris was always laughing and smiling. They had no children of their own and if one of us was brave enough to ask if she minded, she'd giggle and say, 'Mind! How can I mind? I've got you lot, haven't I? What a flippin' shower.' We'd smile at her use of our slang. She would serve us endless trays of sandwiches and sausage rolls and make us coffee from proper Nescafé powder with warm frothing milk. The girls would help clear away and do the washing up, and afterwards we'd join in the raucous singing of 'Oh, Sir Jaspar Do Not Touch Me' which Tony Ford would follow immediately with 'Roll Me Over in the Clover' round the piano in their spacious 'lounge' as Doris called it. Patrick Ling would play or Anne Pallant would sing one of her trembly solos. She sang at Harvest Festivals and Sunday School anniversaries and always took the solo part if the choir sang alone on Sundays. Bert would nod contentedly in time to the music, and beat out the rhythm neatly on his knee, smiling benignly at us, and Doris would join in in her high treble, lisping fiercely on all the words with 's' in them, occasionally stopping to burst out laughing at Ivan who stood beside her and who was mischievous enough to change the occasional word, making nonsense of what we were singing—and their giggles would infect those near them until the whole group collapsed laughing and Patrick would stop playing, to turn round to see what he was missing.

Ivan was a slow thinker and had difficulty stringing a sentence together and Doris would josh him along, supplying his missing words, and we would giggle with her.

Roger wore silly woollen hats with poms-poms on, even indoors, and we laughed at him too and snatched the hat from him, to place it ceremoniously on the head of whoever was singing solo.

'Worship doesn't have to be serious,' Bert would say in his serious way. 'I'm sure it gladdens the good Lord to see young people gathered together like this.'

'What a shower,' Tony Ford would say. He was a trainee bank manager, now he'd left Northgate. He was one of the oldest in the group. We looked up to him with love and not a little awe.

I wanted a Methodist hymn book printed on very fine paper, leather bound, that closed with a zip, like Ancia Pinhorn's who was going to marry Tony and won prizes for her handsewn buttonholes and smocking on her seersucker dresses at church bazaars.

Pat Bennington, who had buck teeth and rosy cheeks, and Gillian Reynolds, who was quiet and gentle, went to Copplestone Road Secondary School while Anne Howard and I were at Northgate, and Rosamund Pinhorn, Ancia's younger sister, went to Amberfield, a private school, but none of that mattered at Alan Road Youth Club. Diane and Arnold's mother was a widow and so was Anne Howard's, but no one bothered about that either. They all knew Gran and asked about her often.

The boys played table tennis but when the girls played they called it ping-pong.

I learned to dance the valeta, the Gay Gordons and the Saint Bernard's Waltz.

The big girls danced with boys while the rest of us had to make do dancing with each other. It embarrassed me to dance with a girl—but I didn't have the courage to complain.

I was too busy watching a boy called Barry Cunnell.

Ros was in love with Arnold Reeve and Arnold's sister Diana was in love with Barry Cunnell. I thought him the best and I thought very unChristian thoughts about Diana Reeve. Anne

Pallant was in love with Norman Peck who was a
lay preacher, and Colin and Merle and Joyce and
Anne taught in Sunday School. Margaret Pallant,
Anne's younger sister, was in love with Ivan
although no one understood why, and Bert and
Doris loved us all and we loved them. I sang till my
voice hurt and laughed till it was reduced to a
hoarse croak.

CHAPTER 15

I coughed. My throat was parched, my body damp
with sweat. The sheet stuck to me. I threw it off. I
stuck to the sheet under my back. I turned on my
side. Then my face sank deep into the pillow.
Feather. Asthma. I turned quickly on to my back
again, splaying my arms and legs so that no part of
my body was in contact with my burning flesh. I
breathed in for seven and out for seven. Lucky
number. That would bring sleep. How could
anyone sleep in this heat? The chirping outside the
window seemed louder than ever in the darkness.

Irritably I got out of bed and went to stand by
the shuttered windows, almost tripping up on the
nightdress that I'd discarded earlier. I was too hot
to care about my nakedness now. Or my mother's
feelings. A dark shape stirred on the floor and
sighed. Bebop. I put my thumb in my mouth
and wondered if he'd let me play with his ear and
snuggle up to him. Better not. He didn't know me.
I'm a stranger, I thought . . .

I stood with my nose up against the gaps in the
slats of wood like a dog breathing in the draught

under a door. The breeze was stirring the trees outside, more than it had done earlier. More air inside the room with the shutters open! Brainwave. I switched the bedside light on and went back to inspect the strange-looking catch that held the windows together. Everything was different here. Even catches on windows. No, it wasn't a window. It was a shutter.

I pushed it sideways hard, hoping it wouldn't make a noise. It hardly moved and I barked my knuckles on the wood. I couldn't pull it down any further. It simply wouldn't go. Trickles of sweat made their way down my neck. In growing impatience I pushed it up. It sprang out of my sticky hand with a jerk and then I saw that it had to be pushed sideways to be released from the metal bar in which it was lodged. The shutters folded back like the pleats in a concertina, revealing the inkiness of the night. An arm's length away from the window, two small trees waved their branches slowly, leaves rustling. Tall bushes near them moved in the opposite direction, like a silent ballet. The air felt so good on my face. It wasn't much cooler, but at least it was moving. I felt the sweat on my neck begin to dry. I switched the light off so that I could enjoy the picture-like quality of the night framed by the rim of the window. Once my eyes became accustomed to the darkness again I could see that the navy-blue sky was crammed with more stars than seemed possible. The moon wasn't visible but I knew it was there somewhere as there was a distant whiteness on an avenue of trees to the right that led away into the distance. A small red light glowed in the blackness. Must be the top of the radio station's aerial that my mother had mentioned. I concentrated really hard till I could almost see the fine black tracery of the crane-like mast that led up to it. The rasping in the bushes stopped and started intermittently now. Even the crickets, if crickets they were, were falling asleep.

I don't know how long I stood there but I was suddenly aware of a cramp-like ache in my knees— my legs were stiff and aching from being in the same position. My eyes felt puffy and tired; but my brain galloped with the jumble of strange new thoughts.

I clicked the light back on and got back on to the bed. The sheets, thicker than any I'd seen at Levington Road, were unbelievably crumpled. There was a damp patch on the bed beside the pillow where I must have sucked my thumb and dribbled.

There was a book on the shelf underneath the bedside table—*Les Malheurs de Sophie* it said. Sophie was the name of the doll that Lolo had taken from me. I pushed that thought away . . . 'mal-heurs': bad hours, my groggy brain deduced. *'Roman Historique'* it said down its spine—an historical novel, it came to me in a flash; that would help improve my French. I determined there and then, my busy brain delighted to be absorbed at last, to read and understand every word. I'd borrow a dictionary; surely they'd have one and I'd write a list of all the words I didn't understand. I'd show them. I'd learn French quickly. That would make them love me.

The opening sentence whirled in front of my eyes. Apart from the occasional *le* or *la* I understood hardly anything.

I flicked through to the back of the book. Some

of the pages wouldn't flick. They felt thicker than the others. I thought at first they were stuck together then I realised the book had been made like that; only the first few pages had been slit open. I sat up in bed and peered down the middle of the pages that were joined together and saw print on both sides. What a funny book. It had to have its pages cut before it could be read. I'd never seen a book like that before.

My face itched. I scratched it, and pushed open some more pages so that I could peer down the middle. Absent-mindedly I scratched my chest, and tried hard to pick out a reasonably familiar word. *Devant*: was that 'in front of' or 'underneath'? I simply couldn't remember. I scratched my ear and then my forehead. It was then that I noticed a buzzing sound coming from near the bedside light. I thought the light was going to fuse, the noise was so loud. Then I saw it. It had wings like a dragonfly and was hovering just above the bulb. It was huge and black and ugly. Crawling all over the lampshade were a myriad of small flies. But they weren't flies. They were hopping and jumping and tumbling over each other in their struggle to get to the warmth. Fleas! My mother's house had fleas! Only really dirty people in Ipswich had fleas. I put the book down quickly, scratching my wrist as I did so, and saw that the sheet under my legs was alive with the same minute insects. I jumped off the bed horrified, scratching and rubbing myself all over. I picked the discarded nightdress up off the floor and quickly put it on.

As my head went through the neck I saw on the ceiling where the walls joined and the lampshade cast a strip of light, the whole corner of the room was alive and crawling with insects and flying things of every shape and size. All of which were strange and unfamiliar. Some of them were banging into the wall, their huge wings making a papery fluttering sound as they collided with it. Panic rose in me.

'Oh, no! Oh, no!'

My voice echoed strangely in the empty room. Bebop had gone without my noticing. Supposing some of them were poisonous? Some of them might sting? Did scorpions fly? I didn't know.

I wished I hadn't put the nightdress on so hastily. I hadn't checked if flies had crawled into it as it lay on the floor. I started to cry and scratch myself more. A huge lump had come up in the place on my chest and another on my wrist. I felt miserable and the more miserable I felt the harder I scratched. The bumps looked angry and red and pin-pricks of blood appeared in their centres under my scratching fingers.

Cross with myself for being so pathetic, I grabbed the book, stood on the bed and began to take great swinging swipes at the creepy-crawlies settling in the shaft of light.

The book slapped up against the bare wall. Sometimes unsuccessfully, sometimes battered wings and splashes of blood and green trickles were revealed when I took the book away. I made sure my fingers didn't touch any of it, and bashed on.

'Janie, Janie darling. What *are* you doing?' My mother stood at the foot of the bed. 'What is the matter?'

Words tumbled out of my mouth while tears trickled into it. I made no sense. I was too upset even to feel silly. I wanted to be back in my bedroom at Levington Road where nothing was unfamiliar.

She put her hands through her silver hair which stood out at unruly angles now, yawned and said, 'Well, of course, *chérie*, if you open the *contrevents* and put the light on, of course all the *bébêtes* are going to come in. *Attends*.'

She crossed to the window and in one easy movement leaned out and pulled the concertina together. She fastened the catch across and down with a practised click.

'I'll go and get the fly-tox—oh, *mon dieu*, look at the mess on that wall . . .'

I turned guiltily and saw the battleground I'd made of the pristine whiteness.

'Papa will be *furieux*. Thank goodness *nothing* wakes him up. Let's hope it will wash off in the morning—now get down off the bed and don't be so silly.'

She came back into the room with something that looked like a bicycle pump with a metal box at the end. She pulled the bed away from the wall. Its wooden legs squeaked across the tiles with an appalling loudness that set my teeth on edge. I hoped Lolo wouldn't wake and come in to witness my foolishness. She pulled the handle out, shot a few deft squirts into the corner of the room and insects fell dead or dying on to the floor. The air was full of a smell like petrol which tightened my chest and made me wheeze, but I said nothing. I scratched the swellings on my arm and wrist surreptitiously.

'Now go to sleep, *chérie, je t'en prie*. You've had a long day and if you're anything like me, Janie, you're good for nothing if you don't sleep. I must

215

go back to bed now or this tablet will stop working and I'll have to take another.'

I noticed that her words were slurred and wondered whether she took phenobarbitone like Gran. Then wished I hadn't thought of Gran. It made me feel heavy inside my tightening chest.

'*Au lit, au lit,*' she said, gesturing towards the bed. I climbed in, and under the pretence of rearranging the top sheet billowed it out to shake off anything that might have landed there. She clicked off the light.

'Now sleep, Janie, for goodness' sake,' she said, her voice tinged with an impatience I hadn't heard before. 'And for goodness' sake don't mention it to Daddy. We'll clean it up in the morning. *Bonne nuit.*'

'Yes, Mummy. Goodnight, Mummy. *Bonne nuit,*' I returned self-consciously.

At least I hadn't had to call him 'Daddy' because he wasn't.

CHAPTER 16

'But I don't want to go back.' Another lie.

'Well, Janie darling, you were the one who didn't want to come and said you wanted to stay in Ipswich. It hurt me terribly, you know.' I felt worse.

The *salle à manger* was filled with the pungent smell of nail varnish remover which I rather liked. My mother was renewing the varnish on her long nails which looked yellow and stained without it. My own short stubs of nails were tinted silver. I watched her fascinated.

'I so love it here.' That wasn't strictly true but I knew she wanted to hear it.

'*Alors ça te plaît ici?*'

'*Oui—j'aime,*' I ventured unsteadily.

'*Ça me plaît,*' said Lolo grumpily.

'*Oui, ça me plaît ici.*'

I drained the remainder of my coffee made with evaporated milk from its large bowl. No milkman called here. No real milk even, it would have curdled in the heat. We drank *lait écrémé* Gloria from the red tin in the fridge, mixed with water from a bottle for our coffee. Or we took great gulps of it neat if Mother wasn't in the kitchen. I watched Lolo dunking her piece of bread into her bowl of chocolate. That was one French habit I wouldn't take up. It was disgusting, all those soggy bits of bread floating around in the bottom. Papa did it too. It turned my stomach. I could shout at Gran for dunking her ginger nut biscuits, but here I held my tongue. I felt like I was turning into two people.

The summer had seemed as if it would go on for ever, but it must be time to go back soon. It must be, but no one had mentioned it. I didn't want to think about not being able to go back.

'Now what are you going to do today, you two?'

'Oh, let's go to the beach.'

'*Oh, ça m'ennuie,*' said Lolo, slamming down her bowl. 'Why can't we go horse-riding?'

There was a picture of my mother and Lolo on horseback in the *salon* smiling happily. They'd taken me once to the English military stables nearby. They were run by a man called Bill whose barracks were in Colchester. It shocked me to hear a Suffolk accent in the blazing sun with flies buzzing everywhere and Arabs mucking out the yard. But I hadn't taken in much of Bill's guffawing conversation when he heard I lived in Ipswich. I was too apprehensive about the horse that I was to mount, who stood pawing the ground and trying to jerk his head out of Bill's grasp.

'No, we can't go to the stables today. Bill's in Benghazi on leave, *chérie*,' said my mother.

'*Oh, j'ai le trac.*'

'What does that mean?'

'She's fed up,' said my mother. 'She so loves horse riding.'

'You got out the wrong side of the bed, my young lady,' said Gran's voice in my head. I dismissed it. I didn't want to think about Gran.

'Oh, come on, please, *petite chérie*,' I said, tickling her gently under her bronzed arms.

'*Arrête! Arrête*, Janie!'

'Oh, come on, I haven't got many days left,' I wheedled, hoping someone would confirm it. No one did.

'Janie darling, you ought not to go to the beach unless your shoulders have healed, you know.'

That was a sore point.

I'd been forbidden to sunbathe for any length of time at first, but I'd disobeyed, sneaking out into the sun at the back of the house while everyone was snoozing in the afternoons—'doing the siesta' my mother called it. I wanted so badly to be brown like them, and I'd managed it—or so I thought. At first I'd gone an ever-deepening red, as if I was blushing all over, and just when the skin on my shoulders was beginning to turn a vague shade of brown little flaky bubbles had appeared under the surface. They weren't like the itchy bumps I had in a rash across my chest, my thighs and the backs of my

218

hands.

'Heat rash again,' said my mother. 'Don't sunbathe any more.'

But I had, and I'd peeled, revealing shiny pink skin in two patches like the epaulettes on Papa's shirts. And then I'd gone in the sun again and the sun had burnt the new bits. For a night I'd been in agony, tossing and turning and sticking to the sheet. Mummy had put packs of ice on my head and cold towels on my neck but I'd been almost delirious with the pain.

Papa had got cross when I'd cried but I'd been given some Veganin which made me feel all woozy and light-headed so it hadn't mattered.

'No, no, they're fine now. I'll go and get the bikinis off the line . . .'

I scraped the seat back, nearly catching Little Girl's tail.

'*Oh, pardon, mon beau chien-chien,*' I said, stooping down to pat her, noticing that Lolo had her bare feet on Bebop's back as if he were a footstool. He seemed to like it as she dug her toes in and out of his fur—or maybe he liked the cool floor under the table too much to move.

'*C'est une chienne.*'

'What?'

'Little Girl's a *chienne*, Janie,' said Lolo impatiently. She had taken on the mantle of main French teacher—apart from Papa, in whose presence I never uttered more than '*oui*' or '*non*' or '*merci*'.

'Don't go into the garden without your flipflops on, Janie.'

'Okey dokey,' I said, repeating a phrase she liked to hear though I thought it old-fashioned. 'Oil jes

219

go owt inter the back yard and fetch them there swimmin' costumes,' I said in a gross imitation of a Suffolk accent. My mother smiled and I thought it a good moment to give her a hug.

'Mind my nails, Janie—they're still wet,' she said, not responding, leaving me standing beside her, not quite knowing what to do next.

'And your flipflops are on the patio—don't forget to put them on. There are scorpions in the garden—remember?'

We'd found a scorpion one day, Lolo and I. She'd told me that if a scorpion sees fire he brings his tail over his head and stings himself to death. We'd trapped one, a yellow evil-looking thing—I'd thought they were black.

'No, no,' Lolo said. 'These are the really bad guys—these yellow ones, they're the worst.'

We'd trapped him in the upturned empty marmalade jar and collected some dried pine needles which we'd placed in a circle around the jar. Lolo had bullied Mohammed into giving her a match, but I could see how anxious he was for her not to tell 'MonsieuretMadameLapotaire', as the words came out in a torrent, as one.

We'd lit the pine needles and removed the jar and watched absorbed, as the sun beat down on our backs. But the scorpion had walked into the burning pine needles and had been frizzled up before we could see whether he'd moved his tail or not. We'd screamed with glee and I'd wondered whether I should tell Lolo about pulling the legs off spiders and putting Smokey down the lavatory pan at Levington Road, but thought better of it.

I liked the sound my flipflops made on the stone floor of the patio. I swung the patio door wide, waiting for the sound of the tinny twang it made behind me, prepared myself for the onslaught and stepped out from the shade of the overhanging bougainvillaea ablaze with its clusters of deep purple flowers into the searing brightness.

The sun hit my eyes and burnt through the light shirt on my back. I was aware how tender the spots were on my shoulders but that wasn't going to stop me. Nobody in IIID or Alan Road Youth Club would ever have seen a tan like mine. The world hardly moved under such heat. Flies busied themselves around the clusters of purple grapes. I stopped to pick several, still not quite able to believe that grapes grew in rows like potatoes did in England. The Landowskis had a lemon tree in their garden. Magda was a pianist and Lolo said Henry was a spy but then she'd also said that Henry was Mummy's boyfriend, but my mind just couldn't get itself round that idea, so I'd dismissed the whole Landowski scenario as preposterous right down to the lemon tree. I'd never seen anyone pick them; perhaps they were just for decoration. Anyway, none of the lemons in the wooden boxes in Fowlers' shop had leaves attached to them. So they probably weren't the same thing at all.

I took the bikinis off the line. Lolo's was pink and white gingham with frills along the top of its wired cups. She rarely wore the top. The bottom was bleached several shades lighter. I had been borrowing one of my mother's which was equally stylish but more conservative. My regulation Northgate swimming costume, an all-in-one itchy black wool thing, had been discarded in the bottom of Bert and Doris's suitcase ever since it had been greeted with looks of dismay from my mother and snorts of derision from Lolo.

I walked back round the house the other way. Mohammed was watering the part of the garden that was shaded by the trees outside my bedroom window.

'Bonjour, Mohammed. Comment vas-tu?'

Mohammed looked away, unused to questions concerning his well-being. Mohammed was the only person with whom I felt sure of my French. His was worse than mine.

'Il fait beau aujourd'hui, n'est-ce pas?' I ventured, more for myself than for him, then stopped myself short by his look of utter amazement. Stupid question, Jane. *Il fait beau* every day.

He made a quaint little bow and kissed his index finger as he did so. *'Salaam aleikum.'*

'Salaam.'

He smiled modestly at me, revealing his brown stained front teeth. He was barefoot, standing in puddles of muddy water amongst the threadbare grass. The bushes on the far side of the lawn were thick with flying creatures. I stopped to see if the caterpillars of an amazing greenness were still hanging under the leaves. They reminded me of the caterpillar in *Alice in Wonderland*, huge and fat with ringed bodies. Just like the man who advertised Michelin tyres in the dirty shed that was the local garage on the road to Tripoli where Papa stopped sometimes for *essence* if he was speaking French, or gas if he was speaking American. I stepped out of the shade over the hosepipe, into the blistering heat again, where swarms of vividly coloured butterflies busied themselves amongst the morning glory which would wither and disappear by the afternoon.

A chameleon, his eyes swivelling sideways to look at me, stopped in his tracks and waited nervously as my shadow passed on the bare patch of whitewashed wall.

Little Girl sat panting in the shade by the patio door and wagged her scraggy sun-bleached tail as I approached.

'She's *enceinte* again,' my mother had said. 'Let's hope it was Bebop; one of the puppies will be yours, Janie bach.'

Little Girl did look fatter than she had done all those weeks ago when I arrived. I stopped to pat her. She rolled over on to her back, displaying a rounded stomach from which rows of pale pink nipples ringed in sand and dirt protruded amongst the sparse fur.

'Little Girl,' I whispered to her enquiring face. 'I want to go home.'

She sat up for a second, tried to lick me. I recoiled. She rolled over again.

I didn't like to stroke her stomach; it embarrassed me.

'Oh, you're full of complexes,' my mother had said.

I looked away if Papa walked nude from the shower to his bedroom. I'd never seen a man naked before. I was torn between an obsessive curiosity and acute embarrassment.

'*Tu es vierge?*' Papa had asked one evening.

'Well, of course she is, Daddy.'

'What?'

'Are you still a virgin?'

Even the word made me blush like the word pregnant. I thought them both ugly clumsy words.

I stepped over Little Girl and the patio door

banged shut again. I liked the patio with its terracotta pots of red and white geraniums. Doors opened on to it from the *salon* where the record player was. We'd dance there on the patio at our parties. As Deedee or Roland or Bob and Gwen Yates-Earl, or Dick Templeton grew tired and resorted to lounging in the chairs in the *salon* drinking quietly, my stepfather (that had become my official name for him) would do his cabaret. He would pirouette like a ballerina, which considering the bulk and the squatness of his frame was absurd, and they would laugh and clap. Or he would stick the feather duster between his legs and shout '*l'oiseau rare*' as on the night of my arrival, and they would laugh some more, or he would sing, holding my mother's chin and looking deep into her eyes in a mocking way, 'Your eyes are the eyes of a woman in love' and they would laugh again. Lolo would sit flicking through the pages of an old *Paris-Match* not joining in, but I laughed, though I didn't know why. We'd had barbecues and *méchoui* where Papa had roasted a lamb whole over the glaring charcoals, and Lolo and I held large pink and white marshmallows on sticks into the flames until the outside caramelised and the inside was warm and runny. We bought them from the supermarket in the town. They couldn't shop at Wheelus Air Force base any more, as they no longer worked there. I loved going to the supermarket. It was the biggest food shop I had ever seen. There were packets of popcorn that you could pop yourself in a saucepan with the lid on, M & M's candy bars, huge bottles of tomato ketchup that Lolo called Catsup, and tall jars of something called Relish that she ate on her hamburgers. 'What's that?' I'd asked Papa. 'Ersatz,'

224

he'd answered and I didn't like to ask again.

The supermarket was surrounded by villas of every design imaginable, most of them much bigger than ours. Every kind of marble had been lavished on the stairs, and intricate mosaics swirled across floors. Huge white curved porches and archways cut vivid shapes against the constantly blue sky. Square pillars supported white turrets ending in minaret-shaped domes like the mosques but the sound that came from these mansions was often the symphonic swell of 'There's a Summer Place' or Laurie London singing 'He's got the whole worrld in his hands', rather than the high-pitched wail of the muezzin calling the faithful to prayer five times a day.

My mother was in the kitchen supervising lunch as I came in from the patio, her bottles of nail varnish carefully stowed in the fridge away from the heat which made them thick and unusable. The French would make a meal out of things that passed unnoticed in England. *Hors d'oeuvres*—I was never sure what *hors d'oeuvres* meant. I knew what a *chef d'oeuvre* was—we'd talked about that in art. *Hors d'oeuvres* were often '*radis au beurre*'—'*De Bretagne*,' my mother would say. I had no idea where radishes came from in England, or if anyone cared, but these were huge crisp bulbous ones that we crunched with salt and ate with the long crispy *baguettes* that Papa brought back from town fresh and warm each lunch-time: I'd got used to lunch being at dinner-time and dinner being supper.

'He used to spend his holidays as a child in Brittany,' my mother would explain. 'He speaks Breton—he can understand Auntie Louie when she speaks Welsh, you know. Brittany's wild and cold—you'd love it, Janie. The Ile de Sein—it's three kilometres wide and five kilometres long.'

I still wasn't sure what a kilometre was; more than a mile or less? Or if a kilo was more or less than a pound. A *livre* was a pound as well as a book and a pound had to be called a 'pound sterling'. It was all very confusing.

'All the women wear black and the *coiffe*: most of their husbands and sons lost at sea. The sea sweeps the island so their downstairs rooms are bare and all their treasures and prized pieces of furniture are kept upstairs. We'll take you there, Janie—it's an extraordinary place. They all know Daddy; "*Vonvon*" they call him in Breton—everybody knows him on the island . . .'

'It has three churches and fifty-four *bistros*,' Papa would add laughing, as if that were more than ample reason for buying only Breton radishes.

My mother was slicing huge tomatoes and arranging them on a plate which would be decorated with sharp green parsley. The only thing that Papa made in the kitchen was the vinaigrette.

'Ze secret is a little sugar,' he said as conspiratorially as Gran told me that the secret of a good Yorkshire was a little drop of water from the tap. 'You are to make it for us soon. If you can't make a good vinaigrette you can't begin to be *une bonne cuisinière*.'

I was determined to be a *bonne cuisinière*, although I couldn't see how I could practise in England. I couldn't imagine Gran wanting a concoction of olive oil, wine vinegar, mustard, sugar and garlic on her salad. She ate her lettuce doused in vinegar and then sprinkled sugar on top of it if she wasn't covering it with Heinz salad cream, but that was a luxury as it was so expensive.

No one seemed to worry about money here. My mother changed her thick gold rings sometimes to match the outfit she was wearing.

'This used to be Grand-mère's,' she would say, pointing to a large chunky oblong of gold inset with an oval filled with small diamonds.

'And it's going to be mine when I grow up, isn't it, Mommy?' Lolo said. I wondered when they were going to notice that I didn't even have a gold bracelet.

Mohammed did the washing-up and swept and washed the floors, did the ironing, made the beds and peeled the potatoes, all under my mother's watchful eye. When we went to the market she pointed out the fruit or fish she wanted, refused to pay the price first asked, left Mohammed to haggle and carry the bags to the car.

'Oh, Janie, they are so stupid most of them,' she would say within his earshot. I kept having to remind myself that he couldn't understand us when we spoke English.

'I told him when he first came to work for us to cook some rice for the dogs. Two packets. I was going to mix it up with some meat left over from a *bouillon* and d'you know what he did? Just that. He cooked two packets of rice. He put the rice, boxes and all, into the saucepan of boiling water. *Mon dieu—tu t'imagines.*'

Papa would make Mohammed laugh when he served us our meals. He knew a smattering of Arabic; Lolo could speak it fluently along with German and Italian. Papa would ask her to sing the Libyan national anthem to us if he'd run out of his silly jokes or was bored at dinner and she would

227

sing something that sounded like:

> Yap pill ardi
> Yap pill ardi
> Wickshta wada whenee

and he always laughed while she sang. I didn't understand why Mohammed would keep his eyes lowered as he cleared up and piled the dirty plates very carefully and quietly one on top of the other, bowing several times as he did so.

'*Tackel halonf*,' Papa interjected. Mohammed would make an effort to smile, unsuccessfully.

'What does that mean?'

'Oh, it's something rude, Janie. It's "Your mother is a pig", which of course is a big insult as Arabs don't eat pork,' my mother would say disapprovingly.

Papa would speak to him in a French I couldn't understand at all.

'*Eh, Mohammed, viens ici, mon vieux,*' which would then be followed by a stream of French in a sharp thin voice.

'What's he saying?'

'Oh, he's talking French like an Arab,' Mummy would say smiling, pouring herself another glass of whisky.

Mohammed would giggle coyly like a girl, his slippered feet shuffling around the table like a loud whisper.

'*Eh, Mohammed, tu veux vivre comme des Français, huh? Tu ne veux pas t'asseoir par terre, tu veux t'acheter de bonnes chaises comme chez nous, huh?*'

'*Si, si, monsieur.*'

'*On dirait un espagnol,*' said Papa, and Mummy and Lolo would laugh.

'*Ce n'est pas si, Mohammed, c'est* oui.'

'*Si, monsieur.*'

'*Oh, qu'est-ce qu'ils sont cons, ces gens!*' Papa would mutter under his breath.

'What's *con*?'

'It's a *very* rude word,' said my mother, offering no explanation.

'*C'est beau mon pays, n'est-ce pas?*'

'*Oui, pour les mouches à merde.*'

'*C'est beau pour les français ici; le sable, la mer—*' Mohammed would begin.

'*Assez! Au travail!*'

Suddenly the mood would be changed. Papa pointed to the kitchen and Mohammed shuffled off, carrying the plates without another word.

It struck me as wrong but I didn't know why. I couldn't imagine Gran talking to her home help like that. On the days when the home help came to clean the house, she got up early to tidy up and dust a bit. 'I don't want her thinking I'm a dirty old woman,' and as soon as she arrived Gran would sit her down for a good half hour and ply her with biscuits and coffee.

Lolo was mixing up pancake dough from a packet with a smiling black woman with large gold hoop earrings on the front. 'Aunt Jemima's Pancake Mix.' We bought it from the American supermarket. The large bottle of maple syrup beside it was almost empty: it was going to be a fight over sharing it out.

'Oh, can I have some?'

'*Je vous jure*, you're always hungry, you two.'

'Oh, please, can I have some?'

'Well, of course, Janie bach—don't whine. If Lolo's making some for herself she'll make some for you too.'

I wasn't so sure of that. Mummy had a habit of endowing us with more magnanimity towards each other than either of us felt.

I hated Lolo because of her clothes and her charm. She never looked tongue-tied or uncomfortable 'in company' as Mrs Whitman would have said, and I knew she hated me because I passed exams. She didn't know what IIID meant.

'I thought we were going to the beach.'

'*Après*,' said Lolo sharply, beating the creamy mixture so hard that her brown legs shook. They were such a lovely shape. I was convinced Gran had tried to make me walk before I was ready and that was why my legs were bandy—my mother's legs were a good shape too.

I didn't like to look at Papa's too often.

From the back they both looked normal but his right leg had a huge scar that ran from his ankle to above his knee. It was livid and dark and had several short scars that ran across it that were scored far into the flesh.

'How did you do that, Papa?' I'd asked one evening after dinner, when Mohammed had cleared away the dishes and gone shuffling home to his wife and son in their little house in Gargaresch. I was half-fearful that he might resent my question, but worried that he might think me uncaring for not asking. I had to think so hard now, before I spoke. I didn't feel like me at all. We were about to play a game of crazy eight—a card game that big fat Bill who worked at the Wheelus Air Force base had taught us. We liked Bill. He always had jokes

230

to tell us, and they weren't rude like Papa's.

'What's yellow and dangerous?'

'Shark-infested custard,' Lolo would shout.

'Why do elephants paint their toenails red?'

'So they can hide in cherry trees,' my mother would say, laughing.

Papa would smile, take a large swig of his whisky and say, 'Bill, you old son of a bitch,' which made Bill laugh.

I'd never found the courage to ask Bill if he'd ever been based in England, but if Gran was right and my father was American then the thought that maybe Bill might have known him haunted me when Bill was around in his Air Force uniform. If Gran was right my father must have looked like this. Bill must've reminded my mother too, but my mother never looked upset or disturbed by him. She was always pleased to see Bill. He brought her whisky from the PX, whatever that was.

'So what happened to your leg, Papa?'

My mother answered before he had time to draw breath. 'He went through the whole war; it was only days before peace was declared. His tank went over a mine, he nearly lost that leg—was in hospital for ages. That's why he got this job because of his war record. That's where I first met him, eh Papa? When he was convalescing in Tunbridge Wells . . .'

I knew my mother had been sent there by Gran in disgrace, to explain my birth to Auntie Louie.

'*Ouf*, Tunbridge Wells,' he said, waving it away with his arm in a dismissive fashion. 'It wasn't as good as Liverpool.'

'He spent most of the war in Liverpool—'

'Not most of it, Louise—'

'He was in the *deuxième* DB. They were shipped

231

out from the Ile de Sein, General Leclerc's Regiment. They had to wait in England until they were given uniforms—the Free French Forces. They don't pay any tax to France now, the Ile de Sein, because of the FFF being there. De Gaulle made a special law about it.'

'Oh, Louise, you get it all wrong. Like all your stories about the war. They're crazy, they don't make sense. Your war was *fantaisie*. I want to know how you and Mary Waller, *par exemple*, manage to be in London with bombs dropping when you were supposed to be nursing . . .'

The atmosphere in the *salle à manger* changed. My mother concentrated hard on fitting a new cigarette in her cigarette-holder. Papa's eyes glittered. He leant forward, and stubbed out his Gauloise so firmly that the cigarette paper split and burning tobacco spread over the ashtray.

'Now, come on, Louise, tell the truth if you *can*.'

I pricked up my ears: maybe I was going to hear something important, something I'd never heard before—something about my father . . .

'*Papa, tu as trop bu.*'

Bu was the past participle of *boire*, to drink, that I knew.

'*Mais* non, *Louise. Au contraire, c'est* toi,' he said very calmly, leaning forward on folded arms as if he were about to interrogate her.

I was beginning to recognise certain tones in their voices that spelled trouble even though I didn't understand what they were saying.

'Tell Janie about Liverpool, Daddee,' said my mother, stubbing out the remains of his cigarette with her own.

'Oh, shit, they were wonderful, those two old

girls.' He smiled at the memory. 'I 'ad bacon and eggs for breakfast, a big lunch, they made all their own cakes for tea. I was as fat as hell.' He laughed, drained the whisky from his glass and reached for the bottle.

'Janie darling, don't stand there in the doorway dreaming.'

'What?'

'I said you'll get fat if you eat all those.'

'What?'

I looked at the heap of perfectly browned circles that Lolo had piled on a second plate for me.

I wasn't really hungry at all after the crusty warm *baguette*, but I wasn't going to let her have all the pancakes. I couldn't imagine Gran mixing pancakes out of a packet. We only had them on Shrove Tuesday—with lemon and sugar—but these, which looked like 'drop scones', we doused with more of the thick treacly maple syrup than was polite or palatable.

'*Lolo, ce n'est pas un bistro ici,*' said my mother sharply as Lolo began to tuck into her pile standing by the oven. Gran's oven was electric. This oven ran on bottles of something I thought my mother called pewter gas until I read the name stamped on the large metal cylinder one day, BUTAGAZ. My mother got cross if it ran out and Papa would complain about having to fetch a new one from the shop in town and roll the empty one into the garage.

'What's a *bistro*?'

'Janie, don't they teach you anything at school in your French lessons? It's a café.'

'Is it slang?'

'No, it's not *argot*—it's everyday French. You're

233

as bad as Papa. When I first met him he could quote lines from Shakespeare but he didn't know how to ask the time.'

I vowed to use *bistro* in my next French essay and impress Miss Reid.

'Oh, shall we go and sit down and eat these, then?'

'*Mais oui, bien sûr.*'

'*Oh, petite maman, chérie*, it's more fun eating them like this,' said Lolo, putting down her plate, and wrapping her arms around my mother and covering her bare brown arms with sticky kisses.

My mother laughed, hugged her back and kissed her.

'*Tu es la plus gentille mère au monde*,' said Lolo returning to her plate.

I knew what that meant, I'd heard her say it so often. I wished I could agree.

I envied Lolo the ease with which she hugged Mummy. I always felt awkward and uncomfortable.

'Now I must go and do my toilet,' she said, opening the door of the fridge which was always packed with food and reaching for a beer, 'or Michael Drew will be popping in before I'm dressed.'

Michael Drew was a family joke. His face was always sweaty and unshaven. The collars and cuffs of his suits were frayed. Even in this heat he wore scuffed lace-up shoes and socks that wrinkled round his ankles. As my mother had said, he was a radio engineer and worked in the small square brick building by the tall radio aerial on the beach, so he had ample excuse to drop in as he passed our villa every day. He would return our hospitality by inviting us to his messy villa for a curry, an invitation which was met with groans by all of us except my mother. Yves thought he was a rotten cook, Lolo and I hated curry, but my mother loved it. It reminded her she said of meals she had had in a place called Veeraswamy's in London during the war.

'Louise,' Yves would say, 'it's not possible that you went to London as much as you say you did. On what money?'

'Boyfriends took me.'

'Your boyfriends are *fantômes* like Little Girl's pregnancies,' said Yves.

'Has Jane's boyfriend been again today?' he would say as he came in for lunch.

'He's *not* my boyfriend.'

'He will ask you to marry him and you will live in a bungalow that smells of curry.' Yves's laughter echoed in my head.

'Lolo, please let's hurry if we're going to the beach.'

'You two are going to the beach, huh? Don't forget to be back for *déjeuner*. Papa doesn't like to be kept waiting. Put your watch on, Janie, so there's no excuse. You're in charge.'

I looked at the white watch-shaped mark on my arm. I kept the watch on in the sun and only took it off in the evening after my shower so I could see how brown I was now compared with how white I'd been. I could show that off to Annette, Deirdre and Rita.

'*Oh, ça m'ennuie d'y aller,*' said Lolo pulling a face.

Ennuyer—that was to be bored.

'Oh, c'mon,' I mumbled, stuffing my last pancake into my mouth, feeling my mother's shorts

235

tighten round my waist.

'I'll come if you sing that song, Janie. Sing some Cockney.'

'Oh, go on, darling—I love it too. It reminds me of Ipswich when you talk like Nana.'

I didn't understand why she wanted to be reminded of Ipswich. She always said she hated it and had she forgotten how far Suffolk was from London? But I liked the smile on her face, and Lolo laughed when I did it. I took a deep breath. My knees always shook a bit when they turned to watch me, but it was worth it because they seemed to enjoy it.

'All I want is a room somewhere . . .
Far away from the cold night air . . .'

How odd, I thought as I sang, the nights here made me sweat almost more than the days.

'With one enormous chair
Oh wouldn't it be luvverly . . .'

My mother took several gulps of beer and smiled happily.

'. . . Someone's 'ead resting on my knee
Warm and tender as 'e can be
Who'd take good care of me
Oh wouldn't it be luvverly.
Oh so luvverly sittin' abso-bloomin'-
Lutely still
I would never budge
Till Spring crept over me windowsill . . .'

236

I screeched, twisting the bikinis corkscrew-fashion in an effort to reach the top note. Mohammed edged past me in the doorway carrying the broom and the brush and dustpan.

'Ssh, Mohammed.' He hadn't said anything, just lowered his eyes again. 'Ssh, Mohammed—*elle chante, ma soeur*,' said Lolo. I liked her calling me her sister, although it wasn't strictly true. Very little seemed to be strictly true any more.

> 'Lots of chocolates for me to eat
> Lots of coal making lots of 'eat
> Warm face warm 'ands warm feet
> Oh wouldn't it be luvverly
> Luwerly
> Luvverly
> Luvverly
> Luvverly
> LUVVERLY.'

'Bravo, bravo, Janie,' said my mother, clapping her hands.

'*Oh, c'est du tonnerre, c'est sensas*,' said Lolo.

'What?' I said, blushing with pleasure but unsure whether it was a criticism or a compliment.

'*Tonnerre*'s thunder—it's an expression—and *sensas*'s short for sensational.'

I blushed more. 'Race you to the beach,' I said and made a dash to the bathroom to change, glowing with embarrassment and pleasure.

I ran—arms akimbo, flying my towel behind me like a flag—and the dogs ran after me. Bebop racing ahead past the notice that said, '*Attenzione ai Bambini*', past the eucalyptus trees that smelled so sharp and pure, past the *cri-cris*, as I now thought

237

of them, chirping in the cool shade of the bushes, my flipflops spraying a fine, glittering dust up the backs of my legs as I ran. The sea glistened at the end of the track, and shimmered in the heat haze which made it difficult to see where it joined the azure sky.

Past the Arab *guardien* who patrolled the beach making sure Arabs didn't trespass, only the privileged of CPTL were allowed to use the beach, his '*Bonjour, Mademoiselle Lapotaire*' distorted by the blood thumping in my head. That pleased me. He wasn't to know. Past the clubhouse and tennis courts, the outdoor café dotted with brightly coloured parasols, round the corner into the deserted sheltered bay. At weekends it was difficult to find a spot to sit on the powdery sand. The company and their wives and children descended in droves with their picnics and wine and gossip. We hardly went then, or if we did, Mummy would insist on sitting slightly apart from the rest.

Shorts and shirt thrown in a heap, flipflops discarded, a quick dash across the burning sand and a belly-flop into the lukewarm shallows.

Peace. Ears full of water, head full of quiet. Sun baking my shoulders as I surfaced and swam. Ahead of me was Italy and Sicily, to the right Greece, far right Israel and along the coast Egypt. Over there beyond France was England. Papa had taken my ticket and my passport to make arrangements for my return journey but still no one had mentioned my going back. I didn't want to think about it. It made my stomach lurch with fear and excitement. Fear that they wouldn't let me go, and excitement at the endless possibilities of showing off my differentness in Ipswich. I seemed to have two opposing sets of feelings for everything these days.

Lolo was donning her mask and snorkel and flippers.

'Janie bach. *Tiens, tiens,*' she shouted and threw mine in after me. We couldn't talk in the water, so we couldn't quarrel.

She swam up to me, her eyes large behind the mask and indicated that I should follow. I thought of the bleakness of Felixstowe beach, the iciness of the water in Pipers Vale swimming pool, the way the chlorine stung my eyes in Fore Street baths and closed my eyes, squinted into the sun and felt superior.

I spat into my mask to stop it blurring up as Papa had shown me, and put the rubbery-tasting mouthpiece of the snorkel in between my teeth. I was always suspicious that I wouldn't be able to breathe under the water even with this tube in my mouth, and, frightened of having asthma, my first breaths were always apprehensive and unsure till I got used to the gurgling sound the air made as I expelled it up the tube to the surface.

Lolo's skin looked paler under the water; hundreds of minute air bubbles stuck to the hairs on her arms and legs. With a flourish of black rubber flippers she swam ahead.

Shoals of small colourless fish swam about just above the sand and, turning to swim out deeper, I could see silver saars and mottled orange rougets darting between the rocks that stretched out from one side of the bay into the deeper blue water.

She was a strong swimmer and could hold her breath and dive down between the rocks swimming into secret dark places. I often lost her from sight

239

for a while but suspected where she was if a shoal of fish darted out from between some rocks in a panic.

'*Un poulpe!*' Lolo shouted, surfacing quickly and dived again. Octopuses frightened me. At first I thought they were jellyfish. Jellyfish terrorised Sunday School outings on the beaches at Walton on the Naze, Clacton and Yarmouth. Here the Arabs pulled the squid out of the water and bashed them senseless up against the rocks until their tentacles hung lifeless and there was no more suction in their pads, and took them home to cook.

They didn't squirt ink like I'd read in books, they just clung tighter to the rocks if we pulled them or tickled them with bits of seaweed until they let go. One had stuck to me once and I still wasn't able to shake off the memory of its clinging sucking pads on the underside of my arm.

I turned and swam in the opposite direction, to where the sea graded from azure to deep greeny blue. Although I enjoyed the speed at which they enabled me to slide through the water, my arms immobile by my side, my flippers made my ankles ache after a while. I trod water and slipped them off, stretching my toes in their new weightlessness into the water below me. My ten silver nails that matched my fingers looked like small darting fish beneath me. Flippers in hand I shuffled along in the water as best I could, towards the nearest rocks and scrambled up. I sat in the sun, hugging my knees, water dripping from my hair, cascading down my shoulders and arms. As the sun began to penetrate, the salt began to dry and make the new skin on my shoulders itch.

My legs were a battleground. Huge raised bumps

of new mosquito bites, old ones scratched until they wept a stream of pus, and then stained red with something Mummy called Mercurochrome. My feet began to tingle and smart. I picked one up and splayed my leg across my knee to inspect the sole. It was pitted with small brown sliver-like specks.

'Oh, no,' I muttered into the blueness. The morning began to take a sharp dip downwards.

*   *   *

'*Ah, non! Pas encore!*' said my mother as she watched me limp out on to the terrace into the afternoon sun. I was still groggy from my siesta and hadn't been sharp-witted enough to realise that she, as usual, would be awake before me. I never understood how she was so tanned; she only ever sat out in the sun at the end of the afternoon with a pile of sewing beside her, a silly shapeless white cloche of a sunhat on her head.

'Oh, Janie darling, you're covered in bites, we've just got you through a bad throat and now *oursins* again!'

I'd hated having the sore throat. The French seemed to stick everything up your bottom if you were ill, cold thermometers and slippery greasy things called suppositories. I failed to see how something stuck up my bottom could make the raging soreness in my throat, which made it impossible to swallow the crusty *baguettes* and even uncomfortable to swallow iced drinks, better, but it did.

'Will I have to have suppositories again?'

It embarrassed me dreadfully to have to pull

241

down my pants and bare my bottom to my mother.

'No, no,' she said, 'don't be silly, but we'll have to get them out with a needle and put Mercurochrome on them. Go and get it. Oh, Janie, you're so *mal fichue*.'

'What's that?'

'Badly put together: *tu es mal fichue, ma fille*.'

'Well, that's not my fault,' I muttered to myself as I limped back into the shade of the house. As I pushed open the bathroom door and clicked on the light there was that horrid scratchy slithery sound again. Cockroaches. With the shutters closed and the bathroom light off, they thought it was night and made their way up through the gaping plughole to bask immobile in the few drops of water that dripped from the shower-head above the bath. They scuttled away back to where they'd come from, to avoid the glare of the light.

'Ugh.' I shuddered, remembering the difficulty Papa had crunching them underfoot, their bodies were so scaly and tough.

'*Mal fichue*,' I murmured again.

'If I'm *mal* bloody *fichue* it's *your* bloody fault,' I said out loud, opening the bathroom cabinet door, surprised at my bad temper. 'Now you've got out of bed the wrong side, my girl,' said Gran in my head. 'Bugger off,' I said to no one in particular. My voice sounded loud in the quiet shaded house. Lolo was sleeping. I could hear the hum of the air-conditioning behind her shut door. Papa's dirty shirt and white knee-socks were thrown in the *bidet*. I now knew it was for something rude, so I liked to see washing in it. He wore a clean set of clothes in the afternoon, so he'd returned to the office. Perhaps I'd had too much sun again. I was hot, my head felt thick and my throat was dry. I swallowed hard.

'If I'm *mal fichue* it's because,' I said, pausing for breath, continuing my one-sided conversation, 'it's because Gran said you never drank milk when you were pregnant with me, that's why my teeth are so crumbly and soft—*and* she had to force you to go for walks around the rec.' The word sounded so out of place in front of a bottle of *'Bien-Etre'* eau de Cologne and the chirping of the cicadas all around me. 'You never took care of yourself, *that's* why I've always got things wrong with me.'

I slammed the glass door shut making the bottles inside rattle. I caught a glimpse of my disagreeable face in the mirror.

'You're a bad-tempered little sod and make no mistake,' I said aloud, surprised to hear Gran's voice now coming out of my mouth. Why was I suddenly thinking of Gran? I'd managed to keep her out of my mind quite successfully for such a long time now. Of course it was because I was going home soon. Or was I? Home. 85 was my real home. Home where the only things that stung were wasps if I tried to swat them when I ate jam sandwiches in the back yard; where the lavatory, however dark and cold and frightening, harboured only silly daddy-long-legs, and not great brown armoured bugs with huge waving feelers; where everyone had white skin all year long and everybody got mosquito bites in summer, not just me. Where nobody said I was 'badly put together' and where Gran would let me sit on her knee and suck my thumb and play with her ear if I didn't feel up to much.

'Well, she didn't want you, that's why she took

243

no care of 'erself,' Gran's voice continued in my ear. She certainly seemed to take care of herself now. She spent ages doing her nails and her face, and she slept every afternoon—I couldn't imagine Mrs Whitman or Mrs Hayward putting their feet up after lunch.

I was cross with her, but I didn't dare show it. And that made me cross with myself. I was a coward. I hadn't dared ask the important questions.

The radio was playing quietly, crackling a bit as it did when she'd tuned into a French radio station. Reception from Wheelus was always clear but they had adverts in between the music which annoyed her. I made my way slowly out into the light again. My mother was singing quietly along with the radio.

> '*Un jour tu verras qu'on se rencontrera*
> *Quelque part n'importe où . . .*'

It was one of her favourite songs.

I knew some of the words by heart now too, '*Guidé par l'hasard . . .*' although I wouldn't sing them when Papa was around. I wasn't sure whether it was '*l'hasard*' or '*le hasard*'. And anyway, whenever he heard me sing he said, '*Tu chantes français comme une vache espagnole,*' which Lolo always found funny.

I settled down in the chair beside her, offering a foot for her to start on. I picked up a book from the table, hoping it would take my mind off the needle probing into the skin. Also it would stop me feeling uncomfortable as I always did when my mother and I were completely alone. My head was so full of the

244

unasked questions, and they buzzed so loudly I was sure she could hear and that made me uneasy.

The book was a novel in French by Maurice West, *The Cardinal*. She'd seen a film of his called *The Shoes of the Fisherman*. It didn't sound a plausible title but that's how she'd translated it to me. Her French wasn't very good at all. That was another thing I didn't understand.

'Ouch!' I flinched as the needle dug deep into my heel.

'Janie, don't be a baby. We've told you about the *oursins* on the rocks. I can't understand how you managed to get them into your feet *again*.'

'What are they?'

'Oh, what do you call them in English? Sea urchins.'

'Sea urchins?'

'They're delicious.'

Papa had brought some home from the market once. They were like completely round hedgehogs but in between their long brown prickles was a mark like a cross which my mother cut into with a knife and opened it up to reveal four orange-coloured segments inside, resting in a little sea-water, which she scooped out with a teaspoon, smacking her lips and making *noises* of pleasure as she ate.

'*Mmm, mmm, que c'est bon, que c'est bon.*'

I shuddered, remembering.

'What's the matter?'

'Nothing—I think someone walked over my grave.'

'Oh. You sound so like Nana sometimes,' she said, not entirely complimentarily. They were evil, *oursins*. They rested on the rocks and looked just

245

like shadows or crevices. They floated away if you caught them with your foot, as they weren't attached, but before they did they left the tips of their spines in your feet. I flinched again.

'Oh, Janie, *voyons! voyons!*'

French was confusing. What did she mean 'let us see'?

I shifted in the chair. The afternoon sun was still powerful and the heat was making my thighs stick to the plastic.

'Will they go septic again?'

'No, of course not.'

'Are you sure?'

'I was a nurse, you know, Janie, during the war, before you were born. I know what I'm doing.'

'A nurse—hmph,' said Gran's voice in my head. 'She weren't a nurse proper. Everybody had to do *something* during the war and she didn't want to be a land-girl, that's why she went nursing at Allington House. If the truth be known she spent more time gallivantin' about with that Mary Waller, goin' to dances and suchlike, than she ever did nursing. She were never an SRN like Betty.'

'Yes, I know,' I said politely, hoping my disbelief wasn't showing, my heart beginning to beat harder, willing her to go on.

'She was a good friend to me, Mary Waller. She came from a proper family; they lived in a big farmhouse, Janie, near Hadleigh, Sonny her brother, her father, her mother. Her mother was always dressed so elegantly—just like a French woman.'

I felt a flicker of discomfort that I'd never thought about 'elegance' before. It seemed suddenly important. I resolved to consider it more

246

in the future, and be it when I was grown up.

'It was a proper family,' she repeated again. 'They were quite well-off.'

Gran interrupted in my head: 'Well off! They made their money sowin' sugar beet when he should 'a been growin' what the government told him to, durin' the war. That's how they made their money—on the black market.'

'Not like 85 Levington Road,' she went on. 'I never liked Pat, you know . . .'

'Oh, no, I know what you mean,' I said with some feeling.

'Horrible, common they were, all of them, Edna, Gladys—though Doris was all right. I always liked Doris.'

'Oh, yes,' I said. 'I like Doris too. She used to take me down to Holywells Park with her boyfriends—Americans,' I added lamely.

My mother's glasses slipped down the end of her nose.

'*Ouf, c'est chaud!*' she said, pushing them back up, wiping her forehead with the back of her hand.

The smell of her perfume caught my nostrils again.

Mohammed shuffled out on to the terrace carrying a small mat, half-bowed and mumbled something quietly.

'*Oui, oui, vas-y,*' said my mother impatiently, waving him towards the patch of grass. Mohammed kneeled down on his mat and began muttering and bowing some more.

'Is he saying his prayers *again*?' I said incredulously.

'Yes,' said my mother raising her eyebrows mockingly. 'It's the hour that the faithful are called to prayer.'

I remembered with a shock that I hadn't said my prayers once all the time I'd been here. Alan Road and Sunday School and the angel with the book of black marks seemed such a long way away. I'd even forgotten to enlist God's help to get me back to Ipswich. My heart missed a beat. Should I ask when I was going back?

'He wants to go to Mecca then he can put "Ben" after his name: Mohammed Ben . . . *quelque chose.*'

'What is his other name?'

'Oh, I don't know, Janie,' she said as if it were a preposterous idea that I should, that she would even be interested.

'Names are funny, aren't they?'

She didn't answer.

'Why is my name Burgess?'

It came from nowhere. I hadn't planned it, I shocked myself.

'Well, because that's my name, silly. You were called after me,' she added, dipping the glass tube into the red liquid and squeezing the rubber cap. Several drops trickled down my instep and splashed on to the table.

'Horace Hubert Burgess,' she continued. 'He was my father.'

Her 'h's came out like guttural sounds as if she had difficulty in saying them, like French people, but she spoke English without an accent. It struck me as odd.

I'd never thought of my grandfather as someone having a name.

'Horace Hubert Burgess,' I repeated slowly, relishing the words. 'Is he still—'

'Of course not. I'm an orphan. He died, Janie,

248

not long after my mother died.'

A grandmother too.

'Then my brother and I were brought to England. But Auntie Louie couldn't look after us. Anyway we had TB; we were put in a sanatorium and my brother died there. So I was put into Dr Barnardo's. Age seven speaking only French. That's when Nana took me, along with Pat and Doris and Edna and Gladys.'

I waited, holding my breath, hating myself for not daring. All this news washed over me in a blur. It wasn't what I wanted to know. It was her story—not mine.

'Is it a French name?'

'No, of course it isn't.'

My fear made me ask the stupidest questions. I knew Burgess came from Burgher, a citizen of a town. We'd learnt that in history.

'No, of course it isn't. Janie darling, do keep your feet still, you're so *nerveuse*, so like me. So like me.' She paused. 'They used to call me Bugalugs at Allington House.' She laughed. 'Do they call you that?'

'Some people in Ipswich call me Louise,' I said. I didn't want to say girls at school called me Bossy Burgess.

She smiled. 'Yes, you're very like me.'

My turn to pause. I looked away through the olive trees that edged the road to Tripoli—hoping my glance would diffuse the importance of the question.

'I don't look like my father then?'

'Tut,' she went, very dismissively, in the way Papa and Lolo did when they meant 'No'. A lot of French people did that, I'd noticed. Gran would've called it rude. 'You're like him in some ways—he loved literature and music. He was artistic too.'

I thought of eagle-faced Miss Hoyle who taught us art in her cold dark art room. She didn't think of me as artistic at all, she disliked me because I painted pictures without people in them. People were too difficult. I only wanted to paint hedges and fields and trees. I sat in the back row and hid behind my easel, throwing paper darts, trying to elicit giggles of approval or talking when I was bored.

'He had an artistic temperament.'

I wasn't sure what temperament meant; it sounded awfully like temper. Gran always said I had a dreadful one. My mother didn't know that though.

'He loved the balalaika.'

'What's a balalaika?'

'Russian music.'

'Was he Russian?'

'No, of course not, Janie. *Tu sors des choses, ma fille!*'

Sors came from *sortir* to go out, *fille* was daughter . . .

'I loved him very much, you know,' she said sadly.

'Oh,' I said, not knowing whether to be pleased for me or sorry for her.

'Is he still—'

'No, of course not, Janie. We were going to be married but . . . he was killed in action.'

A picture flashed into my mind of a man storming the ramparts of a castle carrying a flag which unfurled behind him in the wind. Like in the *Alamo* film we'd seen a while back. My father is

250

brave. My father *was* brave. Odd to have found a family and lost it again so quickly. I wondered where he was buried and saw myself carrying a bunch of flowers sedately towards his grave.

'Don't tell Papa. He doesn't like me talking about your father.'

Hearing her say 'your father' suddenly made him very real. I didn't move.

'Of course Nana didn't approve of him.'

Gran didn't even remember who he was.

'But then Nana didn't approve of most things I did. I was so unhappy there, Janie, can you imagine?'

I couldn't. 85 Levington Road was my home.

'A little French girl of seven uprooted and made to go and live in a dreadful place like Ipswich.'

I suddenly felt rather loyal about Ipswich. It wasn't *that* dreadful really.

'Was my grandfather French?'

'No, Janie.' Again that disapproving tone as if I should have known he wasn't. 'He was Welsh, darling, Welsh. He was a jockey. Auntie Louie's brother. That's where you get your colouring from. Dark hair and white skin—it's Welsh.'

My roots were being changed with every sentence; it was unsettling.

'There, only one more to get out, then you'll be as good as new. I didn't like Nana, you know, Janie. She wasn't like she is with you when I was young. She was very strict and severe. I hated her.'

That shocked me.

'I hated her dirty house.'

It *isn't*, I thought defensively, hearing Gran say, 'We may be poor but we're clean.'

'I hated the people in Ipswich.'

251

That I understood. I never felt I belonged either.

'She always said she loved her girls but she only did it for the money. Barnardo's used to pay her a little each week for every one of us. I thought that was wicked.'

'But that was the only way a widow could live in those days.' I started repeating the explanation I'd heard Gran offer so frequently.

'I wanted to keep you, darling, but I couldn't. She wouldn't even let me pick you up when you cried, she always got there first; it broke my heart.'

My mother's voice cracked and I saw her eyes fill with tears.

I lifted my foot off the table. My leg was stiff from having kept it in one position for so long. I stood unsurely on it and bent to put my arms around her.

It was difficult to cuddle her: she was so angular and bony, my arms never seemed to fit properly. It wasn't a proper cuddle like I could have with Gran. It was more a placing of arms, that I continually rearranged in order to find a better position, and never could.

'I couldn't *fight* her, you see.'

Tears trickled out from under her glasses down her nose with its open pores just like mine.

'I was too young, only nineteen, Janie. I wanted you but I couldn't fight her.'

My head was in turmoil. It was a side of the story I hadn't heard before and I was shocked. Shocked and angry at Gran. I hadn't been told the truth. I felt I'd betrayed my mother all these years. She reached for some Kleenex in the pocket of her shorts. Gran never bought paper handkerchiefs. Our handkerchiefs came in boxes as Christmas

252

presents. They had lacy edges and embroidered flowers on them, or sometimes a G or a J.

'Don't cry, Mummy,' I said, taking the Kleenex from her and beginning to mop her face. 'Please don't cry or you'll make me cry.' That always worked when I said it to Gran.

'You've got nothing to cry about, Janie—you've got Nana. She loves you, she's given you a good home, you're all right.'

I wasn't. I felt bad, but I didn't know why. I lifted her glasses off with trembling hands, catching her ear as I did so.

'*Attention, mes lunettes*, Janie. They're new and very expensive. Papa won't pay for another pair if you break them.'

Why did the French call glasses small moons? I felt guilty that my mind should wander in this way when she was so distressed. My hands shook as I put them down on the table and returned to cleaning up her face.

'No, no, let me do it. You'll smudge my Rimmel and I'll have to do my eyes again.' Rimmel was make-up that Woolworths sold, but she means mascara, my wandering mind chattered on.

I shifted my sore foot off the hot sandy concrete, hoping she hadn't noticed, and eased it back into my flipflop surreptitiously. The cicadas chirped. The sun beat down, as if it was making a last burning effort before disappearing in a blaze of pink behind the sea. The silence made me edgy.

There was a shout and a scream from behind the house which made me jump and made my mother stop peering at herself in the little mirror that she had in her sewing-box.

'*Mon dieu, qu'est-ce que c'est?*'

253

Papa appeared around the corner of the house, his shirt soaked, his sunglasses splashed and dripping water.

'*Quelle salope!*' he said, and heading towards the table, he took off his shirt in a great hurry, threw his glasses down and dropped the papers he'd been carrying into a chair. 'Don't let them get wet—it's Janie's passport and ticket.' His brown torso rippled as he moved; I forgot to look away, forgot to be embarrassed. My ticket and my passport.

'*Cette salope*,' he said, spluttering and wiping the water from his eyes, spilling drops all over us as he shook his head like Bebop after a swim.

'*Cette salope—je vais l'avoir*,' and he ran to the other side of the house and disappeared.

'What's *salope*?' I enquired with renewed interest, relieved that soon I wouldn't have to ask questions about what people said.

'Oh, that's Lolo,' said my mother, not explaining, smiling proudly. I was amazed at how quickly her mood had changed and jealous that Lolo had changed it. There was another shout from the back of the house near the garage.

'Oh, she's got him again,' said my mother, laughing even more.

'What's she doing?'

'She's on the roof with the hose, Janie. She must have been waiting for him to arrive.' Another yell. 'She's got him.'

'*C'est la guerre*,' Papa shouted in the distance. '*Aiee!*'

'Bull's-eye,' said my mother.

Lolo appeared on the flat roof above our heads, stalking her prey, making signs for us to keep quiet and not reveal where she was. She wore only the

254

bottom half of her bikini as she always did. She must have put it on hastily as a wide white band of flesh was visible on one buttock where the bikini was doubled under. That seemed somehow more rude than revealing the upper part of her body which was tanned all over the same deep brown.

My mother pointed silently in the direction that Papa had gone.

Lolo put her fingers to her lips begging us to remain silent and made to turn towards the back of the house, dragging yards of green plastic hose after her.

There was an almighty roar and before she could turn, Papa appeared behind her, fastening her arms to her body so that she dropped the hose which began to squirt water all over the parasol, the table and us.

'*Mais non, chérie, mais non,*' said my mother, laughing and dodging out of the way of the water, grabbing her sewing and retreating away from the growing puddle of water. They fell in a heap on the floor of the roof, almost disappearing from view except for a jumble of twisting brown arms and legs.

'Don't just stand there, Janie, *va! va!* Go and have fun.'

It didn't look much like fun to me. There was something too dangerous in the way they were fighting. I ran to the back of the house. The step-ladder from the garage was leaning up against the wall. Unsteadily I climbed its metal rungs. I didn't like looking through them at the scrubby grass that grew out from the edge of the villa. It reminded me of Derby Road Station bridge. I forced myself to look up, wondering whose side I should take, when the full blast of the hose hit my face. Bellows of laughter came from both Papa and Lolo. They had joined forces.

I spluttered and gasped for breath. It was like being ducked in the swimming pool which I hated. I nearly lost my footing as I removed one hand from the ladder to wipe the water from my eyes.

Lolo screamed as Papa grabbed the hose from her and, putting his finger over the opening, squirted it with double force as he pulled her bikini bottom away from her body and directed the hose down it. She was laughing so much she could barely stand. Oh, so it was fun. I'd never seen grown-ups play with children like this. Couldn't imagine Mr Whitman doing this to Margaret.

I clambered up dripping and gasping while she writhed out of his grasp.

'Go on, Janie, get him, get him; you're bigger than me.'

'If you try,' he said, threatening me with the swipe of water that came nearer and nearer my feet. He was so serious I hesitated.

'*Ne sois pas lâche*,' shouted Lolo, struggling to get back into her bikini.

'What?'

'You're a coward,' he shouted.

'*A l'attaque!*' screamed Lolo behind me. That I understood. We both lunged at him, Lolo trying to unclamp his hands from the hose while I tried to pin back his arms. He was incredibly strong; my skinny arms wouldn't reach all the way round him and my hands couldn't grip his bulging muscles. I resorted to other tactics.

'Ah hah!' he said, his face near mine as we fell in a jumble on the roof, laughing and spluttering.

256

'You fight dirty!' he said in between yelps as my fingers sought out sensitive spots under his arms. 'You fight dirty, just like your mother. Hey hey.' He dropped his voice to a whisper. I could smell the now familiar odour of alcohol and cigarettes on his breath but was too frightened to move my head away.

'Hey, let's get Louise!'

'*Bonne idée*,' said Lolo. 'Ssh . . .'

We slithered along the roof flat on our stomachs.

The road to Tripoli stretched away ahead of us through the palms and olive trees. The sand dunes dotted with small low white houses quivered in a heat haze.

Mummy was inspecting some of the plants that grew on the slopes beside the steps, a glass of whisky in one hand, her cigarette in the other. I could just hear her singing in her croaky broken-voiced way that sounded so like my bad attempts at singing.

'*C'est la guerre*,' said Yves, standing upright and in one movement directing the full blast of the hose at her back. The shock nearly made her lose her balance but she hung on to her glass and her cigarette.

Within seconds her shirt was soaked and we could see the outline of her small breasts under it. I wished I was holding the hose.

'*Oh, ça, non! Alors,* non, *Papa,*' she said, turning unthinkingly towards us. '*Quel salaud.*'

Within seconds her whisky glass was overflowing with water, her cigarette dropped out of its holder and she tried to protect her face from the stream of water.

Mohammed stood under the tree not knowing

257

whether to laugh or go to her aid. Bebop and Little Girl rushed out on to the terrace yapping, tails wagging furiously, stopping every now and then to lap up some of the water that lay in pools by the table. The chairs dripped water, the parasol was soaked and the hose, which Papa had directed on to the garden, was splattering sandy spurts of earth up my mother's legs. Lolo was screaming and hopping wildly from leg to leg.

Papa was merciless. Still the jet of water sought her out relentlessly, however much she tried to avoid it.

My middle ached from giggling and shouting. I had hardly any voice or any breath left but seeing my mother, her mascara making black tracks down her face, her whisky glass and cigarette-holder falling into the mud, and water running off her as if she were under the shower, and regretting only that I wasn't holding the hose, I closed my eyes into the sun, threw back my head and laughed and laughed and laughed.

CHAPTER 17

The morning felt fresh, long shadows sprawled across the rows of vines, pushed by a sun just beginning to make its presence felt on the horizon. The whole world seemed washed and new. It hadn't rained of course, but the night's humidity fell as such heavy dew, everything seemed moist and clean.

The circular fans, on top of their skeletal pylons, were busy pumping water to the fields in the distance. They whirled and spun, changing direction to catch the breeze. I'd never seen them this active before. But then I'd never been up this early; by midmorning, the time I usually woke, nothing moved under the merciless sun. Now the whole world seemed busy and awake. Carts clattered along the road to Tripoli in the shadows cast by the olive and eucalyptus trees. Bees and insects buzzed and whined nearby.

I took great gulps of the morning air, hoping it would still my banging heart and rumbling stomach.

I was going home. I wanted to jump and run and shout. But I knew I couldn't. I had to pretend I was sad to go. I'd said I was. I was getting good at pretending one thing while feeling another. But the pretence unsettled me. I was never entirely sure that my pretence was convincing and couldn't be seen through. Soon, though, I wouldn't have to pretend any more. I could just go back to being my old self. Bert and Doris's suitcase had long since been packed and shut down, and soon, so very soon, but not soon enough, Bert would be carrying it for me across Liverpool Street Station to the Ipswich train. I'd had to slow down getting ready for fear it would be obvious how much I wanted to leave. I wanted to leave so badly my stomach lurched with excitement, and my heart banged faster. I could see it against my mother's black blouse. The horrid green suit lay well and truly packed at the bottom of the suitcase never to be worn again. Gran wouldn't know. It was easy to hide things from her, easier than it was here.

I rubbed my hand against my churning middle and smoothed down my mother's black and white cotton skirt. My bare legs were almost brown beneath it. It was September in England. It's September here too, silly. But a different kind of September. I wasn't going to wear ankle socks though. Ankle socks were babyish.

A row of large ants busied itself along the terrace wall. Half-heartedly I moved to see where they were going to. Bebop shifted from his position under a bush, his tail smacking against the leaves as it wagged.

'Ssh,' I said. 'Bebop, ssh.'

Little Girl ambled out to join us, her stomach bigger than ever, a crust of bread retrieved from our meal on the terrace the night before held firmly in her salivating jaws.

She gave a quiet warning growl as Bebop approached her.

'Ssh, Little Girl—ssh, *tais-toi*,' I ventured. She stopped and looked at me, not relinquishing the bread.

'*Ta gueule*,' I tried emboldened, essaying Yves's French. '*Ta gueule*, Little Girl.' Miss Tait would be surprised at how colloquial my French was now.

'Don't talk to the dog like zat,' came Yves's voice from somewhere behind me. 'She 'ave done nothing to you.'

I jumped guiltily, an explanation on my lips—but he disappeared with my suitcase around the back of the villa. It was early, even Mohammed hadn't arrived to start his day or he would've been asked, told, to carry it.

Little Girl waddled after him, the soggy lump of bread discarded. I wondered when my puppy would be born. I wouldn't be there to see it but even that thought couldn't dampen my spirits. I squashed the lump of bread underfoot into hundreds of crumbs. Soon the ants on the wall would find it and make a detour, and I wouldn't be here to see that either. Again my insides lurched with something that I supposed was joy.

'*Viens ici, prends ton petit déjeuner,*' shouted my mother. Soon I'd have proper breakfasts, Gran's porridge with golden syrup on top. Porridge made with real milk. It was difficult to relish the idea of porridge really as the sun was beginning to heat through the cotton blouse, warming the space between my shoulder blades, and moisten my forehead under my fringe.

'Janie, come and eat.' My mother's voice more insistent this time. It was going to be difficult to swallow anything with all this excitement churning away inside me, but I'd have to force it all down somehow; my huge appetite was a family joke. They'd notice if I didn't eat my usual amount. They noticed everything. Everything except what I felt inside.

'Ja-anie.'

I let the terrace door bang behind me and thought, next time it shuts behind me I'll be leaving, I'll be on my way home . . .

*   *   *

I said goodbye at the barrier, clutching my passport to me like a talisman; as long as I had that, I was all right. I could go. Nothing could stop me now. I kissed Yves on both cheeks and even gave Lolo a hug I was so happy to be going. At least while I was busy doing that I didn't have to notice the tears that had gathered in my mother's eyes.

I should be crying, I thought worriedly. I should be crying like her. I tried hard to squeeze some water from my eyes as she bent to embrace me. Once more I was enveloped in that heady scented aroma encircled by her bony arms, our bony cheeks pressed together. She wiped her eyes as she stood up and blew her nose hard.

'Oh, Louise, *voyons*,' said Yves impatiently. 'Come on, let's get the hell out of this bloody 'ole of an airport.'

'G'bye, Janie *chérie*,' she said, swallowing back more tears.

'Goodbye, Mummy darling,' I said, overdoing it, the word 'darling' feeling unnatural and flaccid in my mouth.

'You won't forget me, will you?'

You forgot me, a voice said somewhere in my head. I felt nothing and was frightened by it. I turned away and swallowed an imaginary lump in my throat, hoping that would convince her of my share of sadness at this parting and I put what I hoped was a relevant expression on my face. Lolo and Yves had already wandered away towards the door marked *SORTIE* and *USCITA*.

She made one last lurch towards me and hugged me again.

'Louise! *mais viens!*' echoed Yves's voice from across the almost empty departure hall.

'I do love you, you know, *chérie*,' she said, tears spilling down her nose. The back of my throat began to sting and tickle which startled me. I wiped her tears away with my fingers hoping that concentration on this would stop mine. 'You will come back, won't you—won't you?' she added pleadingly.

Tears rushed up my throat. I couldn't stop them now. Looking at her swollen sad eyes just made it worse. I liked her like this. She didn't seem so frightening now. Just sad. And for some unaccountable reason that made me sad and angry too that I was sad. It had all seemed so simple just a short while ago. I was going home and had been happy. Now my feelings were all churned up, I gulped back a sob and made a funny half-grunt half-groaning sound.

'Don't worry, Mummy darling, I'll be back. I *will* come back I promise . . .' and I meant it.

*   *   *

I opened my eyes and looked at my watch. It wasn't even midday. I felt exhausted and wondered what time it was in England.

The plane wasn't very full. A few fat Italian *signoras* dressed in black, a few Libyans, some in suits, some with red hats and robes, sat scattered about the droning plane. No schoolchildren. Of course boarding schools had longer holidays than grammar schools. That's not fair, I thought. Then remembered it would have meant a few more weeks in Tripoli. I didn't want that. Or did I?

There was a kind of dragging feeling inside me now. It was a sort of ache resembling what I'd felt at the beginning of the holidays when I'd thought about Gran. I hadn't ever missed anyone before.

How could I be missing them already?

I didn't even like them.

And worse.

I wasn't sure whether they liked me.

Anyway it wasn't worth thinking about them

263

now. I was going home. I tried to feel excited again but nothing stirred inside me. Nothing except that nagging ache. I brushed it aside and tried to concentrate on the air hostess coming towards me carrying a pile of newspapers between gloved hands. She stooped over me.

If I asked for the *Daily Mirror* I could surprise Gran by knowing all the news she'd read if Russell had brought the *Daily Mirror* for her today.

'They're yesterday's of course,' she said smiling, 'but would you like a newspaper?'

I couldn't see a *Daily Mirror*—anyway, if it was yesterday's there was no point. Odd how I was thinking of Russell too, now. As if moving nearer to England in the space above the clouds where the sun always shone brought with it English thoughts that had been absent from my mind for such a long time.

'A *Times*, please,' I heard my shaky voice squeak above the hum of the engines. I felt very important as without a word she handed me the unfamiliar newspaper.

Only sixth formers read *The Times*. I hadn't thought much about Northgate lately either. My second year, this term. Maybe I'd be elected form captain. Maybe—I couldn't count on many girls' votes. Delia and Vivienne would vote for me; I couldn't be sure of the Valerie Plummer gang or Anne Deal and Valerie Woodward, they were a law unto themselves, and as for the dreaded Annette, Deirdre and Rita—what would they say about my silver nails and my brown midriff? I hoped they'd be impressed, but knew they wouldn't. It didn't bear thinking about.

I glanced through the pictures in the paper

264

noticing how the black print had left grimy patches on my fingertips. I'd go to the toilet soon. I didn't think of it as a lavatory any more and I'd clean my hands with the Elizabeth Arden toilet water. I wished I had an empty bottle to take some home for Gran. I had nothing for her. I'd been too scared to ask Yves for money to buy her a present. Fearful that he would have made some unfunny joke about the money he sent us as it was, and I wouldn't have had the courage to tell him it often didn't come or never came on time. When it does come next time I'll buy something 'chic' to wear, I thought and stopped. Would he have sent July and August's money? Or would he have stopped it as I'd been living with them—and if he had, how long would it take to start the whole process over again?

I thought of Barclays Bank and how I hated going there. It took so much explaining.

Gran had a cheque book that she had to sign that frightened her, as anything official did. I had to take the cheque book with a letter to the bank.

'Account's in the name of Grace E. Chisnall?'

'Yes,' I would say weakly.

'And you're . . . ?'

'Jane Burgess.'

'And the money's coming from—where?'

'Tripoli.'

'Where?'

'Tripoli—Libya.'

That bit of explanation at least would now be easier. Now I could picture it in my mind.

'And who's the money coming from?'

'Yves Lapotaire.' That bit of the picture wasn't so easy. It sounded such an outlandish name, but I couldn't understand why English people had such

265

trouble with it. You said it like you wrote it. What was difficult about that?

Then I'd push the letter under the glass window that separated me from the cashier.

'It's all explained in there,' I'd say, glad to be rid of the problem.

All that was bad enough. But it was worse after what seemed hours facing an empty cashier's seat to be told on his return, 'I'm sorry, there are no funds in this account at present, the money hasn't arrived yet.'

It would be there. Of course it would. I needed a hockey stick of my own this term. I wasn't going to play with one of the battered old school ones, not this term. Not now I wasn't a first-year any more. Resolute about my new hockey stick I turned back to the paper. There was a small article on the left-hand page that caught my eye. 'MALTA' it said in bold print, 'from our correspondent'. I didn't bother to read the article; I peered through the window of the plane at the blue sea miles below dotted about with little dollops of land.

A steward with blond hair whom I'd noticed earlier because he reminded me of Bob who served in Fowlers' shop came slowly towards me behind the drinks trolley. I'd have a Coca-Cola. I still couldn't quite believe I didn't have to pay for it, which was just as well considering I didn't have any money. For a second I panicked. How would I buy my train ticket? Bert and Doris would have to lend me the money. No, Gran would have organised all that, surely. I felt a surge of anger that my mother, in spite of all her tears, hadn't even bothered to think how I would complete the end of my journey. I was glad I felt cross, it stopped that nagging ache

266

in my chest.

I put on my sweetest voice and said, 'A Coca-Cola please, with ice—and can you tell me what that is down there?'

He poured my drink on to the chunks of ice; that's probably the last ice I'll have, before I go . . . I go back there, I thought. He pulled the little table out of the back of the seat in front of me. I was cross I hadn't remembered to do that for myself—it looked like I hadn't flown before—and he leant across me to peer out of the window.

'What—that, young lady?' he said, pointing to a larger island that was appearing under the wing of the plane. 'Oh, that's Malta,' he said, with great conviction.

I looked down at the newspaper on the empty seat beside me. 'MALTA'—the big print caught my eye again.

'And where are you off to?'

'I'm going home,' I said proudly and beamed at being able to speak the word with relief at last.

'Have you been on holiday?' The word sounded strange, all the Lapotaires called it a 'vacation'. 'You're very young to be travelling alone.'

'Yes,' I whispered, sickening myself at the way I melted under his concern.

'And where did you spend your holiday?'

'Gargaresch,' I said, hoping he would need me to explain further.

'Oh. Just outside Tripoli,' he said knowledgeably. 'And what were you doing in Gargaresch?'

'Visiting my . . . mum'—the word sounded odd, I never thought of her as mum—'My mum and my . . .' I hesitated, not wanting to explain it further. I coughed, swallowing the rest of the sentence.

'Oh,' he said. 'And now you're going *home*?' He looked quizzical.

'Yes,' I said with some finality, hoping that would put paid to any further questions.

'And where's home?' he said kindly.

'Ipswich, Suffolk,' I added explanatorily.

'My goodness me.' He smiled. 'I come from Woodbridge. Small world, isn't it?'

He disappeared with a dull clunk of plastic glasses. I didn't look round. Coming from Woodbridge diminished his attractiveness somehow. I looked down at the newspaper, then out of the window. I was reading about Malta in *The Times* and there it was, almost underneath me.

Only six weeks ago, North Africa had seemed like the edge of the universe, and I'd been there only—what was it now—an hour ago. Now here I was above Malta.

The steward from Woodbridge was right.

The world was very small.

*   *   *

Bert called me his little globetrotter, Doris admired my silver fingernails. 'You'll have to wear rubber gloves when you do the washing-up,' she said, and chuckled gleefully as she dared me to show her my brown middle. 'You'll have to put some cream on that,' she said caringly, lifting my mother's blouse out of my mother's skirt, 'or you'll peel . . .'

'Not where people can see, dear,' Bert said gently. 'She's a big girl now, aren't you, Janie dear? You'll have to tell us all about your adventures one Sunday evening at Youth Club, won't you?'

For a second I felt a stab of panic. I couldn't tell them Yves drank whisky and my mother an even bigger quantity of wine, and how could I explain the way Yves talked to Mohammed? My spirits dipped for a second but I was too happy to see them. I hoped everyone in the railway carriage would think they were my mother and father, but most of all I hoped everyone would notice the BOAC label swinging from their suitcase in the overhead rack as the train made its seemingly slow way after the speed of the plane towards Ipswich.

'Black,' said Gran disapprovingly after I'd hugged and kissed her. 'You look like your mother. What are you wearing black for at your age? 'As somebody died? Now move out of the way so Bert and Doris can get by—they can go into the *front* room,' she said emphatically. 'I've got the kettle on. Now don't stand there shivering in the doorway, Jane, we don't want the whole street to know our business. And why in't you got something warm on, I don't know—no socks and a thin cardigan like that tha's daft. It's September, you know, not the middle of summer.'

'Well, it was boiling hot this morning,' I started.

'Not here it weren't,' she said gruffly. 'In't seen the sun for weeks. Now let Doris sit in the armchair and don't slam that front door—the paint's flakin' off as it is. Can't get the landlord to do a damn thing these days,' she said, swallowing the swear word as she remembered Bert and Doris's presence.

'I'll come and give you a hand with the tea tray, dear,' said Doris, bustling along the hall after Gran.

'Oh, thank you, dear'—I just caught Gran's words as she disappeared into the living-room—'All

269

this coming and goin' is downright unsettling, my hands are shakin' like a leaf.'

I sat down in the coldness of the front room, breathing in the smell of Brasso and Johnson's Lavender wax furniture polish, trying hard to remember what the air had smelled like on the terrace early this morning.

'She's pleased to see you,' said Bert, filling the silence. He must have sensed my spirits dipping.

'What?' I muttered, dazed by it all.

'Gran, she's pleased to have you back, you know.'

I didn't know and thought wickedly, she's got a bloody funny way of showing it. Then I felt bad. I'd wanted to see her so much for so long.

'And I bet you're pleased to see her, aren't you? You're glad to be back too; this is your real home, isn't it?' before I could answer.

My mother's well-made-up face, blotched by tears, danced before my stinging, tired eyes.

'Oh, yes,' I said obediently. Why did grown-ups think they were helping by telling you what you ought to feel and didn't? I thought of having to get a bus to school, no more car rides, no Mohammed to pick my clothes up off the floor, no more swimming in the warm blue shallows, no more barbecues, *méchouis*—I stopped myself. I felt perilously near tears but I didn't know why—I hadn't been happy over there. I swallowed hard.

'Oh, yes,' I said, putting on my brightest smile and my most obedient voice. 'Oh yes. I'm glad to be home.'

CHAPTER 18

Caught between reluctance and pride I lifted my blouse out of my gym slip and bared my middle, hands shaking.

'Yes,' said Rita noncommittally, 'that's *quite* brown.'

'What else?' said Deirdre, half-hiding behind her, a smirk playing about her lips.

We were supposed to be changing into our house shoes before morning assembly. The cloakroom was cold and deserted. Rows of shoes and empty shoebags hung by their laces from the pegs. Vivienne and Delia were friends with each other this week, and not with me. No support there, or safety in numbers.

'What else then did you get?'

'They're buying me a gold bracelet.'

'Oh, yes,' said Annette, her voice full of disbelief. She had smudges of mascara around her eyes from her night out the night before. She wore a ring on a chain round her neck that her boyfriend had given her. She boasted that she went the whole way with him.

'A gold bracelet, like Lolo's,' I said unthinkingly.

'Lolo?' Rita screeched. 'Lolo?'

'It's short for Laurence,' I said defensively.

'Laurence is a boy's name, isn't it?'

'Not in French,' I said.

'Burgess doesn't sound French.'

'My real name's Lapotaire.'

More laughter.

'Lapo what?'

271

'Lapotaire.'

'Why aren't you called Jane Lapotaire, then?'

'I am in Tripoli.'

Each name came out sounding more ridiculous than the last.

'Brian's getting me a bracelet for Christmas,' said Annette, patting the ring that hung just above the crease where her breasts met. She always wore the top button of her Northgate dress undone to show them off. I knew mine would never be big enough for that.

Heather Syrett joined us chewing gum. 'Have you got a boyfriend, then?' she said accusingly.

'Of course I have.'

'What's his name?'

'Michael Drew,' I said.

'What's he like?'

'He's tall and blond and ever so good-looking. We go snorkelling together.'

Hoots of laughter.

'Snogging?'

'No, *snorkelling*—underwater fishing with masks and guns . . .' My voice trailed away.

'What's his job, then?' said Rita. 'Mine works for Ransomes Sims and Jeffries,' she said proudly.

'He's a radio engineer.'

'Does he work for Radio Rentals?'

Sniggers

'No, he works for the company that transmits radio messages to the rigs in the desert,' I said, repeating my mother's words exactly.

'The desert? What desert?'

'The Sahara.' There was a pause.

I could hear singing from the assembly hall. I realised we were late. That meant trouble. More

272

trouble even than this.

> I bring fresh showers for the thirsting
> Flowers from the seas
> And the streams.

'The Sahara,' I repeated more boldly.

Each fact sounded more preposterous than the last.

I was panicked that they wouldn't believe my lies, and frustrated that they thought the truth ridiculous.

'My father works in the desert sometimes.'

'I thought you said you hadn't got a father.'

'My stepfather.'

'What did you say your real father did again?'

'He was a pilot,' I said. 'He was killed in the war.'

'You said he was killed on a boat last term. How can a pilot be killed on a boat?'

Deirdre giggled into Rita's shoulder. I found the buckles of my sandals difficult to fasten with shaking hands.

'No, I never.'

'Yes, you did.'

'No, I never.'

'She did, didn't she?'

'Yeah,' they chorused.

'She probably never went to Africa at all,' Heather Syrett whispered. 'Spent her holidays in Great Yarmouth,' she added and they all sniggered.

'Oh, come on, we'll be late again. Anyway this is boring. She can't even remember what lies she told.'

'Killed in action my foot,' said Gran. 'I bet he didn't even know she was pregnant.'

'Well,' I went on, 'she said—'

'Who's she? The cat's mother?'

'Mummy . . . my mother said . . . they were going to get married.'

'A likely tale,' said Gran, trying to get the remaining bit of rice pudding out of the corner of the Pyrex dish.

'That's enough, Gran, I don't want any more.'

'What's the matter, gone off your food lately? If you don't eat you'll have to have some Bengers or arrowroot. I s'pose it's just my cooking's not good enough for you now.'

'I'm full up.'

'Don't say full up, it's rude. Your mother'll think I've brought you up with no manners at all. Married,' she muttered. 'He were probably married with kids of his own back in America if the truth be known.'

More half-brothers and sisters. I hadn't thought of that.

'Was he American?'

'Well, if it's the one I think it was, he was.'

'What was his name?'

'Oh, Jane, I don't know!'

'You must know.'

'I've told you before there were so many.'

'But there must have been one who came here more than the others.'

'Well,' she said, hesitating. 'Oh, I can't remember—my memory's gettin' something dreadful; I'm not as young as I was, you know. I

274

can't remember things.'

'But you must remember this . . .'

'Strikes me you should have asked your mother—you've had plenty enough time with her all this summer.'

I wasn't going to admit to Gran I had been too frightened to ask. I barely admitted it to myself.

'We were too busy doing things. Going to the cinema, barbecues, swimming, dancing parties.'

'Living the life of Riley, I reckon. Who do she think she is, your mother, Lady Nevershit? I know I shouldn't say these things in front of you, but 'at try my patience, all this fuss, 'at really do. She's no one, you know, no more are you.'

'C'mon, Gran, don't change the subject. You must remember!'

'Oh, dear, Jane, I can't.'

'Please, there must have been *one* . . .'

'Well, there was one, I s'pose, who used to come here more than the others.'

'What was his name, can you remember his name?'

'Mmmm . . .' She scratched her head and readjusted her glasses. 'Mmmm. I think it was . . . he was a . . . Clark Leigh,' she said.

Clark Leigh. So that was it. At last. Clark Leigh.

'Or Lee Clark,' she added.

*   *   *

'I can't see what I'm doing if you keep your hands there. Anyway you're not supposed to wear silver nail varnish at school, are you?' Pat wiped the beads of sweat from her upper lip with the back of her hand. It wasn't warm at all; it was late

September. I tried not to shiver.

'I'm form captain.'

'Well, I'd 'a thought you're supposed to set an example, then.'

I tried very hard to concentrate on what she was saying but it was difficult with her bending down in front of me and me with no knickers on.

'You'd better sort it out, Pat,' Gran had said. 'It's beyond me, all these new-fangled things. We used to cut up bits of towelling and then boil them in the copper afterwards.'

'What, wash them out and use them again?' I said aghast.

'Well, of course,' said Gran. 'We didn't have none of this disposable truck that you girls have nowadays.'

I shifted uneasily from foot to foot, chilled and nervous.

'Now, I won't look,' said Pat, which was ridiculous, considering she was busy attaching a sanitary towel to a white belt which dangled confusing loops around my waist.

'What's this white mark along here?' she said, looking above the spot where my pubic hair had just started to grow.

'That's my bikini line,' I said proudly, forgetting that she'd said she wouldn't look.

'Bikini?' she said disparagingly. 'How do you manage to keep it on? It's that small. It must be bloody difficult to swim with that on, there's hardly anything to it.'

'You shouldn't swear.'

'Practise what you preach, young lady,' she said in her prim thin-lipped way.

I concentrated hard on my silver nails which I

276

was regarding at arm's length in order not to feel embarrassed by her proximity.

I thought I'd cut myself when I'd seen blood in my knickers earlier in the morning. We'd skirted over menstruation in biology but I didn't connect the two. I'd said nothing as I felt no pain but wondered how I could be bleeding from a cut but feel no soreness.

Now I felt it all right.

'Keep still,' Pat said, puffing a bit. I wondered how she'd heave her huge frame up from this kneeling position. I wished she'd hurry. 'There now,' she said. 'Next time you'll have to do it for yourself.'

I pulled my knickers up hastily. I was pleased but for the nagging pain low down in my stomach. No, it wasn't my stomach. It was lower down—a part of my body that I hadn't been aware of before.

'Now, I'll leave you a packet of my STs but you'll have to buy your own from the chemist after that.'

Trust her to call them STs. Those abbreviations were the butt of jokes at school. I determined to call them sanitary towels, ugly cumbersome things, and I'd make sure there was no one else in the chemist when I went in to ask for them, of that I was certain.

'Don't walk like that,' she said, opening the door of my bedroom, 'or everyone will know.'

'Well, it's hard to walk properly with this great wodge of stuff in my knickers.'

I wanted to feel relieved that at last I was part of the select group of girls in Upper IIIA who had their periods but it was difficult to feel anything at all with this griping pain nudging my thoughts.

'Why are you pulling such a face?'

277

'It hurts.'

'I never get period pains.'

'Well, I'm not you, am I?' I snapped, hoping the superiority wasn't too evident in my voice.

Gran was tying a cloth round a suet pudding as we returned to the kitchen. That seemed somehow vaguely distasteful considering Pat had just tied something round me.

'You mustn't talk to boys now you're . . . like that,' said Gran, hesitating over the last two words.

'Why on earth not?'

'Or wash your hair,' added Pat, 'or walk around on cold lino without any shoes on.'

'Why?'

'Because,' said Pat in her dumb way.

I felt I'd been only half initiated into the world of women. Their closeness and refusal to explain things completely left me with a frustrating sense of exclusion about the rest of it.

I couldn't wait to tell Delia. Then I remembered that Delia had been best friends with Vivienne last week. Maybe Vivienne would be *my* best friend this week. I was never sure. It changed so rapidly all the time.

'Now what's the matter?' said Gran crossly.

I couldn't understand why she wasn't pleased. When girl after girl came to school triumphant, I'd begun to wonder if there was something wrong with me as I was one of the last in the class to get my period. Now I knew there wasn't anything wrong. Not that sort of wrong.

'I've got pains here,' I said, cupping my hands around myself.

'Curse pains,' said Pat.

'What?'

'Oh, I don't like that word,' said Gran, quietly.
'What—the curse?'
'Yes.'
I didn't like it either; it sounded vulgar.
'It's more of a curse if you *don't* get it,' said Gran sharply, lowering the pudding into the strainer.
I wanted to ask what she meant.
'I've left a packet of Dr White's upstairs for her, Mum.'
I hated the way Pat talked about me as if I wasn't there or didn't count.
'What do I do with them when they're . . .' I hesitated, 'used—finished? Do I throw them in the dustbin?'
'Good gracious, no,' said Gran appalled. 'That's not hygienic.'
'You'll have to roll them in newspaper and then burn them all together when the dustbin's empty. Leave them in the grate in your bedroom, that's what I used to do when Doug and I still lived here.'
I knew. She'd done it several times when she visited Gran. Sick of being ridiculed for being one of the few in class who still hadn't got her period I'd taken one into school to show Deirdre, Rita and Annette, pretending it was mine. They couldn't refute the evidence, but I was never sure they were convinced.
I squirmed inside at the memory still.
'Do I *have* to wear these? Isn't there something smaller? I mean how am I going to ride my bike to school with this awful lump in my knickers?'
'Well, you'll have to go on the bus on days when you're—like that.'
'You can't wear anything else until you're married,' said Pat mysteriously. 'Anyway, I don't

think it's right to go pushing them things up you—they wouldn't do for me anyway, I'd be through them in no time at all.'

'I used to have terrible floods!' said Gran under her breath.

'I have to use two on certain days,' said Pat, equally conspiratorially. That confirmed that I wasn't being included in this secret group at all in spite of my initiation.

'It hurts,' I whined.

'You mustn't let it get the better of you,' said Gran.

'Oh, take an Aspro,' Pat interrupted. 'Or a Phensic.'

'We've got none,' said Gran. 'Take a bob out of the ornament on the mantelpiece, and go to Fowlers and get some.'

'But he'll know, won't he, if I ask for Aspro?'

'Oh, for goodness' sake, say you've got a headache,' said Gran as if it had all become too much trouble for her. 'Anyway, he's not in the shop now, not since he's been made Mayor, and Mrs Fowler talks down to you as if she were Lady Muck,' Gran added, rubbing the bottom of a saucepan with a frayed piece of metal scourer.

'I'll go up to the chemist's in the Felixstowe Road then I can change my library books and get an airmail letter from the post office on the way back.'

'I'm not made of money,' said Gran. 'You bought an airmail letter only last week.'

'It's nearly the first of the month. Yves's money will be here soon.'

'So will Christmas,' said Gran disparagingly. 'You've always spent it before we've even got it and why you're changing your library books again, God only knows. I've never seen anyone get through books like she do,' she continued to Pat with a curt nod in my direction. 'She can't read them proper. She just skimp through them. She must do. She read at such a rate. Now I read—'

'And inwardly digest,' I said before she could get the words out.

Stupid phrase. It sounded like eating.

'We're taught to read quickly at Northgate.'

'I don't know what you in't taught there; too much for your own good I'll be bound.'

I turned to get my mac from the hall.

'Don't walk like that, silly, walk normal.'

'And don't be gone ages or this steak and kidney pudding'll go heavy and I want it all cleared away before *In Town Tonight*.'

'Once again we stop the roar of London's traffic—violets, lovely violets.' I aped the announcer but she wasn't to be won.

'Strikes me there must be boys up at that there library. You're always gone so long.'

'Oh, Gran.'

'And if she in't up there she spend hours with her nose stuck in a book; makes me think she's sickenin' for something.'

Lorna Mayon-White's house was full of books— I'd been there once. Everyone read books in her family and even talked about them after. Inside I chalked up another unfairness.

'I won't be long.'

'I daresay.'

I'd found *The Well of Loneliness* by Radclyffe Hall. I didn't dare bring it home, so I read all the interesting bits standing by the history section so

281

the librarian would think I was studying. Annette and Rita had a boyfriend. I didn't. I cried if Delia was friends with Vivienne for too long. Or if Vivienne didn't want to be friends with me. Perhaps I was lesbian. I didn't know what lesbians did or felt. Perhaps Radclyffe Hall would give me a clue. Clues had become important.

'G'bye, Pat,' I said, hoping she'd be gone before I got back. I hated it when we rowed in front of her.

'Can I take the extra ninepence for an airmail letter, then?'

'Time was, I had to force her to write to her mother. She's changed her tune now,' said Gran, swilling the water from the saucepan down the sink. She scattered Vim liberally over the pockmarked white china sink, and began to scrub vigorously.

'I'll do that when I get back. Gran, you always used to let me.'

It had been a special treat as a small child to stand on the stool and clean the sink with Vim. I liked to see the stains dissolve especially if she'd been cooking beetroot or had emptied the teapot into the sink. It was magic to see the red and brown tide marks disappear as I scrubbed.

'Oh, it's done now. Anyway, Vim'll spoil your nails,' she added disapprovingly.

I found the money in the ornament along with the usual several Kirbigrips, a few yellow Divi Co-op receipts, a wooden peg with one side missing and a brooch with 'Mother' picked out in coloured glass, saw Gran's purse next to the alarm clock, took half-a-crown from it, and replaced it with two sixpences from the ornament. I'd spend the money on an Everlasting Strip or some peardrops. I

282

planned to take the Aspros at the chemist to get rid of the pain as soon as possible. I'd ask for a glass of water like really ill people did, as soon as their prescription was handed over. I'd pretend I'd got flu and sniffle and cough a bit like the time I'd had to sing 'Unto Us a Boy is Born' at the Girls Life Brigade Christmas concert.

I hadn't been able to reach the high notes on 'King of all cre-*a*-tion' so I'd cleared my throat and spluttered a bit to fool them into thinking I had a cold. I'd done it on the same line every verse. I squirmed at that memory too, and my face burned anew, shaking my conviction that although I'd fooled them, which didn't matter now, I hadn't fooled myself.

If *The Well of Loneliness* wasn't there, I'd walk back slowly eating the sweets, hoping to bump into someone who I could impress with my news. Then I'd write and tell Mummy. She would be pleased, I thought, not like these two. A plate dropped on to the kitchen lino and smashed.

'Oh, drat the bloody thing,' Gran muttered darkly from behind the half-closed door. 'I don't know what's the matter with me these days, I'm all fingers and thumbs.'

'I'm going now,' I shouted.

'That's right, you clear off,' she shouted back. 'She's never in these days—she worry the life out of me, she do, Pat. She in't the same since she's been traipsing over *there*. She'll turn out like her mother, you mark my words.'

I waddled up the road unaware of everything except the lump between my legs, the nagging pain and a disquieting sensation of occasional wetness. It wasn't like peeing, because I could tighten a muscle and stop that. This wetness I was powerless to control. It frightened me, but made me proud too, at the same time. Contradictory feelings, I knew, but I was getting used to contradictions.

I thought of what Pat and Gran had said and felt ashamed. Could people see? Would they know? The street was deserted so I couldn't tell—no sign even of the man who sold shrimps from a bike with a large basket on the front. He rang a large handbell to catch our attention. Probably September was too late for Harry shrimps. Shrimps from Harwich. The sky was grey and overcast. I shivered again and thought of the Mediterranean sun, the lukewarm sea. I pulled my mac around me and surreptitiously rubbed myself where the pain was, my hand hidden in my pocket.

A period was something Lolo didn't have. But she did have the car and barbecues and fun.

It wasn't fair.

It wasn't fun either. I allowed the truth to seep in just for a second, before I elbowed it away. I looked around me. The houses seemed smaller now, and somehow drab and dull. My mother was right. Ipswich was awful.

Why did I have to live in such a—I toyed with the word 'grubby' but Gran's voice in my head dismissed it with her usual, 'we may be poor but we're clean'—threadbare, that was it, a threadbare hole. Anyway, I wasn't poor. The Lapotaires weren't poor and I was a Lapotaire really, I pretended. I had a right to live with them. Not with this old lady who wasn't even a relation—who had hairs on her chin and gnarled corn-ridden feet, and ... I felt a second's worth of guilt thinking of Gran like this. New horrid hate-filled thoughts tumbled

284

into my head. I seemed powerless to control those too. But she didn't understand how pleased I was about my period and that wasn't fair! So it served her right. Mummy would understand my period; she'd give me a cuddle and then I'd feel . . . I couldn't quite complete the picture. I wanted to go back to be with her again. An uneasy feeling mushroomed somewhere above the pain. I wanted to feel warm inside when I thought of her; instead I felt as I had years earlier about the drawing of the skeleton of a prehistoric monster in the *Girl Annual*. The dark outlines of the bones half-hidden in shadow both alarmed and thrilled me. I knew which page it was on, so I could have chosen to avoid it, but every time I opened the book something compelled me to turn to that well-thumbed page and force myself to have a look.

I shivered again remembering and suddenly felt tired.

Why were Pat and Gran apprehensive? Why hadn't they been proud?

My mother would have been, and if she wasn't, I'd make her. I'd make her proud of me.

She's like her mother. Gran's voice pierced my thoughts. Well that's all right by me, I rallied in my head. I wanted to have tanned skin, golden rings and long red nails and—why didn't they have the courage to say what they meant? I knew what they were frightened of—but I wasn't going to get pregnant and have a . . . I dodged the word. Anyway, I hadn't got a boyfriend—and I missed Delia or Vivienne, whichever one I didn't have, so much, so—so that was that.

Rex Roberts wheeled his bike across the pavement in front of me as a stab of pain shot above my groin.

'Hallo,' he mumbled gruffly. I blushed and stared down at the cracks beneath me, faint hopscotch marks in red brick writing hardly visible on the slabs of concrete. They belonged to a world I'd inhabited a lifetime ago.

I didn't answer. He swung his leg over the crossbar and prepared to cycle off. I wished girls had crossbars on their bikes. That swing was so much more stylish than the way we started pedalling. I pictured myself doing it in my head, and then remembered my present state.

'Cat got your tongue?' he mumbled.

I strengthened my resolve and walked on in what I hoped was a proud and elegant manner, wodge of cotton wool permitting.

I'd do everything they said. I'd show them, all of them. I wasn't going to be afraid of anything. Yves's bronzed craggy face flashed before my eyes, laughing, ridiculing my news. Well if I was afraid, I half-conceded, I wouldn't let them see it.

CHAPTER 19

The sun wasn't shining. It hid frequently amongst banks of high white cloud that seemed to scud along as fast as the car. No suntan this time. The dry gutter that carved its fickle way between sandstone rocks along the road to Gargaresch now flashed bright with water. Yves flung out a reply in response to my gasp of astonishment. I understood only 'rain' and 'Christmas'. My spirits sank on both counts.

'Rain equals river,' he repeated in English, insisting that I understand. 'What do they teach you in geography at your school?'

I thought of Miss Currie and her coal deposits in the North of England, alluvial plains and oxbow lakes, and said nothing.

He chatted to me persistently in French which I punctuated with sage-like nods, understanding barely half of what he said, desperate not to be drawn into the conversation or, worse, questioned further.

My face I hoped I'd arranged in a serene and comprehending expression. My hands, half hidden, their nails newly bitten, clutched the edge of my seat to counterbalance the erratic swerving of the car as he avoided an untethered goat, a child rolling a car tyre like a hoop and a group of women carrying water-jugs on their heads or shoulders.

The car slowed suddenly and I glimpsed ahead of us a group clustered around a set of traffic lights.

An accident, I thought, although I couldn't see anything to indicate that it was. There was a truck, its driver standing beside it deep in conversation, his American peaked cap at odds with his Arab trousers, with a boy on a bike and several pedestrians. I couldn't see a policeman's smart khaki uniform anywhere.

Yves pressed the horn of the car and the group, who looked startled initially, slowly began to disperse so that he had room to overtake.

Amid much swearing and scorn I detected that they'd simply gathered to watch the traffic lights change colour. That, apparently, was preferable to something called Ramadan which caused them to wander like *fantômes* all over the road.

287

I realised wryly that I understood the French for damn and blast and shit, and worse, but couldn't get my travel-stained brain round the sentence to ask why he'd come to pick me up at the airport all alone. It wasn't just his way of correcting my French, when I was brave enough to utter any, with a sudden stinging flick at my face or arm that set me on edge; somehow it was worse when his hand settled on my knee and he simply smiled at me.

He confided that Libyans were *malins* and very pro-Nasser, and I pretended I understood why, and faked a share in his annoyance that they'd slashed all the car tyres outside the French Embassy one *Reveillon*, whatever that was, some two years earlier, during the Suez crisis. I was just about to chip in with an 'Anthony Eden', wishing fervently that I'd listened to the news more often, and less to *Educating Archie* or *Life with the Lyons*, when he interrupted with a 'de Lesseps'.

We drove in silence for a while.

I said nothing.

'Built by a Frenchman, Suez. Panama too . . .'

I nodded, confirming what I hadn't known and dreading that this was going to turn into a geography test.

' 'Ow far are you from the sea in England?'

'Pardon?' I'd heard and understood, but played for time; after all, the reputation they'd given me for intelligence was at stake.

He repeated himself as to an idiot, then inhaled deeply on his cigarette.

'Well, Felixstowe is about twelve miles away, I suppose. I've never cycled it . . .' I trailed off.

Shouldn't have mentioned the bike. If he asked, I'd have no defence. It was much more difficult to lie convincingly to him than to Gran. He had a way of looking at me with disbelief before I'd even conceived the lie.

' 'Ow far is it from the sea?'

'Oh,' I said, understanding more clearly what he was trying to say, but hating the way he frequently blamed his bad English for my lack of understanding. It almost made me wish he was talking French.

' 'Ow far?'

My brain went blank.

'You 'ave lived in England for 'ow long?'

'Fourteen years.'

'You are fourteen?'

'No, I *will* be, this Christmas coming.'

Stupid of me to mention Christmas again. If he asked me directly why I hadn't come the last holiday I knew I wasn't brave enough to deflect his question with, 'Well, you and Mummy didn't remember my birthday, so.'

'Eighty miles,' he said triumphantly. 'You are never more than eighty miles from the sea in England.'

'Gosh,' I said like someone else.

'Gosh, cor blimey,' he said, mimicking me. I began to wish my mother and even Lolo had come to the airport to meet me. Conversation was easier when I wasn't alone with him.

'If you 'ave a . . .' He walked two fingers in the air inscribing a circle.

'A compass?'

'If you draw a circle in the middle of England with a . . . compass—this distance . . .' he waggled his fingers again and swerved to avoid a donkey cart loaded with crates of orange Fanta, keeping one hand on the steering wheel, '. . . you are never more far away from the sea than *eighty*.'

'Well I never,' I said, knowing he wouldn't see the sarcasm in the phrase used more by Gran than me.

'Never more than eighty!'

'There *is* the sea!'

Across the sand dotted with rocks and scrubby bushes topped with startling new green leaves, a wide strip of blue began to accompany the speeding car.

'*En français.*'

'*Voilà la mer,*' I said, my excitement halted not only by the dread that I had got the definite article wrong again but by my ever strengthening need to slap him back when he hit out at me.

'*Oui, la mer*—but talking of *ta mère*, she is not very 'appy with you!' A riposte from the Youth Club slunk into my head. Tell me news not history.

'She was very *déçue à Noël*.'

Was that 'deceived'? How did they know I'd deceived them?

'*Déçue?*' I ventured, panicked I'd been found out.

'Disappointed.'

'Oh—well you see Gran—'

'Gran?' His dislike of her was so evident just in the way he said the name.

'Nana.' I reverted to my mother's name for her. 'You see Nana's old—and Walter died at Christmas time . . . so I felt . . . I had to stay.'

'Janie, don't be a liar like your mother, just say ze troos.'

Could I explain that I'd chosen the excitement of singing carols under lampposts in the cold night air with the Youth Club, or the challenge of rattling my Dr Barnardo's Homes tin furiously in lighted doorways to elicit the greatest amount of money— and the deliciousness of Doris's mince pies rather than a trip to Libya? I'd thought, too, that Gran would feel happier if I didn't go *every* holiday. I'd done it for her and it had pleased her. Now Yves looked anything but pleased. The fact that I'd chosen her, instead of them again, hung in the air between us.

'Ze troos . . .'

At any other time I would have smiled at the trouble he had saying it. 'Th' sounds were impossible for the French. Lolo had challenged me once into daring to ask him to say 'Smith's potato crisps', when his persistent correcting of my French had made me cry. It was a phrase that was full of unmanageable amusing hurdles for the French. 'Smitt'—this was difficult enough, but having survived that, and been relieved at the relatively easy 'po-tay-toe'—the final word was a stumbling block of unpronounceable 'criss-tu-pers' or 'crith-per-thers', which provoked great mirth if my mother challenged him with it after the third apéritif, but I'd never dared.

'So. Say ze troos, Jane.'

He swung the steering wheel right as far as it would go, to avoid a battered truck that was lurching towards us in the middle of the road loaded with empty petrol cans. We bumped over the dirt track that led down to the beach at the same speed that we'd been driving along the sandstrewn tarmac road, forcing him to brake sharply to avoid overshooting the path that led round the back of the house to the garage.

291

The car slowed down with the now familiar squeal of brakes and accompanying cloud of dust—which brought, almost instantaneously, the dogs out to bark at us. My attention was caught by there being more wagging tails than I had seen before. I had no time to pursue my curiosity as he continued, 'Don't be a liar like your mother, Jane—*tu m'écoutes?* Just say you didn't want to come.'

*   *   *

'Isn't he a lovely present?'

'He's called Buster Brown and he's yours.'

No gold bracelet. Another lie for Rita, Deirdre and Annette. The puppy had sandy-coloured feet and a matching patch over one eye; the rest of him was dark brown. He scrambled over the comatose Little Girl and staggered towards me, wagging his unruly tail which in turn wagged the whole of his rotund body. He seemed very taken by the smells that clung to me from England, and sniffed the edge of my skirt, my scuffed shoes, and dirty ankle socks; until a small feather lifted by a puff of wind caught his wet-nosed attention and he scrambled over my feet, his brothers and his sisters, to pursue it.

'Can I take him back to England?'

It was a stupid question and it failed to ingratiate me into my mother's noticeably restrained affections.

'Of course not, Janie, you know there's six months of quarantine—he wouldn't recognise you at the end of that. Anyway, he's a North African dog—he couldn't support the cold in England. Now come and eat or *la soupe va froidir.*'

A young brown face shuffled in from the kitchen beaming.

'*Salaam aleikum.*'

'Where's Mohammed?'

'*Ouf,*' said Yves, waving away my questions. 'This is Ahmed—*voilà la fille numero uno.*'

'Papa, how can he understand you if you mix up your languages like that?'

'*Chut*, Louise,' said Yves, waving away her interruption too. He then rattled off something in high-pitched Arabic-sounding French. Ahmed smiled and bowed and smiled some more, revealing a gold tooth. I didn't understand how so many of them could afford gold teeth, working as houseboys.

'We're invited to his sister's wedding,' said Lolo, leaning towards me, breaking up her bread as she did so.

I would never get used to not cutting it with a knife or putting it on a plate. Everyone ended up with a pile of crumbs on the table in front of them, but that seemed to be polite.

'But we're going to the cinema first, aren't we?'

'Oh, you and your cinema,' said Yves mockingly.

'Tell Janie what film you said you saw last week,' interrupted my mother.

'Leslie Caron was in it. She was Gigi—you know.' I didn't. 'It was called the doctor's dilly mama with subtillities in French,' said Lolo in a way that I guessed she had said it many times before to evoke a charmed response.

'What?' I said.

'The doctor's *dilemma*,' my mother explained quietly, putting a cigarette into her holder, 'with *subtitles* in French,' she said, smiled for the first

293

time that evening in Lolo's direction.

'Oh,' I said and laughed hollowly.

I didn't find her muddled English cute. No one found my mistakes in French cute and I didn't get praised for being correct either.

A hot wave of injustice crept up my neck.

'You have to take a jacket with you to the cinema, Janie. The air-conditioning's very strong, you'll catch cold.'

'That's funny,' I said in a surly manner, 'in England you have to take your coat *off* in the cinema.'

I'd been to the cinema a lot. On stolen money. I'd seen Danny Kaye in *The Court Jester*. I'd seen *South Pacific* twice, and *The King and I* three times. I knew all the words to 'Shall We Dance' and once, in an argument with Gran, I'd uttered Deborah Kerr's winning words in a row with Yul Brynner: 'You have no heart.' Gran had stopped in her tracks, horror-struck, and without saying a word had marched next door to get Joan Holden to deal with me. I'd no idea why what I'd said had been so devastating. I was just being Deborah Kerr. And wanted to render Gran speechless as Anna had the King of Siam.

'We're not going till tomorrow night, Louise.'

'Aren't you coming, Mummy?'

'Tut,' she answered with a shake of her head. *'C'est comme tu veux, Papa,'* said my mother uncharacteristically acquiescent.

'Come and see the new American *poupée* that big fat Bill bought me from the States, Janie— *viens.'*

'Wipe your mouth on your napkin, Janie, before you leave the table.' I'd never got used to napkins either.

'Isn't she cute?'

'What's wrong?' I said, shutting the door to her bedroom.

'Oh,' she said, clicking her tongue as they all did when something was not worth considering. 'Papa has a mistress.'

'What's that?'

'A mistress—you know.'

'Oh,' I said noncommittally, knowing what it was, but in the face of the ease with which she accepted it, my surprise made me feel gauche. 'Oh, dear. I suppose I made things worse by not coming at Christmas?'

Lolo went on removing the doll's fringed leather jacket, cowboy hat and loud check shirt.

'Did I? Did I make it worse?' She didn't answer. 'By not coming?'

'Oh, Janie, you always think that everything bad that happens is your fault.'

'Poor Mummy,' I said with more sympathy than I felt.

'Poor Mummy, my foot,' said Lolo, tugging at the doll's thick blonde hair with a wide-toothed comb. I wondered what had happened to my doll, but she was nowhere to be seen amongst the rows of cuddly animals and soft toys arranged on several chairs round the room.

'Look, I can give her a bouffant—like Brigitte Bardot—*très à la mode*,' she said, engrossed in backcombing the hair on the crown of the doll's head, unmindful of how much came out in the comb.

'Look,' she said, 'I can put lacquer on it.' She turned to me, wanting me to be impressed. 'Don't

295

feel sorry for her, Janie—she's had lots of boyfriends, it's just that this time he's got one and she hasn't. *Tant pis.*'

And with a shrug of her shoulders she picked up the plastic bottle that contained the hair lacquer I'd seen my mother use, and squeezed it hard at the doll's head. The doll's eyes closed under the blast and little blobs of sticky lacquer stuck to the end of her eyelashes.

'Did you have a nice Christmas?' I asked my mother as she was folding up washing into a neat pile in my room ready for Ahmed to iron. I was sleepy, having trouble keeping my eyes open. The washing hadn't been kept in my room before. I was trying unsuccessfully to read but she kept coming in and out of the room carrying clean shorts and table-cloths, not saying anything. My question was asked out of discomfort with the silence between us, and not from genuine interest.

'*Comment?*' She stopped for a second, and the ash from her cigarette fell into a clean shirt. '*Oh, ça alors.*'

'I hope you did . . . have a nice Christmas.'

I was rendered helpless by my recently developed ability to mention exactly those subjects I'd promised myself to avoid. I was convinced they could see what I was hiding, and that conviction made me blurt out everything I didn't want discussed.

'Don't be a hypocrite, Janie.'

'Pardon?'

It sounded such a terrible word I was sure I was one, even before she began to explain.

'You say one thing and do another.'

I was shocked. That was true. It felt wrong. But I

296

didn't know how to put it right. I squirmed under the sheets, and made pretence of straightening them.

'I'm sorry about Christmas, it's just that Gran . . .' I mumbled.

'Oh, Nana . . . she's had her life, Janie.'

I did hope not. If anything happened to her I would have to come here and live. Live here all the time. Lolo didn't like Tripoli College; she said it was a stupid school and anyway it wasn't Northgate. Nobody had to pass an exam to go to Tripoli College. Although it would mean that I could get away from Annette and Rita and Deirdre, of course. For good. There was that. Things had been easier with them since I'd been form captain. I felt that my position protected me from them in some way. Anyway, if I was popular enough to have been chosen by the majority of the form then their baiting and dislike of me almost didn't matter. Almost.

I determined there and then to be elected form captain many times.

'I'm form captain,' I started, realising again that I'd spoken my thoughts out loud. She either didn't hear or chose to ignore it.

'I've done everything I can to make you feel *chez toi* . . . at home here . . . The *grille* is finished, the air-conditioning's in . . . Papa had to fight so hard with the company to get this room built . . . he really wanted you to come.' It sounded as if she didn't. 'The house was so small with just the two bedrooms . . .' Now I wasn't sure whether it was me or the room that was wanted.

'Thank you for the air-conditioning,' I mumbled. It felt odd to be grateful for such a cold metallic thing.

'You don't need to use it this time of the year . . . it's not . . . hot enough.' She stumbled over the words.

I was out of bed, trying to put my arms around her, which was difficult as she insisted on continuing to fold a table-cloth.

'I hoped *le bon dieu* had made me suffer enough . . .'

'Um . . .' I'd never heard her talk about God before.

'I should never have left you with Nana but I didn't have a choice, Janie—'

'Louise!' came sharply from the dining-room. 'Louise!'

'Oui, Papa,' she shouted hastily and sniffed back the beginning of tears.

He shouted something else that contained the word *con* which I knew was very rude.

'He's so *autoritaire*, Papa, you know,' she said confidentially. *'Il me fait peur*, Janie.' She began to cry afresh and I noticed her breath smelt very strongly of whisky as she sighed, and held my arm in a surprisingly friendly fashion. 'Do you know what he does sometimes? It's terrible . . . he . . .'

She bent towards me confidentially, and I wiped away a tear from under her eye with my finger, then wished I hadn't. The salt in it made the chewed skin round my nail smart.

'Ssh, ssh,' I said as comfortingly as I could. I was relieved the conversation had switched from me to Yves, although the unease between us hadn't quite evaporated.

I put her cigarette in its holder down safely on the edge of the old Formica table that had been put

298

there for the washing. It had several cigarette burn marks along it already. I didn't want it in my new room, but said nothing. I managed to put my arms around her as Yves wandered into the corridor.

'*Oh, les deux anglaises,*' he said mockingly.

'*Je ne suis pas anglaise,*' said my mother almost firmly, turning her back on him to clean up her face without him seeing.

'Is she telling you 'ow terrible I am?' he said accusingly.

'No,' I stammered. 'We were just . . .'

'She is full of shit. She tell you more lies, huh? Like the lies she tell you about your father?'

'No, we were just . . .'

'She make up so many, not even she remember what she say.'

So we were alike in that way too.

'*Daddee, je t'en supplie.*' Under the words I could hear her insistence that they talk in French. So could he.

'But, Louise, she should know, your precious daughter.'

'Don't listen to him, Janie.'

'It's all right—it's all right,' I said, embarrassed, wandering aimlessly between the two of them, confused as to how things had escalated to this state.

'She doesn't like you,' he said to my mother, waving his whisky glass in my direction so that some of the whisky plopped out on to the floor. He spread it about with his bare foot.

'Oh, that's not true . . .' I started, shocked that he'd voiced the unspeakable. 'I'd better get a cloth,' I mumbled, having no idea where floor cloths were kept.

299

'*Non, non,*' he said. 'The boy will do that tomorrow. So you *do* like your mother?'

'Well, of course she does,' she snapped. 'I'm her mother.'

'That has nothing to do with it.'

'Of course it has something to do with it. Blood's thicker than water,' said my mother with great conviction. She picked up what remained of her cigarette and made to leave my bedroom.

She hesitated, unsure of herself, and as she drew level with him, she stopped. 'Now let me pass, please.'

I thought it odd that she should have to ask. He straightened himself slowly, holding her gaze. I stopped breathing. She edged past him nervously— as if she expected a retaliation. 'I'll get you some water, Janie.'

I hadn't asked for any.

'Water?' he repeated incredulously, slurring the word. Then paused to raise his arm in a threatening way behind her retreating back.

'Janie, I give you some advice about water,' he said chuckling, ambling towards me, inviting me into the curve of his outstretched arm. I went reluctantly. He laughed some more, wiped his moustache with the back of his hand that held the glass, and slopped more whisky on to the sparse grey hairs on his chest.

'Oh, shit,' he said, watching it drip on to the floor. 'Never drink water,' he resumed, holding me uncomfortably close. 'Fish fuck in it.'

300

CHAPTER 20

The noise of the women's high-pitched wailing was as persistent as the cicadas.

'*Que disent-elles?*' I managed after several moments of careful construction.

'Speak English,' said my mother surprisingly. 'Then there's no way they can understand you.'

'What are they saying? It sounds like "pilli-pilli-pilli".'

'They do it when there's a death or a marriage,' said Lolo.

'It drives you crazy,' whispered my mother. 'They keep it up for hours on end.'

The compound of little white houses was ablaze with light from several small fires.

'Where's Ahmed?' I said.

'We won't see *him*, silly,' said my mother. 'He'll be with the men. We're only allowed to see the bride. We're women,' she added, as if that were somehow less.

We hovered in the entrance, uncertain where to go, until two women appeared out of the darkness and beckoned us to follow. Our walk was accompanied by murmurs and whispers from the dark on either side of us. We were shown into a low rectangular room, with a mud floor, lit by small oil lamps, full of bales of brightly coloured material, and many women. They were all barefoot, the soles of their feet stained dark orange. Some had bangles round their ankles that jingled as they scurried about.

'What's that?' I whispered, pointing to the feet.

'It's henna,' said my mother.

Several of them pulled their veils coyly over their heads and across their faces as we sat down. Others, bravely bareheaded, whispered behind their hands and giggled in our direction. Their black hair coiled and plaited was intertwined with beads and ribbons, its oily sheen caught by the light of the flames.

'Look at that one,' said Lolo, pointing to a young woman who had a babe in arms and a toddler climbing over her.

'She's only about fourteen,' I gasped. 'She's got children already.'

'Look at her hair, her hair,' Lolo nudged me. 'She's sitting on it. It's right down to her *derrière*.'

'I wish I had long hair,' I whispered.

'I don't,' said Lolo. 'I'm going to have mine cut really short. Like Jean Seberg's in the film.'

We'd just seen *Bonjour Tristesse*. I hadn't understood much of it, although it had been in English. But there were French subtitles along the bottom of the screen and I'd spent most of the film comparing the English I could hear with the French I could read and consequently I had been several beats behind the story.

I'd followed enough to know that the father's girlfriend had died. I understood why the daughter had hated the girlfriend so much. It was very sad and I'd cried.

Lolo, amused by my tears, had nudged Yves and pointed at me. He'd said as he cast me a cursory glance, '*Elle pissera moins.*'

'What?' I'd whispered in the dark of the over-air-conditioned Cinema Rex.

'The more you cry the less you'll pee,' Lolo had

302

answered smugly.

Some of the women had dark blue dots across their foreheads and on their knuckles.

'Those are tattoos,' said Lolo. 'Bedouins or Berbers up from the desert for the wedding. They live in tents in the Sahara.'

'Nomads,' I whispered knowingly. 'Where's the bride, then?'

'She's the one sitting very still over there, cross-legged on the high cushion,' said my mother.

'They have to sit like that for three days,' said Lolo. 'Tut! *Imagines*. I heard once that a bride was bitten by a scorpion and died sitting there; nobody knew she was dead until the bridegroom came to take her away.'

'That's not possible,' said my mother, brushing the dirt from her immaculate trousers. She'd insisted we all wear trousers as a protection against creepy-crawlies.

'It is possible,' Lolo insisted. 'Maria told me.'

'Oh, those *Siciliens*,' said my mother disparagingly. 'They're vagabonds—gypsies. *Disgraziato*. You know I don't like you mixing with them, *chérie*.'

They lived near us, in a clutter of ramshackle sheds. The father grew groundnuts in neat vivid lines of dark green and their mule, which Lolo tried to ride, carried pots of water slung across his back up and down between the rows.

I sat down gingerly on a brightly coloured mat, checking discreetly to see if there was anything crawling between the busy patterns. I didn't want to cause offence.

The two older women who had met us at the entrance were busy by a little stove in the corner where a brass teapot emitted a steady jet of steam from its blackened spout. One of them upturned the pot and held a small glass tumbler way below it. The glass filled up with a yellow foaming liquid.

'That's mint tea,' said my mother.

The contents of the glass were then poured from a great height into a similar tumbler, with not a drop being spilt, backwards and forwards until most of the liquid had changed to foam.

'We have to drink it,' said my mother.

'What if the water isn't boiled?' I said, proudly remembering basic North African hygiene.

'Ssh,' said my mother. 'The Arabs have been making tea longer than the English.'

As the elder of the two women came towards us my mother held out the small package wrapped in tissue paper that she had brought as a gift for the bride. They offered tea to my mother and me.

'Don't I get any?' said Lolo.

They took the package with much smiling and bowing to the far end of the room where the bride was sitting as immobile as ever.

In the gloom I thought I could detect the flicker of acknowledgement on the bride's face as the gift was added to a pile of brass plates, jugs and mats at her feet.

'What did you give her?' I whispered.

'Oh, some old poppet beads,' said my mother. 'You know, those plastic things that you can snap into each other and make the necklace long or short. She'll like that.'

Pat and Doug had had a whole canteen of cutlery, a set of Pyrex dishes and a dinner service— all their wedding presents had been on display too. A string of plastic beads seemed a rather small present.

'Oh, no!' groaned Lolo. 'Look!'

Two women approached us with plates of steaming food.

'What is it?'

'It's couscous and we have to eat it.'

'I'm not hungry,' whined Lolo.

'I suppose you had popcorn at the movies?' said my mother enquiringly.

'And delicious ice-creams after that,' I added innocently.

'Jan-nie,' moaned Lolo quietly beside me, 'you weren't supposed to say that. Now she'll know Papa stopped off with us at a café for a whisky on the way home.'

I'd had three different-flavoured scoops of ice-cream, *gelati* Yves had called it, not *glace*: pistachio, mango and passion-fruit, none of which I'd seen before, from the best Italian café in Tripoli. We'd sat for ages watching people wandering about, shopping and talking. It was very odd that the shops stayed open at night.

'It's cooler, silly,' Lolo had said disinterestedly. Most of the shopkeepers were Italian. Yves had replied curtly to my question. 'It was an Italian colony before the British took it over and put Idris on the throne. A puppet king,' he added.

I'd never seen so many beautiful leather bags and shoes. High heels, better than the ones I'd persuaded Gran to let me buy from Curtess Shoes in Tavern Street. They were black, with short clumpy heels and a cut-out pattern on the toe; here were suede, lizard, crocodile and snake, shiny leathers and coloured patents. My gasps of amazement and delight as I stopped to look and point on our way to the café only elicited: 'They are beautiful and expensive. *C'est fait pour ça, les Italiens.*'

I ached to have a pair. I yearned too to have a ride in one of the horse-drawn carriages that trotted up and down the Promenade des Anglais. '*Garries*' Yves called them. 'No, you can't,' he'd said. 'They're for tourists. We live here.' I don't, I wanted to add, but didn't.

'You have to eat it,' repeated my mother, jolting me back to the present. 'They'll take offence if you don't.'

I smiled and took the hot tin plate and placed it carefully on the mat in front of me.

'Don't spill anything on the *tapis*, Janie, for goodness' sake.'

My clumsiness was by now a family joke. A small brass bowl containing something that looked like ketchup was offered me. I poured it liberally over what resembled meat stew resting on a bed of semolina, and took a hearty spoonful. At first there was a tingling in my mouth as if my lips and tongue had pins and needles. Then the burning began. As my eyes began to water and the heat in my mouth grew to unbearable proportions I reached hazily for the glass of tea in front of me.

Both Lolo and my mother spluttered with restrained laughter.

'What is it? What have I done?' I managed to gasp, as the food dribbled uncontrollably out of my mouth which was now ablaze.

'Oh, Janie, it's fel-fel.'

'What?' I said as I sipped the welcoming sweet tea which was too hot for my tender mouth.

'Fel-fel—it's like neat chilli. You shouldn't have

306

taken so much,' Lolo giggled.

'It's agony,' I gasped. 'Why do they eat it?'

'They're used to it, it makes you sweat and cools you down,' said Lolo. 'Anyway, it's to make the meat taste better.'

I pushed the red-stained meat to the side of the plate and dug into the semolina underneath that was sauce-free. I'd never eaten semolina at Northgate, horribly grainy stuff sweetened with milk and sugar. Now I was grateful for it.

'Actually the meat's not bad,' I said, finding a chunk that wasn't red and trying to put a brave face on it and smiling through my tears at the women sitting nearer us. 'It's really very tender . . .' Better than the stewing steak Gran gets from the Co-op, I thought. 'What is it?' I said swallowing.

'It's probably goat,' said my mother.

'Or horse,' said Lolo.

*   *   *

'Please make an effort to look chic for once,' said my mother. 'And clear the table while you think about it.'

'But I haven't got anything to wear.'

'*Oh, les femmes. Fais-moi mon café, Lolo.*'

'Oh, that's not fair,' she grumbled, sliding her chair out from under her so hard it fell and clattered on the floor. 'Janie's going out, so I have to do the coffee. Again.'

'*Marche ou crève comme à la guerre,*' Yves said and smiled.

'Oh, Daddy, it's not the war now,' said my mother irritably. 'I sometimes think you wish it was.'

307

'Yes, I do,' said Yves meaningfully.

I was relieved to be released from the nightly tyranny of Yves's coffee. Gran made coffee by simply adding hot milk to the Camp coffee essence—but Yves's coffee pot was a nightmare of a tin puzzle. I was never sure which bit to fill with water, I often forgot to put the lid on the section that contained the coffee so even if I managed to dodge the spurt of boiling water that shot out in a spiteful stream from a little hole between the two sections and caught my bare legs with its stinging heat, when I turned the whole complicated gadget upside down I was eligible for even more punishment as I poured it, afloat with grounds, into his cup.

'Oh, Janie,' said my mother impatiently, 'when I'm invited to a party I make my mind up and get dressed quickly.'

'But that's because your wardrobe's full of clothes,' I complained, thinking it unfair that they should comment on my looking so English and *'pas chic'* and not do anything to help me look better.

'Why don't you wear that suit of Mommy's that you wore when we went to that barbecue at the Landowskis,' Lolo suggested unhelpfully.

'She spilled ketchup down it,' said my mother, 'and Ahmed hasn't washed it yet.'

I bet nobody else is going to Susan Fowler's party wearing their mother's clothes, I thought to myself, getting dangerously near tears.

'Dad Fowler must be crazy. All these kids in his villa . . .'

Mr Fowler, a tall American who worked for Esso, was great friends with Yves. I didn't really know his equally tall daughter Susan who was at school in the States, but I guessed Yves had elicited an invitation for me.

'Will they *all* be American?' I said, leaning across to fold Yves's napkin up and put it back in its ring.

'So what's the problem? You speak English, don't you?'

'But I won't know anyone,' I whined.

'Oh, Janie, you're so full of complexes,' said my mother.

Anything I'm full of must be your fault, I thought as I collected up the little oblongs of petrified wood that we rested our knives and forks on between courses. Yves had brought them back on one of his many trips to the rigs in the desert. They didn't look like wood at all, more like sombre stone. They were cold and dead and unpleasant to touch. Unlike the *roses de sables* which were dotted about the villa: small clusters of sandy pink stone eroded by thousands of years in the Sahara which had gathered themselves into petal-like formations. He'd given me a little bronze age arrowhead from the desert too, that he said I could make into a pendant. And where's the money for *that* coming from, I'd like to know, said Gran in my head. He'd given it to me because Lolo and Mummy didn't want it.

There was a banging of metal from the kitchen followed by a loud '*Merde*'. I smiled to myself. Lolo hadn't managed to avoid the spray of hot water either.

'*Oh, ta fille—tu sais, Louise.*' I noticed we were always Louise's daughters when we did something wrong.

'*Ton café*,' said Lolo, banging the tin pot down

309

on the table beside his coffee cup.

Every night he would incline his head towards the coffee pot and we would all have to be quiet so that he could hear whether the water had finished dropping through the coffee.

'No, *c'est pas encore prêt*,' he said satisfied, settling back into his chair. 'Where's the newspaper? Let's do *le jeu des sept erreurs*.'

'I'm off to play with Maria . . .'

'Papa, tell her not to go.'

'She is your daughter, Louise—you tell her.'

'*Tu reviens tout de suite*,' said my mother in a vague way.

'*Oh, Louise, sois logique*. If she is going it's *stupide* for 'er to come back *tout de suite*.'

'*Tu deviendrais un vrai voyou*,' said my mother— barely casting a glance in Lolo's direction.

'*Deviendras*,' said Yves emphatically.

'What's a *voyou*?' I asked.

'You see, she learn French, Louise. Not like you. 'Er accent is good. Better than yours.' I liked it when he praised me. But I felt uncomfortable that my praise was earned inevitably at my mother's expense.

'A vagabond, a gypsy,' said my mother, standing up to pour his coffee, glaring down at him, and then at me. He put three lumps of sugar into the small cup. Sometimes he'd let us rest a sugar lump on the edge of his slanted brandy glass and watch the brandy slowly drain into the sugar. We had to catch it quickly before it disintegrated into the brandy and spoilt it, but he always seemed pleased if we asked to have '*un petit canard*'. I didn't like the taste of the brandy but I liked crunching the cubed sugar. I'd never seen sugar lumps at

310

Levington Road, but I had seen a pair of sugar tongs once at Bert and Doris's. Nobody used sugar tongs here though.

He stirred his coffee vigorously until all the sugar disappeared. I leaned across my mother to pick up the bottle of wine from the table.

'*Non, non, laisse, chérie*, leave it,' said my mother, putting the bottle firmly back on the table.

'Ouch!' I screamed as a burning sensation on my thigh made its presence felt.

'*Oh, Janie, tu m'as fait peur*,' complained my mother, putting her hand to her heart.

'*Aiee, aiee*,' I said, copying what Lolo did when she was hurt. '*Tu m'as fait mal, Papa.*'

'*Très correct*,' said Yves smiling. 'You speak French very well.'

'Oh, Janie, you should know better than to go near him wearing shorts when he's stirring his coffee.'

A small spoon-shaped red welt began to appear on my leg. I licked my fingers and tried to cool the burning spot with my spit. Lolo stifled a laugh from the doorway of her bedroom.

'*Tu t'en régales, huh?*' he said looking up. '*Méfie-toi—ça sera ta fête démain.*'

'*Fête*. Is that birthday?' I said, limping away from him collecting the rest of the cutlery. 'Her birthday's not till November.'

'Oh, he just means—he's got it in for her.' Odd. Another of Gran's phrases from my mother's mouth.

'Where's the paper, Louise?'

Every night the same question—every night the same response.

'I don't know—where did you put it?'

311

He never read the newspaper, ever. He just played the game of comparing two cartoons and finding seven differences between the two drawings. I'd never seen him read a book. I had seen a book once on his side of the bed. *Le Deuxième DB* was the title, but I never saw him open it. I don't think that the pages were cut. 'Papa was in the *deuxième* DB during the war, I've told you before,' my mother had said crossly when I'd enquired about the book, so I didn't like to ask what DB stood for.

'Oh, it's in the kitchen with your car keys,' said Lolo. 'You left it there when you brought the new gas in—I'll get it,' she said, uncharacteristically helpful. Buying time with Maria, I thought meanly, as I passed her on her way out of the kitchen.

I threw the knives and forks into the sink, and took a quick guilty swig of neat evaporated milk from the fridge to help lift my spirits before I returned to the dining-room.

Lolo, having put the paper down in front of him, bent to kiss him. She squealed loudly, and backed away from him so fast she nearly knocked my mother out of her chair.

'*Oh, Lolo, je t'en prie,*' said my mother, brushing cigarette ash off her bare legs. '*Qu'est-ce qui te prend?*'

'He gave me a horse bite,' she wailed.

'You 'ave to be quicker than that,' Yves said, pleased with himself, downing his coffee in one gulp.

Lolo rubbed the inside of her thigh where he'd pinched the tender sensitive flesh and where red fingermarks were beginning to appear.

'*Marche ou crève comme—*'

312

'We are *not à la guerre*,' said my mother quickly.

'They 'ave to learn to be smart.'

'Papa, they are your daughters, they are girls. You talk to them sometimes as if you were down on the rig.'

'He's bored, that's why he does it,' said Lolo, brushing away tears. 'When do you go back to the desert, Papa?'

My mother beckoned Lolo to her.

'Not soon enough,' he said brusquely.

My mother stood up, humming a snatch of a song that was becoming familiar: *'Je t'aime beaucoup plus quand tu n'es pas là'*, gave Lolo a hug, tidied her Jean Seberg haircut, and said kissing her on both cheeks, *'Va chérie, va jouer.'*

'You will ruin her, Louise. She will despise you when she's older—you'll see, *ma vieille.'*

'Oh, tais-toi,' said my mother sharply. My heart sank. Now there really would be a row. I knew the signs. She'd be too upset to let me borrow a dress and he'd be too cross to drive me to the Fowlers' villa in town. I didn't really want to go, but it would be an evening away from them.

'Ssh,' said my mother. 'What's that noise?'

There was a scuffling noise the other side of the door that led on to the patio.

'It's Buster Brown,' said Lolo. 'He wants to come in.'

'He can't. He begs for food when we're at the table.'

The dog pleaded with us, his eyes wide and watery.

'He's got something in his mouth . . .' He lowered his head and scrabbled at the door anew. 'It's a dead bird or something.'

313

'Oh, he's been scavenging about again in the trash pit at the back of the house,' said my mother, moving towards the door.

'Shoo, Buster Brown, go away; *va faire cou-couche*,' she said.

'*Va coucher*,' Yves corrected her.

Buster Brown stayed resolutely with his nose up against the glass in the door, wagging his tail with no inclination to move or relinquish the bloodstained mess he clutched between his jaws.

'*Va coucher*,' Yves said sternly. The dog wagged his unruly tail even more firmly.

'Oh, ignore him and he'll go away,' said my mother. 'I can't think what he's caught now.'

In a flash I realised.

'Oh no,' I groaned, 'oh no.' My face burning with embarrassment and shame. 'Oh no—it's mine.'

'What is it?' said Lolo.

'It's mine,' I said crossly. 'It doesn't matter what it is—I'll deal with it, I'll deal with it.'

I tried to edge out of the door without letting the puppy and his offensive find into the drawing-room, by jamming one foot in between the gap, and grabbing him by the scruff of his neck.

I grabbed him so hard he yelped.

'Don't hurt him, Janie,' said Lolo.

I had no time to consider her natural kindness to animals at this moment. I was determined that he wasn't going to sneak past me with his treasure and parade it in the dining-room for all to see. They'd seen enough already. I readjusted my hands to hold him properly as Lolo had shown me and he promptly dropped the offending article on the terrace floor. I put him down almost as fast.

'What is it, Maman?' Lolo insisted.

314

'She's got her period,' I heard my mother say as I grabbed the soggy mess and ran, cheeks aflame, to the back of the house. Why didn't they have dustbins here where I could've burned the stupid thing as I did at home? I buried it deep in the pit by the garage in a tin marked '*Pomodores*', rushed to the standpipe where we connected the garden hose and washed my hands over and over again.

I stood for a while breathing in the cool night air, hoping it would quieten my burning face.

A few cars went by along the main road in the opposite direction to Tripoli. It led to Tunisia, Yves had said, and then on to Morocco. Sometimes the Ghibli, a hot wind that blew from the Sahara, would bring with it so much sand that the narrow strip of tarmac would be covered and the road almost impossible to distinguish but for the line of telegraph wires that straggled along beside it.

A beam of light swung across the denuded vines to the right of the house. A car engine grumbled and coughed, then silence. The lights went out and a tinny door banged shut. It had to be Michael Drew; no one else came up the beach road at this time of night.

Now Yves could embarrass me with a captive audience. Now I wanted to go to the party whatever I wore. I wanted to get away.

I slunk round the side of the house and pushed the kitchen door open gingerly. My mother was in the kitchen making fresh coffee.

'Michael Drew,' she said, confirming my worst fears. 'It's all right. I've told him you're going out,' she said with her back to me. 'Have a shower quickly, Janie, and get ready before Papa has so much whisky he won't be capable of driving you.

You can wear that black top of mine with the white beads, you look nice in that, and the little white *talons haut*,' she added as an afterthought.

'Oh, thanks,' I said, grateful that she was avoiding mentioning my recent embarrassment.

'Don't I get a kiss?' she said, turning towards me with a bottle of whisky in her hand. I kissed her on her brown cheeks and she smoothed down my Jean Seberg haircut and said, 'It really suits you, your hair like this, Janie.'

'I don't know how I'll manage at school, though—I haven't got enough hair left to keep my beret on. It gets jolly windy cycling up Caudwellhall Road sometimes, you know . . .'

'I can imagine,' she said, struggling to open the bottle top, not paying attention.

'Let me do it,' I offered.

'No,' she said, proprietorially protecting the bottle from my reach.

' 'At's those North Easterlies 'at blow right across from Felixstowe Dock,' I said in my broadest Suffolk accent. ' 'At's all I can do to keep my knees from gettin' them darned old chilblains.'

She laughed her throaty cracked laugh as I hoped she would, poured a glass of whisky, took several gulps of it and said conspiratorially, 'Ssh, don't tell Papa.'

I waited for her to tell me what it was I shouldn't reveal, then she hid the opened bottle behind a tin tray that leaned against the wall near the cooker.

She smiled at me. Nervously I smiled back.

'I'm so glad you don't have a Suffolk accent,' she said. 'It makes me laugh but it is so ugly.'

She swayed slightly and supported herself against the cooker.

316

'Thass right common 'at is.'

She laughed again and I joined in.

'Now why didn't you tell me you'd got your period?' she asked sympathetically, as I'd hoped she would.

'I . . . I . . .' I stammered, pleased at her concern, but I had no feasible explanation.

'You are silly,' she went on, 'I'm your mother. And fancy wearing those terrible old-fashioned bulky things—we'll get you some Tampax.'

'Oh, but I can't wear Tampax, can I?' I was alarmed at her brusqueness. 'I mean I'm still—I mean I haven't . . .'

'Janie darling, you're not going to sit around the beach all summer in that terrible heat and not swim! That's silly. Anyway everyone will know why you're not swimming. I use cotton wool but that won't do for you. We'll get you some Tampax from the supermarket, then you can swim.'

'But won't that hurt?'

'Not with all the horse-riding you've been doing. You won't even notice it. I'll help you.'

'But . . . I . . . I mean—won't he know?'

'Who?'

'When I'm married . . .'

'Oh, you're so—"Ipswich" sometimes, you know. *Dépêche-toi*—go on, get dressed—*fissa, fissa.*' That was Arabic for quick; she said it to Ahmed all the time.

'Bravo, bravo,' said Michael Drew as I pirouetted in front of them. The *salon* had a pervading smell of his rancid sweat that I could detect above the cloud of Elizabeth Arden 'English Lavender' that I had taken from the BOAC toilet on the plane.

'Your eyes are the eyes of a woman in love,' Yves sang, mimicking Maurice Chevalier whose records he wouldn't have in the house because he'd sung for audiences in Germany during the war.

'You're going to a party, then, are you?' said Michael Drew with his infallible ability to state the obvious.

'Perhaps Michael should go with you,' said Yves wickedly. 'As an escort.'

'Oh, no, no, I wouldn't want to impose—anyway I've just come from work as you can see,' he said wiping away the beads of sweat that glistened above his walrus-like moustache. 'I'm not dressed . . .'

I didn't think he looked much different when he was.

'May I get you another drink?' I said, quickly changing the subject, remembering my reprimands for lack of social graces. I was 'intelligent, but clumsy, badly dressed and English', Lolo was 'stupid, never passing her exams, but charming and adorable and chic'.

'Well, that's very civil of you, Janie,' he said. I didn't like him calling me that. My mother's high heels clicked on the tiled floor as I moved past Yves and bent over to take the glass from Michael's hand. Yves made an attempt to pinch my bottom but was foiled by the amount of petticoats I had on under her black and white checked skirt.

'Papa,' I said, flushing scarlet.

'Oh, pardon,' he said, 'pardon, I forgot you 'ave—'

'Papa,' I pleaded, praying he wouldn't go on. 'That's rude.'

'That's rude,' he said, mimicking me.

318

'She's trying to be polite, Daddy, looking after our visitors as you asked her to.' My mother smiled, pleased.

I put some whisky into the glass and looked round for the ice.

'Why don't you have a treble whisky, Michael? Blimey, my daughters make me—'ow you say?—broke.'

I was flattered to be called his daughter but nothing I did seemed right and I was cross with myself for even wanting to please him.

'Is this too much, then?'

'Too much? You pour whisky like grenadine!'

I thought poisonous thoughts about not being asked to pour whisky often in Ipswich but said nothing. I didn't want to jeopardise my lift to the party.

'That bottle is almost empty, is there another one?' Yves asked, holding up his empty glass.

'No,' said my mother quickly without looking at me. 'No, there isn't. Put some ice in Michael's glass, Janie.'

I picked the ice out with my fingers.

'*Oh, ça alors!*'

'Well, how am I supposed to get it out?' I said querulously, wiping my wet hand surreptitiously on the skirt.

'Oh, that's fine, that's absolutely perfect, Janie, thanks,' said Michael Drew, beaming at me. 'You poured it beautifully.'

Yves winked but I chose to ignore it.

I sat down, carefully arranging my petticoats around me so that my knees were covered.

'So what are you going to do at this party?'

'Oh, well, you know—dance I suppose.'

'What do you dance to?'

I thought of Rosamund Pinhorn and myself boyfriendless at Alan Road Youth Club and said, 'Bill Haley and The Comets—we jive.'

'The same as the jitterbug,' said my mother, topping up her glass from what remained in the bottle.

'*Vieille croulante—soixante dix-huit tours*,' muttered Yves at her.

'He's calling me a seventy-eight,' explained my mother, presuming I would understand.

'What sort of music do you like,' Michael Drew intervened, 'apart from rock and roll?'

I stared blankly.

'What sort of music do you play at home?'

'In England?'

'Yes.'

'Well, I don't have a record player.'

'Everybody has a record player.' He laughed in disbelief. 'My goodness, I shall make you one. What music would you play if you had one?'

I said the first impressive thing that came into my head. Barry Cunnell had mentioned it at Youth Club once: ' "The Rites of Spring".'

'I always knew you were a girl unlike the others,' Michael Drew said, slapping his well-fleshed thigh. 'How many girls her age would choose Stravinsky?' I'd never heard the name before. He beamed in my direction. Yves winked at me again and grinned.

'I'm going back to England on leave soon. I live in Marlow, Bucks,' he said. I had no idea where Bucks was but hoped it was far from Ipswich. 'I'll come and visit you and that's a promise.'

I dreaded the embarrassment of him seeing Gran's house but pushed it to the back of my mind.

'I'll drive her to the Fowlers', Yves; it's not far from my place. It'll be a pleasure.'

Yves hummed the 'Wedding March' quietly under his breath as Michael Drew took his leave of my mother.

'You look lovely, *chérie*,' said my mother, slurring her words slightly. 'You'll be the belle of the ball—of course we danced to Glenn Miller when I was young . . .'

Yves mimed playing a violin. '*La vieille* 'as 'er souvenirs—two minute silence for the youth that 'ave passed.'

'Don't start, Yves,' said my mother sternly. 'You'll have a lovely time, darling, I just know it.'

Everyone was wearing jeans or shorts. There was a banner stretched across the entrance to the house that said 'This is a dilly'.

Whatever a dilly was I didn't have it. They played slow music most of the evening so that couples could neck. Not one of the tall boys with blond crew-cuts asked me to dance, which was, I supposed grudgingly, just as well as my mother's shoes hurt my feet as they began to swell.

There was no Bill Haley and The Comets either, just stringy violins playing 'There's a Summer Place', over and over again.

It isn't summer, I thought irritably. I hated the party and I hated having periods . . . And I hated having to come to Tripoli . . .

'Hey, it may never happen,' said some girl rushing past me laughing. She looked like Debbie Reynolds in her matching shorts and headband. I smiled guiltily, shrugged off envy at her mood and outfit, and stared across the rooftop of the villas below through the starless darkness that hung over

321

the Mediterranean. I tried to ease my weight surreptitiously from one pinched foot to another, blaming my mother for not offering me tablets for my period pains, and blaming Gran for the shabbiness and poverty of 85 Levington Road that I would soon have to explain to an unwelcome Michael Drew.

CHAPTER 21

'Freight train freight train goin' so fast,' I hummed under my breath. 'Do you feel bad?'

'No, I'm all right if I don't look down.'

'Move your foot a bit, I can't get at the hard skin underneath.'

'No. Leave that, just do the nails.'

> 'He lost his reason, lost his life
> He killed his friend in mortal strife . . .'

I picked up her other foot from out of the soapy grey water and surveyed the yellowing grey claw-like nails. Most of the toes were bent and twisted and the large one overlapped the two next to it. Some of the nails were so long they had begun to curl over the edge of the toe and make their way underneath it.

'Gran, they're terrible.'

'Oh, I know, dear. I should've had that shiropodist from the Co-op in to do them but 'at make me feel so bad. I don't like strangers mucking about with my feet.'

'Chiropodist, Gran,' I said. 'You pronounce it

with a "k".'

I sliced at a chunk of nail with a pair of silver rusty nail clippers that my mother must have left one visit. There was a harsh slicing sound and a chunk of nail flew past my face into the hearth near where I was kneeling, next to the plastic washing-up bowl that contained Gran's feet and a rapidly diminishing bar of Sunlight soap. It landed on one of the rungs of the grate and sizzled.

'I don't know what train he's on
Won't you tell me where he's gone?'

'Oh, what a terrible smell.'

'I've nearly done. Are you sure you don't feel bad?'

'No, I'm all right dear. I feel bad I have to ask you to do these things; but perhaps you wouldn't mind turning the wireless down just a bit—'at is rather loud. We don't want the Holdens complaining, do we?'

'Oh, but it's Nancy Whisky,' was on the tip of my tongue but I swallowed it back, stood up and obediently lowered the volume.

We were in a state of truce and I didn't want to spoil it.

'Shall I do your face now?' I said, bending to dry her feet and sprinkle the toes liberally with Pat's Avon talcum powder.

'Yes, but not with that foul-smelling stuff. What's it called again?'

'Veet?'

'Ooh, I don't like it—'at's meant for under your arms anyway.'

'I know, but it takes the hair off right at the

root—it's the best thing for it, you know.'

''At makes me feel right faint. Use the scissors, there's a dear.'

'But scissors make your moustache more noticeable, Gran. I know, I've got a razor upstairs that I pinched from my mother.'

'From your mother? What on earth does she use a razor for?'

'Oh, you know, to shave your legs and under your arms.'

'Well I never. What is the world a-comin' to?'

'I shave, Gran, when I'm going to the beach; hair's awful on women's legs.' I'd read that in *Elle* magazine.

'That's the first I've heard of it,' I heard her say quietly as I charged upstairs to my bedroom. Shaving's nothing, I thought, what would she say if she knew about my mother's promise of Tampax? I stopped to squeeze a spot on my nose, and applied a generous blob of tinted Clearasil cream to the red raised bump that I'd caused. Made a mental note to get some more when I bought my sachet of Vosene Medicated Shampoo for my Saturday afternoon beauty treatment session in the kitchen before going to Youth Club. This week I might even buy a Christie's Lanolin Face Pack, as a treat.

'There you are,' I said as I blew the last remaining grey hairs off her chin. 'Anything else, Modom?'

She chuckled and said, 'You'd better get on with that there homework or I'll be gettin' into hot water with your teachers keepin' you away from your work. You've got your School Sustificate soon, in't you?'

'It's *cer*tificate—anyway, we don't call it that any

324

more; it's GCE O-levels. I have to choose what subjects I'm going to do next term when I'm in the Lower Fifth.'

'*Lower* Fifth?' she asked disapprovingly. 'Why, are they putting you *down* a class? You got good reports, didn't you?'

My school reports had been as they always were, middling—except for English at which I liked to think I excelled.

'No, Gran, *everyone's* in the Lower Fifth—then we move into the Upper Fifth the year we take them.'

''At's all beyond me. I'd already left school at your age. I was in service by the time I was fourteen. Young people don't know the half of it nowadays.'

'Well, it's all different now.' I was beginning to lose the little patience that I'd mustered. It was hot kneeling by the fire, and my back began to ache from bending over her face with the razor, although I was pleased with the results. Her moustache had almost disappeared, although there was a faint trace of clipped hairs around the lump of skin that grew above her upper lip which I couldn't get too near for fear of cutting her. 'Shall I do your fingernails now?'

'No, get on with your work. I'll empty the bowl and take up that powder with the brush and dustpan. My hands are all right.'

'Your thumbnail's long.'

'Yes, but tha's the peculiar one I shut in the window—can't cut that. You get on with your work.'

'I want to finish knitting that pullover for the Youth Club outing.'

325

'Knitting?' she asked in disbelief. 'Well, I s'pose if you're sittin' at home knittin' you won't be gallivanting off to that Smith girl's house; that'll make a nice change. You've been television mad of late.'

The Smith family watched everything on television, even the advertisements, which I liked, and Mrs Smith gave me large slices of caraway seed cake which I didn't. Secretly I'd decided my father looked like the man in the 'You're never alone with a Strand' advertisement. A trilby; coat collar turned up; mysterious under a street light, waiting.

'We play chess too—we don't watch television all the time.' That wasn't quite accurate.

'Chess!' she said derisively. 'When did you learn to play chess, pray?'

'Valerie's father taught me; she's adopted too, you know,' I added, and then wished I hadn't.

'In't he got nothing better to do than play games? I thought he had an allotment to keep up?'

'Chess isn't *that* sort of game, Gran. Anyway, Valerie's very bright, she works really hard. She's in IV*A*,' I said to convince her—and then hoped she wouldn't make the connection with my being in IVC.

'Well, you ought to be workin' hard instead of knittin'. I thought you'd given up on that ages ago—it's been trailing about in the bottom of the sideboard for I don't know how long. How much 'ave you got left to do?'

'I've got to finish the back and do the sleeves, that's all.'

'At the rate you knit you won't 'ave it finished by Christmas.'

'I will,' I said determinedly.

326

'Why do you want to wear it all of a sudden?'

'I want to wear something new.'

'Well, you've got all that stuff your mother sent you. For your birthday supposedly—arrived in the middle of June, din't it? What's wrong with that?'

'Oh, Gran, that's three years old now. Anyway, I can't wear a taffeta dress on the beach at Thorpeness, can I? Anyway I hate it. It makes such a noise when I walk—and I hate all those petticoats underneath.'

'I thought 'at was all the rage—petticoats that make your skirts stick out?'

'Well, it is, but they're a nasty net—they scratch and hurt my legs. Anyway I've cut them out.'

'Ooh, what'll your mother say, Jane?'

'Well, she won't know, will she?'

'Aren't you taking them with you—next time you go to . . .' she always avoided saying the word '. . . over there?'

'No, I'm not!' I said emphatically. 'I'd die in the heat wearing taffeta.' I thought I sounded quite the seasoned traveller.

'Well, what about the other one?'

'The one with cherries on with that stupid collar. I'm not wearing that either—it would've been all right for Sunday school, but not for church.'

'Well I don't know, I'm sure. It's a red-letter day when your mother do remember to send you something—but strikes me I in't the only one that can't get nothing right . . .'

I wasn't going to let that train of thought continue—things had been going so well.

'You see I'd hoped to be able to buy something new with Yves's money this month but—'

'Well, you in't a goin' down that there bank

again; you got to keep some pride, my girl. I bet 'at's not that he in't got any—the devil always shits on the biggest heap . . .'

I tried again to control the situation.

'It's difficult, Gran, you don't know how slow things are—out there—'

'No, I don't, and I've got no wish to know, and thass a fact.' I had tried many times to share something of what my life was like in Tripoli, carefully omitting my fear of my mother and my resentment of Yves and, worse, their dislike of Gran.

'What've we got for supper?' I thought it politic to change the subject.

'Well, thass poor lookout tonight—'

'Walk round the table and have a nag's pie?' I chanted before she could say it.

She smiled. 'Thass pension day tomorrow. I'll ask Mrs Murrills to get a piece of fish while she's up Felixstowe Road—'

'Not that awful yellow haddock, Gran, please!'

'The other girls 'ad to eat what was put before them, you know. I'm too soft with you—they say I'll rue the day. Still, what do you fancy, hausers? I've got some suet I in't mixed up yet. They'll take no time at all to steam.'

'Rock eel?'

'You've got extravagant tastes, my girl, just like your mother. Anyway, I 'spect Russell'll bring something when he comes for his dinner tomorrow and that'll do me and him. He's good to me, that boy.' She heaved the bowl off the fireside mat, grunting as she did so. 'I'll go and get the supper—I saved some dripping from that knuckle o' pork we had on Sunday. Pork drippin' on toast suit you?'

328

'Oh, yes,' I said, 'scrumptious.' I loved it, but I was uncertain about how beneficial it would be for my spots. I did so badly want them to go by Saturday night. My eye had been even more firmly fixed on Barry Cunnell of late.

'You'll 'ave to ask your mother and Yves to kit you out when you go over there.'

'Fat chance of that,' I said. 'They still haven't bought me the gold bracelet they promised.'

'I s'pose you're goin' agin this summer.'

'Well, I don't know yet.' I took a deep breath. 'But I thought I might go this Christmas instead.'

There was a stunned silence from the kitchen as I'd expected.

'What, and be away for your birthday?' she asked incredulously. 'You've never been away on your birthday before, all the years I've had you.'

'Well, I'd like to see what it's like at Christmas,' I said, failing to add that I couldn't risk their displeasure at my missing Christmas in Tripoli again.

'They won't make the fuss of you that I do on Boxing Day, I bet.'

'I expect you're probably right,' I admitted ruefully.

'And what'll I do about the tree? You always do the tree.'

'Oh, Gran, it's only May now, we've got plenty of time to sort that out. I'll decorate it before I go.'

'Well, it won't be the same, Christmas without you here,' she said, clattering the grill pan, so I could barely hear. 'I s'pose I'll have to ask the Holdens if I can go and sit in with them.'

'Gran, Russell won't let you be here on your own, you know that,' I said, sorting through the junk in the sideboard cupboard to find the other knitting needle. 'He'll take care of you.'

'Strikes me I need someone to,' she mumbled under her breath. 'Course no one wants you when you're old.'

'Gran, you're *not* old,' I interjected. 'You were only seventy last birthday.'

'Sixty-nine!' she said defiantly.

'Gran, if you were born in 1888 you're *seventy*.'

'Oh, I don't know, I'm sure. I must get Russell to hunt out my birth sustificate. Thass up in the front bedroom somewhere in one of them tins.'

There was an oblong navy-blue tin with Crawfords Assorted Biscuits in faded yellow writing on the front and the other had housed chocolates of some description. I'd loved looking through those tins on rainy days when I was small.

There was a sepia photograph of Gran and Walter on their wedding day: Walter, with his walrus moustache, in a high collar and waistcoat, and Gran almost hidden under a wide-brimmed hat laden with fruit and feathers, her waist pinched in by tight corsets under the boned, shaped bodice of a smart striped dress that reached all the way down to her shiny button boots. She held a frilly parasol rather shyly in one hand; her other hand was slipped through Walter's arm in a very formal pose.

'I'll get Russell to hunt it out. I swear to God I'm only sixty-nine. You always want to make me older than I am. The time pass quick enough as it is—it were only yesterday I had you as a baby and look at you now—fourteen this Christmas; not that I shall see it, of course.'

'I bet you a bob I'm right,' I joked, hoping to change her mood.

'And where are you goin' to get a bob from, I'd like to know? You're not to go asking Russell for money, you tinker.'

'He'll probably have a bet too,' I joked. '*He* said you were seventy as well. Don't you remember?'

'Oh, he were just pullin' my leg.' I could hear she was almost smiling.

I'd resented Russell at first, now I was grateful for his daily visits.

Getting his dinner before he arrived from the garage where he worked near St Augustine's Church gave her something to occupy her mind, as she put it, while I was at school. I left at eight thirty every morning and often wasn't home before six, especially if I had netball practice. I'd been chosen for the school team, which was a matter of some pride to me. I liked Catherine Roberts and Anne Kerr who were so good at games they played hockey for the school teams too. Listening to them talk about team co-operation and gamesmanship was a world apart from the bickering that went on between Delia, Vivienne and me, or the persecution I felt I experienced at the hands of Rita, Deirdre, Annette and Heather.

Mrs Brady didn't call in much any more, I guess Miss MacVean was satisfied with her success in getting me to visit my mother, and they felt they didn't have to monitor my development so carefully. I smiled wryly to myself when I thought of what Miss MacVean would make of my stepfather having a mistress, and, if Lolo was to be believed, of my mother having boyfriends.

When I'd mentioned Russell to her in Tripoli, she'd smiled a knowing smile and warned me to be careful of him. I'd found that hard to believe—

331

happily married Russell with his red face, cloth cap, and garage dungarees. It had seemed so preposterous an idea that I'd mentioned it to Gran in passing, who'd dismissed it with, 'Oh, your mother always thought every man was after her, but in truth it was probably the other way round.'

Russell brought Gran, or Chisy as he called her, lots of little presents, newlaid eggs, or small bottles of scent, bath cubes although she was no longer able to get into the bath, but she crunched them up in her washing water in the plastic bowl. I knew he paid her generously for his dinners because they'd often have a mock fight over her trying to hand some of the money back by slipping it into his pocket, which he would dodge and adamantly refuse.

'Now, have your supper; put that knittin' down or you'll get grease all over it, and that'll be a right lookout.'

'Look, I said I've only got a few more rows of casting off to do for the raglan armholes then I can start the sleeves.'

'You'll be up all night if you want that done by Saturday, you know.'

'Yes, but I don't mind.'

'Well, I do. You'll be goin' to school with even darker circles under your eyes than you've got now; people'll think I'm ill-treatin' you.'

'Oh, don't be so daft, Gran,' I said, jumping up to give her a squeeze round her middle. 'I'm going to finish that pullover, you just watch me.'

'You're right pigheaded when you set your mind to something, sure as fate is fate. Now sit down properly, there's a dear, and eat your bread and dripping.'

CHAPTER 22

There were grey jelly-like blobs in upturned shells which turned my stomach. 'Oysters,' my mother explained with delight and relish, and then a roast of anaemic-looking meat—'veal,' she added. I ate very little and tried not to think of roast chicken, sage and onion stuffing, Brussels sprouts and Christmas pudding with sixpences hidden in it. The chocolate-covered log cake with a solitary robin perched on the top was the only item in the meal that was vaguely reminiscent of Christmas.

Magda Landowski played us some Chopin as we sat drinking our champagne. She was a brilliant concert pianist in her own country, Yves whispered, and later my mother said, 'Henry is a journalist,' and then in some seriousness added, 'They're both exiles.'

There was an air of other-worldness about both of them. Henry peering through his thick round rimless glasses and Magda with her untidy dark hair, and her look of wanting to be somewhere other than where she was. Especially when she played. Tossing and dipping her head in time to the music. Their villa was huge—almost bare but somehow the sparseness seemed untidy. 'It's good they 'ave a chef,' said Yves. 'Magda play the piano better than she cook.'

Their son Lee was as pale and owl-like as Henry. He sat quietly watching his mother as her flourishes became more extravagant, and her unruly hair flew about her burning face as she lost herself in the rhythm.

'Don't you sing carols at Christmas?' I asked Lolo later in the back of the car as we sped towards the Uaddan Hotel.

> '*Minuit chrétien*
> *C'est l'heure solennelle*
> *Où l'homme dieu*
> *Descendit jusqu'à nous,*'

Lolo obliged. Yves, who was as full of bonhomie as alcohol, joined in, in his gravelly rumble:

> '*Peuple à genoux*
> *Attend la délivrance*
> *Noël noël*
> *Voici le rédempteur*
> *Noël No-ee-ee-el—*'

This line provided great opportunities for exaggeration and embellishment.

> '*Voici le rédempteur—*'

'Ssh,' said my mother playfully, disapproving from the front seat. 'Daddee, Lolo, Janie, ssh—it's a holy song.'

'Oh, she turn religious in her old age, *la vieille,*' said Yves.

'Papa, concentrate on where you're parking so we don't have trouble getting out when we leave.'

He slammed the car door and gave a few piastres to the boy who had signalled us into the parking space. He looked smart in his white baggy trousers and white crochet cap. 'No wash,' Yves said emphatically. '*Non toccare a la macchina.* No

334

touch car. *Si tu touches*,' he said, waggling his finger in the boy's face. He drew a line across his throat and squawked a death rattle.

A strong breeze rustled the palm trees that edged the sea. 'Ooh,' said my mother, 'it's chilly.' I tried hard to think of Ipswich on Christmas Eve. Rain lashing down, wind, snow perhaps. Christmas carols under lampposts. The picture wouldn't come.

There were lights everywhere and people chatting, laughing and dancing. Jewellery sparkled and silks and satins caught the light.

'Oh, good, there's Dick Templeton, he'll ask me to dance,' said Lolo pointing to the red-bearded Scotsman in the distance, easily seen, as he was head and shoulders above the rest of the crowd.

'*Profites-en*,' said my mother. 'He's going to England to marry his fiancée soon.'

'No more bachelor gay for you, old boy,' said Yves, clapping him on the shoulder and guffawing.

Dick laughed and bent down to pick Lolo up and, admiring her dress, spun her round till she shrieked with glee.

'Louise, will you dance?' said Dick, clicking his heels—and my mother, having given me her handbag, was led away wreathed in smiles, patting her hair and rearranging her necklaces, looking around her to ensure she was being watched.

'Where are the Landowskis? I thought they were following us,' I asked, more out of embarrassment at standing there with no invitation to dance than genuine concern.

'*Ouf*,' said Yves dismissively, 'they are probably 'aving a discussion about politics or philosophy or some shit like that.' It struck me as odd that these

335

four should be friends with so little in common.

We settled at a table near the sea. Fairy lights swung high above my head in the wind, all around us family groups chattered in Italian, German, French and English. There was a white-jacketed orchestra and waiters with gold braid on their shoulders like soldiers, hurrying about carrying champagne or curiously shaped glasses containing green and red liquid.

'Can I have a grenadine, Papa?'

'Sure,' said Yves, full of bonhomie, lighting another cigarette and surveying the scene. 'Janie?'

'What's the green stuff in those glasses?'

'*Crème de menthe, ma chérie*, and don't bite your fingers,' he said, delivering a sharp tap on the back of my hand.

'One of those, please,' I said pointing, as a reaction to hide my embarrassment, and hopefully distract from the blush that I felt.

'Very good *digestif*, but you 'ave nothing to digest—apart from your nails. You eat like a sparrow—you are off your food—in love, eh?'

I giggled at the suggestion, hoping it would deflect further questioning. It was beyond me how anyone could swallow those grey blobs of slime.

'Normally you eat like a . . .' he paused, '. . . a 'oover.' I had to think hard before I eventually laughed. 'You 'ave your—'ow you say it?—period?'

'Daddee,' said Lolo, 'ssh, people can hear you. Don't talk about those things.'

'Oh, *mademoiselle ni-touche*,' said Yves, making a mincing gesture with his hand. 'Wait till you get it—no more climbing trees with the *Siciliens* then.'

The Landowskis wandered in, caught up with the dancers who were making their way back from

336

the dance floor to the tables. They waved vaguely in our direction before disappearing again, swallowed up by the crowd.

Lolo excused herself hurriedly to dance with Dick Templeton as soon as my mother returned to the table, or rather she danced *on* him as she placed her feet on his and he danced for them both, her arms clasped about his waist, her head just reaching his stomach. It reminded me of how I used to dance with Doug—I was too old for that now, I supposed. I felt slightly sad and very envious. I dug into the bowls of pistachio nuts, peanuts and fat black olives.

'Daddee, where's my whisky?' my mother said, patting the back of her neck with a Kleenex.

'I haven't ordered it yet, Louise! *Patienza!* They are so slow in this goddam 'ole.' He clapped his hands smartly twice. I couldn't believe that no one would take exception to this, especially the harassed waiters. But no one did.

'*Ça va, chérie?*' said my mother, studying her face in her powder compact mirror.

'Oh, yes. Gosh, I think it's wonderful,' I said, mimicking Lorna Mayon-White.

'Oh, gosh,' said Yves, mimicking me.

'Leave her, Daddee—she's having a good time. Can you imagine the *changement* for her from Ipswich?' Having reapplied her lipstick she pressed her lips together, surveyed her face in the mirror again with some satisfaction, snapped the compact shut and looked up.

'Oh, there's Dad Fowler and Deedee and Roland.' She waved enthusiastically to somewhere behind me and dashed off in that direction.

I felt awkward and gauche and uncomfortable in

337

another of my mother's dresses. This didn't seem like Christmas at all. Dressing up and going out on Christmas Eve. We'd had our presents already or at least Lolo had. More dolls and toys and several matching T-shirts and shorts 'from *France*' my mother had said proudly as Lolo unwrapped them. I'd been promised a trip to her Italian dressmaker.

I drank the cool green-looking liquid in great thirsty gulps. The glass rattled with broken ice which I crunched with great relish and stared about me.

'Missing Michael?' said Yves, interrupting my train of thought which had dresses of every colour and style dancing before my eyes, and a little Italian lady clapping her hands with delight as I paraded in yet another *ensemble* before her admiring gaze.

'What?'

'Don't say what, it's rude.'

'Pardon.'

'Missing Michael Drew?' he said, so seriously I had to consider for several moments before replying.

'Oh, Daddee,' I said, not thinking.

'Don't call me that. I don't like it—Papa is best.'

'Oh, Papa,' I said not quite so playfully and tapped him on his bronzed arm in a mock remonstrance.

'*C'est beau, l'amour,*' he said, not really in my direction. I followed his gaze to the dance floor where my mother and Henry Landowski were dancing very close. The atmosphere had changed, most of the crowd had gone home. My mother had taken off her shoes and was singing '*Arrivederci Roma*' loudly in Henry Landowski's ear as they shuffled past our table, no longer really dancing, just walking and swaying in time to the music. Henry's bow tie hung undone about his neck. Yves had removed his tie completely and sat as he did at home, with his shirt unbuttoned almost to the waist revealing an abundance of greying hair on his chest, which I didn't like to look at. Magda was dancing with a tall rather stiff Italian in a cream jacket, his hair slicked back. She still seemed oblivious to all around her, especially him.

Lolo had long disappeared, having seen several friends from Tripoli College, and they were occasionally visible as they darted in and out of the bushes that edged the dancing area. Intermittent squeals would distract people nearby eating or dancing and heads would turn momentarily, but no one paid them much attention.

With a great yelp from the floor, my mother rushed towards Yves. 'Listen, Daddee, listen,' she said between spurts of laughter; her lipstick was smudged and she had dark marks under her eyes from mascara. 'Listen!' Over the sound of tables being cleared and bursts of laughter from the remaining stragglers, the orchestra was playing 'Your Eyes are the Eyes of a Woman in Love'.

'Listen, Daddee!' she exclaimed again, her voice high-pitched and cracking over-excitedly. 'It's your song, Daddee, we must dance to it.'

'Don't call me Daddee,' he said quietly for the second time that evening, and, turning away from her, grabbed my arm, and added brusquely, 'Come, Janie, we dance.'

'And how they give you away,' he croaked into my ear. We were exactly the same height which I found rather disconcerting.

'Janie, you dance like a 'orse.' I had just about managed to follow the steps he was doing, and thought I was dancing rather well in spite of his occasional 'uh-huh' when one of my feet caught his. This dance was unlike anything I'd learned at Alan Road. It wasn't a valeta, a Gay Gordons, or even a Saint Bernard's Waltz. Just when I thought it was as simple as walking in time to the music, he executed a sneaky change of weight from one foot to the other in double time, which left me a few steps behind, blushing and wanting to disappear into the shiny marble floor.

'Well, what am I doing wrong?' I said exasperated, using it as an excuse to stop dancing and break away from him.

'Don't stick your *derrière* out like that.' He mimicked my posture much to my embarrassment. I stared at the floor. 'Dance like this.' He grabbed me and held my body in contact with his. 'You put your legs 'ere,' he said, clamping my knee between his. 'Don't they teach you anything in England?'

I danced, hardly daring to breathe, my whole concentration focused on the front of my body which was in acute proximity to his.

'Your eyes are the eyes of a woman in love,' he murmured, completely out of time and out of tune with the orchestra.

As we turned I could see my mother, her head thrown back laughing, wildly pulling Henry Landowski on to the dance floor yet again.

'We go after this, yes?' he asked, pulling away from my shoulder, looking me squarely in the face, 'and 'ave a game of chess, huh?'

'What about Lolo?'

'Oh, Templeton will take 'er back—or someone

340

. . .' He didn't seem concerned.

'And Mummy?' I asked lamely, hoping to avoid several hours in the house with him alone while he struggled over the different moves between a rook and a knight.

'*Ouf*,' he said, shrugging his shoulders. '*Ta mère, tu sais*, she break my feet.'

I smiled at this literal translation. 'She gets on your nerves—*elle te casse les pieds*?' I ventured.

'*Exact*,' he said simply, with no further comment on my adventurousness with French.

'Gosh, it's nearly two in the morning.'

'So?'

'It's late.'

'So, you tired?'

'Oh, no,' I said. I couldn't remember having ever stayed up so late before.

'You can sleep tomorrow.'

'But it's Christmas tomorrow,' I said horrified.

'So, you can sleep,' he said, putting paid to any further discussion, adding wickedly as an afterthought, '*if* the bloody goats don't wake you up.'

Mickette and Bickette lived outside my bedroom window tied up under a tree. Yves had brought them back from the rig as presents for Lolo. Bickette had two small bumps between his ears, a mere suggestion of horns. Lolo and I took them both to the beach on dog leads and washed them in Omo at the water's edge. They brayed loudly all the time and Mickette lowered his head in a mock menacing way. Lolo had let go of him once and we'd had to chase a wildly complaining foaming goat all round the beach till we cornered him with our flapping towels.

Even when the Ghibli howled and whined round the house and the unfastened shutters clattered against the walls, Yves would sleep through it. He was never disturbed by the goats. Except at lunchtimes. If the day was exceptionally hot with no wind, the bathroom shutters would be left open to create a *courant d'air* through the house and he could hear the braying then quite clearly.

'*Ces sacrés chèvres!* I tell you—we 'ave goat steak for dinner tonight.' On cue Lolo would rush out, untie the goats from the tree and pull them round the house two or three times, returning flustered with a 'They've run some more, Papa—too tough to eat now.' Everyone would laugh. But behind my eyes nothing moved, except envy.

*   *   *

'Happy birthday,' said Lolo as I bumped into her coming out of the bathroom. A wintry sun was high in the sky, shafts of slatted light were splayed across the bathroom floor. The sun rarely shone on my birthday in England. 'I haven't wrapped your *cadeau* yet. I'll give it to you later on,' she said in an offhand way. 'Brrr, it's cold. I'm going back to bed.'

'Cold? It's not cold,' I said, sounding like Gran. 'Sometimes it snows on my birthday in England.'

'I've never seen snow but I'm going to the *sports d'hiver* when *I'm* fourteen.'

'What's—'

'Oh, skiing, Janie, silly.'

I thought, you're not supposed to call me names; it's my birthday.

She stopped and came back into the bathroom.

'Anyway, I have a saint's day *too*.'

342

'What?'

'A saint's day; everybody has one in France. So I get two—November 29th and St Laurence on August 10th. Two, you see, two birthdays.' I'm not getting one, I thought.

'Where's Mummy and Yves?' I asked as I sat on the toilet watching her clean her face with Mummy's skin tonic which was, as Yves would have said, '*verboten*'.

'Still sleeping off Christmas.'

Gran was always up before me on my birthday and my presents would be waiting for me in the same large pillowslip in which I'd found my Christmas presents the day before. It was one of the many ways she made up for my having a birthday at such an awkward time. 'Thass all because your mother had a gin and it, or I don't know what, with her Christmas dinner—you shouldn't have been born till later.'

'I'm going back to bed,' she said and disappeared.

Little Girl and Bebop wagged their tails and Buster Brown, the one remaining puppy, half-crawled, half-slid along the floor after me to my bedroom.

I opened the suitcase my mother had lent me and took out the envelopes from Russell, Pat and Doug and Gran. Russell's, with a picture of a vintage car and a Labrador dog, contained a pound as I guessed it would. Pat and Doug's, with a large blank-looking poodle on the front, contained a two-pound book token from WH Smith's and Gran's contained five pounds which she could ill afford from her pension. The picture of a teenage girl in a dirndl skirt and a blonde pony-tail holding

343

hands with a rather wooden smart clean boy opened up to reveal the verse on which she set much store:

> On this your special day
> May joy and laughter come your way
> And happiness throughout the year
> Be yours many happy returns dear.

She'd written underneath in her sloping looped hand:

> With love from Gran
> PS I shall be thinking about you.

Well nobody else bloody well is, I thought, kicking the suitcase shut.

I padded back into the *salle à manger* to place the cards on the dining table. They had pride of place on the mantelpiece at Levington Road and usually there were more than three.

'Janie, Janie bach.' My mother's thick morning voice came from their bedroom. I could hear Yves's snoring running quietly away with clockwork regularity. '*Viens—viens ici. Joyeux anniversaire, chérie,*' she said, raising herself up on her elbow. The atmosphere in the room smelled thick and musty. Old cigarette smoke, 'Shocking', and traces of Yves's sweat. I had to step over his Y-fronts discarded on the floor. I avoided looking at them too closely.

She kissed me on both cheeks and then cupped her hand round my face.

'Fourteen years old,' she said. 'My goodness.' I detected last night's whisky on her breath amongst

344

the odour of stale cigarette smoke that even the pungent smell of 'Shocking' couldn't hide.

I smiled shyly, pleased.

'No one believes I've got a grown-up daughter, you know,' she said, stroking down my hair. I could see dark stubble in her armpit, and there was a coffee stain down the front of her *chemise de nuit*. It was odd how I'd begun to think of certain things only by their French names as they all did.

'Well, that's because you look so young,' I said, pleased to please her.

'Well, I'm only thirty-three, darling—it's not old,' she said defensively. Yves shifted in his sleep next to her. In the darkened room I could just make out the glint of gold teeth inside his opened mouth. He snorted and swallowed and then the snoring resumed in a different rhythm and tone. *'Sois gentille—apportes-moi le café, s'il te plaît*. Nescafé will do.'

Gran always made me a special breakfast on my birthday. This wasn't right at all.

She drank it thirstily, a trickle of coffee escaping from the corner of her mouth and making its way down her chin till she caught it with a screwed-up lipstick-stained Kleenex that she found amongst the empty peppermint wrappers on her bedside table.

She lit a cigarette, blowing the acrid smoke in my direction as she turned to move the pillows behind her into a more comfortable position. The smell burned my nostrils and made my eyes smart. I waited to hear about the plans for the day.

'You know, darling,' she said, settling herself, coffee bowl in one hand, cigarette-holder in the other, 'they're so *méchantes*, some of the wives of

345

the *compagnie*.' I was never sure whether her odd construction of sentences was affectation or whether living with Yves's bad English for so long had simply rubbed off on her. I'd heard her complimented on the charming English accent with which she spoke French, and guessed that was why she would never relinquish it. 'One of them told me that she'd seen Papa coming out of the cinema with a young woman.' She tutted under her breath and two streams of smoke trailed out of her nostrils. I didn't know whether to commiserate with her or if, by ignoring it, it wouldn't seem so real.

'Oh well,' I said, floundering out of my depth, not knowing whether I should let her know I knew about their *'affaires'*, as Lolo called them. 'Lots of people have *affaires*,' I said, echoing Lolo's words, trying to be worldly-wise, although I found it impossible to picture Mrs Kerridge on some other man's arm, and Doris with anyone other than Bert was unimaginable.

'Oui, oui,' said my mother philosophically, and then laughed in her dark throaty way.

'*Ta gueule, Louise*,' said Yves without moving or opening his eyes.

'What *does* that mean?' I whispered.

'It's a very rude way of saying shut up.'

'Like shut your gob?' I asked helpfully. Such an Ipswich phrase sounded so out of place.

'Don't listen to him. It's Janie's birthday, Daddee,' she said, pushing his bare shoulder. 'Say "happy birthday, Janie".'

'Happy birthday, Janie,' he said. 'Tell your mother to shut her gob, will you?' He moved further away from her in the bed and within seconds was snoring again, a rumble in his throat

346

that ended in a whistle from his nose. I guessed he was naked under the bedclothes but didn't want to think about it. I hadn't seen them often in bed together and I found it embarrassing and slightly shocking.

'No,' she said, 'it's very *drôle* . . .'

My mind skipped a beat and halted in its wandering. 'Droll?'

'*Drôle*—funny, darling.'

'What is?'

'That Suzanne should tell me about Papa.'

'Oh,' I said regretfully. I hoped Yves's intrusion would have made her forget our conversation and prompt her into telling me what special things we were going to do to celebrate my day. 'Why was it funny?' I said. 'Because you already knew?'

'Well, of course I knew, Janie,' she said irritably. 'It was *you* . . .'

'What?'

'You went to the cinema with Papa last week, when Lolo was at that party and I wasn't feeling *en forme*. It was *you!*' She laughed some more and drained her bowl. 'Now, *va te coucher*,' she said, stubbing out her cigarette with some difficulty in the overflowing ashtray. 'We'll get you fixed up with the dressmaker soon—when all this Christmas palaver, as Nana would say, is over. Now *va te coucher*,' she said in the same tone that she used to Bebop and the dogs. 'We've got nothing to do today, at all. No rendevous, no parties—so go back to bed now and catch up on your beauty sleep.'

*   *   *

'Navy-blue?' she said sighing. 'It's such a *triste*

347

colour.'

'No, no, *bene, bene*,' said the *signora*, her mouth full of pins as she knelt to adjust the hemline. She squirted little puffs of chalk from a small rubber bulb attached to an upright ruler on a stand.

'Why didn't you choose a gay happy colour, red or green?'

I shuddered at the prospect. I didn't like my mother's choice of garish colours. I didn't want to be that noticeable.

The *signora*, whose fat pale arms bulged from a sleeveless black dress that had rings of dried white sweat under the armpits, heaved herself up with some difficulty and surveyed her handiwork through critical squinting eyes, framed by dark hollows.

The dress was cut square across my chest, shoulderless but for two dainty straps. The skirt was gathered at the waist and the silk rustled as I moved to accommodate the *signora*'s pinnings.

As the *signora* moved around me my mother spat discreetly into a crumpled Kleenex and wiped the sand dust off the toes of her high-heeled shoes.

'It goes with the coat, Mummy.' I'd reckoned on having several dresses but my delight in the fluffy pale lemon-coloured overcoat of nylon fur made me forget that the navy-blue dress was the sole offering.

'I don't know what Papa will say about the coat.'

'You said I could have it . . .' I started defensively.

'Janie, don't talk to me like that.'

I blushed, grateful that the *signora* couldn't understand me any more than I could understand her.

'I've spent more money on you than he said, *chérie*,' she said firmly, straightening her hair so that her gold bracelet jangled.

One measly coat and one measly dress, I thought murderously; you spend more than that on one beastly blouse.

'*Ecco*,' said the *signora*, standing back and folding her fat arms. '*Bella, bella*,' she said smiling, wiping the beads of sweat from her upper lip where dark hairs threatened to suggest a moustache.

'She says it's beautiful, you're beautiful.'

I grinned, then remembered from my sessions with the bathroom mirror that I looked better when I kept my lips together when I smiled. I offered her a winsome smirk. Now I wouldn't feel out of place at the Uaddan or at Beach Club parties—and what an impression I'd make at Alan Road on Saturday nights.

The *signora* walked towards me, no longer smiling, and said something that sounded like 'Formaggio'.

'Cheese?' I queried. 'Why's she talking about cheese?'

'*Dommage*,' my mother said. '*Domaggio*.'

The *signora* thrust her pudgy hand down the front of my dress in between my small breasts. I wore no bra. The directness and the intimacy of the gesture shocked me. She flapped her hand about under the material.

'*Domaggio, domaggio*,' she said sadly in pidgin French, turning towards my mother.

My mother uttered a sentence that sounded something like French with lots of 'o's and 'io's attached. 'She says the dress is beautiful.'

I smiled, trying not to mind the hand that still

349

flapped about next to my skin.

'*Grazie, Signora, grazie,*' I managed haltingly.

'The dress is beautiful,' my mother repeated, 'but she says it's a pity—'

'What, what is?'

'—about your *gou-gouttes* . . .'

I hated that silly word. Little Girl had *gou-gouttes*. That word was all right for rows of nipples for dogs. I had breasts.

'What's wrong with my . . . breasts?' I managed shakily.

'They spoil the style of the dress, she says. It's a pity they're so small.'

CHAPTER 23

When I went to church Sunday morning and evening, I now stuffed socks into my empty bra to make an impression on my best Sunday coat, and hopefully on Barry Cunnell too. He didn't turn up at Youth Club as regularly as the rest of us because he was often out with the Reverend John Blamey, but I didn't see our parson as a hindrance to my designs on Barry at the time.

We went to Methodist Youth Club rallies at the Albert Hall in London. We piled into the bus laughing and out of the bus laughing, seeing nothing of the city. We wore green and yellow striped scarves and sang songs written by Steve Race as part of a mass of assembled youth club choirs, in four-part harmonies. I veered between the baritones and altos and hoped no one would notice:

So now goodbye it's nearly time to part
No memories die held closely in the heart
And for all time to be
Let the memories linger
Like a melody
From a lovely singer.

I looked across at where Barry Cunnell stood singing with the baritones and hoped he would notice I was singing it to him.

The renegades Tony, Ancia, Dingaling, the Pallants, Peck and Kindred sat in the back of the bus and sang 'Ten Green Bottles and a Stick of Dynamite Hanging on a Wall' or 'Lloyd George Knew My Father'. I didn't know who either of them were but didn't like to mention it.

We went on Methodist Youth Club weekends at a large country house called Roxawa near Cromer and sat in the back of the bus and sang some more. The quiet ones sat in the front and admired the flatness of Norfolk while Doris passed round acid drops.

Bert once asked me to make a statement of my beliefs at a Youth Club meeting. I refused point blank, mostly out of terror at the prospect of having to talk publicly at a formal meeting. Sunday Youth Club after church was a serious time. Probation officers, almoners, or prison warders were invited as guest speakers, or a panel chosen from members would debate such topics as 'Why I am a Methodist', 'No sex before marriage—discuss'. We would sing here too, but this time we stayed demurely in our rows standing in front of the wooden Sunday School chairs, that most of us had sat on since the age of four. Clasping our hymn books we voiced full-throatedly:

> What a friend we have in Jesus
> All our sins and griefs to bear
> What a privilege to carry
> Everything to God in prayer.

I had prayed more, recently. I'd prayed for a gold bracelet like Lolo's soon so that Rita, Deirdre and Annette wouldn't find me out. I prayed that Barry Cunnell would stop being in love with Diana Reeves and would begin to notice me, but mostly I prayed that Gran and I wouldn't row so much, and that things between us would be as before. None of my prayers had been answered, but I didn't tell Bert that that was also why I declined his offer. 'I can't speak in front of people,' I whined.

'You managed very well when we did that little play last year.' I'd played a North Country maid in a thriller with more relish than was probably tolerable and more accent than was accurate. He smiled, patting me on the head with a 'mustn't hide our light under a bushel.'

> I love you a bushel and a peck
> A bushel and a peck and a hug around the neck

went through my head but I didn't mention it to Bert. It was probably sacrilegious to think of popular songs while talking of faith—or in my case lack of it. A double wrong.

Bert being Bert I made the speech anyway. He helped me write it so it ended up being more of a statement of his beliefs than mine, but I read it

352

with great meaning and almost convinced myself.

I hadn't found Jesus, or more importantly, I didn't think Jesus would ever bother to find me.

Bert took us in prayer and thanked God for something called the Communion of Fellowship; while I thanked God briefly for Barry Cunnell who now cycled to school with me sometimes, if I lurked in the passage till I saw him turn the corner of Clapgate Lane; and while I was on the subject I added an impassioned plea for the spot on my chin to disappear before next Saturday's Youth Club dance, and for God to remind Yves to send the money this month as I'd seen a tight check skirt I wanted to buy.

Sometimes I'd remember to ask the Almighty to forgive me my bad treatment of Gran and at the same time to help me like my mother more, but often I didn't remember. At Youth Club and church I was happy. There, I didn't have time to think of Levington Road or of Tripoli Libya. When I did, wherever I was, I wanted to be in the other place.

CHAPTER 24

'Say I can wear it . . .'

'You'll get pneumonia—with these March winds.'

The thought of a hot poultice on my chest or, worse, a dose of Liquafruita or Ipecac cough mixture almost halted me.

'Say I can wear it . . .'

'It's for your own good, Jane—why don't you

listen to what I say? Don't cast a clout till May is out. Now be a good girl and open this door!'

'Not till you say I can wear it.'

'Oh, dear, you do make me feel bad. I'll have one of my blackouts shut in here.'

'Say I can wear it, then.'

'Oh, all right, have it your own way. If you get a cold and it go down on to your chest, don't come running to me to rub your back when you've got asthma.'

'So I can wear it then?'

'Oh, wear what you like—just let me out of here.'

Her voice began to falter as if she was on the brink of tears. Once she'd agreed I allowed my conscience to get the better of me. I slipped the little brass catch into its upright position and the cupboard door eased itself open just a fraction. I sat down in the old utility chair next to the wireless.

'C'mon, there's a good girl, let me out, enough's enough.'

'It's open,' I said contemptuously as if she should have known.

Her face was red and her eyes were moist. She wiped them with the corner of her dirty apron, and held on to the nearest chair.

'You are a little sod,' she said. 'I don't know what's got into you lately. You'll be the death of me. What'd the Holdens say or Miss Brady if they knew you'd shut me in the cupboard?'

She'd gone in to fetch the bread in the middle of our argument and it had come to me in a flash of inspiration—to shut her in until she agreed to my demand.

'I don't care—' I started.

'Don't care was made to care—'

'Oh, shut up.'

'Don't you talk to me like that. I don't know who you think you are—'

'I'm Jane Burgess-Lapotaire.'

She looked up startled. 'Oh, and who's she when she's at home?'

'And I'm wearing my navy-blue silk dress to Youth Club Saturday night because you said I could and if you change your mind I'll shut you in the cupboard again.'

'You try it, my girl, and I'll go and get Joan Holden in to you.'

'I'm not your girl and I'm not scared of Joan Holden so you can go and get her for all I bloody well care.'

'Oh, dear,' she said faintly, easing herself down into one of the upright chairs by the table. She always sat in one of those if she had to fight for breath. Her large frame shuddered under the strain of a repressed sob and the roll of fat around her middle heaved as she settled down. I noticed her moustache had grown again and her fingernails were black from peeling potatoes. My mother's girl-like frame and immaculate varnished nails flashed before my eyes.

'What language! What would Bert and Doris say if they heard you talk like that? I've tried to do my best by you, but you're not the same girl lately and that's a fact. Your mother's at the root of all this, I'll be bound.'

'You shut up about my mother. What do you know about her?'

'A damn sight more of the truth than you do. I brought her up for twelve years.'

355

'She said she wanted to keep me and you wouldn't let her, so there; she said every time I ran to her you got in the way and if I fell down you wouldn't let her pick me up.'

'Oh, that's just a barefaced lie,' she said, rallying. 'How could you run to her, pray? You weren't even six months old when she left you.'

'When she came *back* I mean.'

'You didn't even know who she was then. She's just poisoned your mind against me. I knew no good would come of you gallivanting halfway round the world every school holiday.'

'I don't go every holiday. I knew you'd say that and anyway I'm going to Paris this summer. That's *not* halfway round the world,' I said, despising her lack of geography.

'Oh, no, of course,' she said. 'I don't know anything. I'm just a dirty stupid old woman not good enough for you now you've got your precious mother. She's always been a bad piece of work. She was more trouble than the rest of the girls put together.'

'Well, of course she was. She had a terrible life. Her father committed suicide, her brother died of TB when they arrived in Dover, she was in a sanatorium for ages and then shoved into Dr Barnardo's in Stepney because Auntie Louie was in service and couldn't look after her, and she came to you at seven, not speaking a word of English, and having me at eighteen must have been a terrible shock.'

'Eighteen!' she said incredulously. 'Where did she spin that yarn? Along with all the others, I suppose. She were nearly twenty when she was carrying you—I should know, I saw her birth date on the papers from Barnardo's . . . and on her ration book,' she added as an afterthought. 'Eighteen my foot.'

'So it's not surprising she didn't like it here,' I ended triumphantly. The unspoken 'and I don't like it here either' hung heavily in the air between us.

'Oh, please, God, take me Home, take me Home,' she moaned into her handkerchief.

I felt sick at what I was doing but I was set on a course and was powerless to stop.

'I've always treated you like my own. Pat and Doris always said I'd rue the day I spoiled you. Well, I know about it now and no mistake.'

'Oh, shut up about Pat and Doris. They're nothing to do with me—they're no relation.' Some shred of conscience just stopped me short of saying 'and neither are you'.

'You didn't say that when Pat and Doug bought you *Pears Encyclopaedia* for Christmas; she's been very good to you, Pat, and you always liked Doris. You've changed your tune—you get more like your mother every day.'

'Well, of course I do; it's only natural. I am her daughter after all.'

This produced a silence out of which flowed a fresh stream of tears. I was past apologising, had said more than I'd ever intended and much more than I really meant.

'Be sure your sins will find you out,' she snuffled.

I stood up, slammed the living-room door, grabbed my Northgate mac which I'd flung on a kitchen chair, and went out, slamming the back gate too for good measure behind me. A stolen half-crown jingled next to a stolen shilling and a

357

threepenny bit in my pocket. Enough to catch a tram up the Nacton Road as far as the airport and walk to Suggy's stables for an illicit half-hour ride.

CHAPTER 25

Grand-mère Lapotaire's feet had badly varnished nails that protruded from battered slippers with stubby worn high heels. The sound that these made on the wooden floors of her dark little apartment in the rue Brown-Séquard, Montparnasse, punctuated her breathy, high-pitched singing as she shuffled about from the minute, dark and rather dirty kitchen to the equally dark *salle à manger*. Yves said that the place had remained almost untouched since the day his father, generally accepted by the few remaining members of the family to have married beneath him, had come home, tired from work and, sitting down in the worn ornamental chair with its bow legs by the fireplace, had quietly died. The dust everywhere seemed to confirm this. On every conceivable ledge and shelf there were sepia-tinted photographs of her husband: in his stiff white collar and bowler hat looking not unlike Walter with the same droopy moustache; of Yves, as a sturdy-looking child with two strong beautifully rounded legs, dressed in curiously feminine-looking smocks edged in lace, of Yves on his motorbike at eighteen delivering messages during the early days of the war with the Eiffel Tower dimly in the background, a swastika hardly visible on some building, of Yves bent double over an ice-hockey stick playing for France

358

with 'Lapopo' scribbled underneath, all caked with dust and cracked in several places from old age.

She'd decamped to sleep on the uncomfortable-looking chaise-longue in the *salle à manger* so that my mother and Yves could share the equally sombre bedroom with its gargantuan bed made of some dark wood that rose in curves at the head and the foot. The sheets, made of coarse white linen, had a generous band of intricate lace edging made by hand, by her. The same lace pattern edged the napkins and the coffee-stained table-cloth that graced the vast table in the *salle à manger*. It occupied most of the room.

Her fingernails, long and curved like talons, had the same vestiges of nail varnish as her toes, and where the varnish had worn off the nails were yellow. She had an untipped Gauloise permanently drooping from the corner of her mouth. The hair on her upper lip was as yellow as the hair above it on her head that escaped in wisps from a badly pinned chignon. She sang snatches of opera that Yves derided constantly when he wasn't complaining about the dirtiness of the place. She called him Vonvon, spoke to him in snatches of Breton and looked at him with constantly adoring eyes as if his abuse of her simply didn't exist.

She adored Lolo too, being the youngest Lapotaire, barely spoke to me and when she did she addressed me as *'L'anglaise'*. The English marmalade and tea that my mother had suggested I bring had been accepted in a gruff manner with much examining of the writing on the box of PG Tips and had not softened her attitude to me one jot.

I never saw her dress or go out. She spent the

359

day in a worn velvet dressing-gown with stains down the front tied haphazardly round her middle by a frayed rope-like belt. A woman from the flat above who ran the 'Cinéma Gloria' did her shopping when we weren't there.

There was a *boulangerie* on the street below, and it was a daily treat to run with Lolo down the dark curving stairs into the spring light. All stairways in Paris emitted a particular smell unlike stairs anywhere else. We'd return with several sticks of bread which we would demolish for breakfast. Grand-mère, with her yellowing stubs of teeth, broke her bread and dropped little bits into her coffee and retrieved them with a spoon. It reminded me of the bread and milk Gran made me as a child, each spoonful named after someone that I knew, to get me to eat it all up. I had to look away when Grand-mère ate hers.

I had no idea why they were in Paris and had little opportunity to ask, as Grand-mère, as I was told to call her, spoke no English at all so every conversation was conducted in French.

I thought Paris magical, the elegant buildings topped with cone-shaped turrets like witches' hats, fronted with balcony railings that looked like metal lace; the Jardin du Luxembourg with its formal flower-beds and sandy pathways that covered our shoes with dust, and the cafés. Best of all were the cafés; I could buy one coffee and sit all morning behind the empty cup watching the people go by. I'd escape whenever I could, buy a copy of *Le Figaro* which was far too difficult for me to read, and with it folded under my arm, its print leaving smudges on my fingers, I'd choose another seat near another corner, and stare and stare. I wanted to be French more than anything in the world, I wanted to be like Parisian girls with their hair piled high in bouffant hair-dos, their black-outlined eyes, black-stockinged legs in the highest of stiletto-heeled shoes, and their ghostly pale pink lips, who sat laughing and smoking surrounded by admiring men.

I'd never been anywhere remotely cold with the Lapotaires before and was dismayed when my mother took exception to my wearing a fashionable roll-on girdle, of which I was extremely proud, and my stockings. I was made to go bare-legged which I found chilly and embarrassing. My legs were shockingly white. I could understand my mother never wearing stockings in Tripoli; it was unheard of even in winter and here in Paris her legs were still so brown there was no need. I suffered the torment of my two white legs until, led on by Lolo, I bought a tube of tan leg make-up from the nearest *pharmacie* and thought my problem solved until my mother, as interested and discouraged as ever by what I wore, gave me, in desperation, a white pleated skirt of her own which I had to roll over at the waist many times as it was too long. The make-up came off, of course, on the inside of the skirt, and every time I sat down I contorted myself into a stooped slumped posture in order to hide it. It seemed that every woman I saw had that chic that I'd heard my mother talk about for so long and dressing up to go out was an agony for me. I felt English, ugly and very unchic.

We visited the Gallous, Celia and André, whom Lolo had befriended on a Moroccan beach years before. She was chatty and vivacious. He, tall and balding and gentle. 'He's the kind of man I should have married,' my mother confided in me, 'but he has a bad maladie . . .' My heart went out to the quietly spoken, mild-mannered man. '. . . he gambles. He took some money from his company and lost it all. He's having to work to pay it back.'

I found it hard to imagine André leaning over a green baize table, checkered with black and red squares like the one I'd seen at the Casino in Tripoli. Papa, annoyed once by my winning all the matchsticks in a game of roulette at home by playing on the seven, had taken me to the Casino, and done the same and had lost all the money he'd bet. I couldn't imagine André driven by anything other than gentleness and was vaguely shocked.

The Marcous, René and Ghislaine, were artists and devout Catholics, their much respected and highly successful work reflecting their personal beliefs, especially in Ghislaine's case. I imagined them living in an attic crammed with canvases and artistic muddle, and it was a surprise to see their large paintings stacked neatly on an immaculately polished parquet floor in a smart ordered apartment, where the curtains that were draped from the tall windows to the floor matched the material with which the elegant chairs were covered. Ghislaine never wore make-up, her grey hair was parted neatly and hung straight down the sides of her face. Her only decoration, a large wooden crucifix strung on a leather thong around her neck. She looked more like a nun than an artist. But I liked her, she was kind and made a quiet determined effort to converse with me in the little English that she knew.

Yves and René laughed a lot together. Again my mother confided in me that René, who was Yves's godfather, was one of the few people in the world that he, Yves, respected, and if René criticised or commented on Papa's behaviour in any way Papa accepted it. René became awesome in my eyes.

We had *gouter* at four o'clock; I wasn't allowed to call it tea. I didn't like the *petit pain au chocolat* that my mother insisted *all* French children ate; it seemed such an odd combination to me, bread and chocolate, so I was allowed a *pâtisserie* instead, a *chausson de pommes* or a *millefeuille* with its layers of cream filling that oozed out from stratas of flaky pastry when I bit into it. Better even than the lemon curd tarts from Newsteads on the Felixstowe Road.

I acquired a taste for goats' cheese which I'd never had before and was more vocal about my enjoyment of it than was strictly genuine as this pleased Papa. I loved *charcuterie* shops with their trays of sliced meats and pâtés set in amber aspic. Although my readiness to sample unknown dishes became a source of family amusement, I drew the line at *quenelles* which looked like pale sausages and shocked by tasting of fish—and *boudin blanc* which *was* sausage but a bloodless rubbery one.

Allowed to stay up later than Lolo, much to her dismay and, not that I would admit it, often to mine, as I was worn out with walking the streets of Montparnasse and exhausted from envying all the chic around me, my nerves frazzled by gusts of self-dislike at my clothes and my Englishness, the three of us would end up sitting round the table late into the night talking, my mother slopping whisky and Yves dropping cigarette ash on to the table-cloth whose lace never ceased to impress me. I found it hard to accept that Grand-mère's gnarled hands

363

had been capable of such delicate beautiful work. *'C'est fait pour ça, les Bretonnes,'* said Papa. As Yves objected to buying more than a bottle of Orangina a day I'd drink half a tumbler of wine that I didn't like and I'd top up the wine with water from a bottle and try to obliterate the sourness in my mouth with a feeling of sophistication. No one drank water from the taps in Paris, I was told, and I was then suspicious of the half-hearted trickle that came out of the shower, in the musty mildewed alcove that my mother called *la douche* when I went for my rapid daily wash. At least the toilet, although dark and smelly, had a proper wooden seat unlike the two holes in the ground with foot-shaped mouldings either side which dogged my visits to cafés. I never managed to pee without it splashing up on to my shoes, and would spend anxious moments in those dark cubby-holes waiting for the tell-tale marks to dry before venturing to reappear.

They seemed almost happy together, and had it not been for Grand-mère's marked ignoring of me, I might have been so too.

'Ouf,' said Yves with the familiar shrug of his shoulders when I replied to his question about my long face, 'She'll die soon—*elle crèvera bientôt, dieu merci.'*

'Daddee, you mustn't talk like that, she's your mother.'

'Oh, it's very easy to open your legs, any woman can do it. You don't 'ave to 'ave special talent to be mother, eh Louise?'

I studied the heaviest stain on the table-cloth with great interest.

'So how are you, my two bastards?' he said,

smiling at us, following a train of thought that was a mystery to me.

I looked up, fearing the conversation was about to take its familiar turn for the worse.

'I know I'm a bastard—' I said bravely.

'Janie, *je t'en prie*,' said my mother.

'She is a realist, your daughter,' said Yves.

'But I didn't know Mummy—'

' 'Orace 'ubert and 'is wife were not married until after your mother was born,' he said laughing. 'We found it out on 'er birth certificate so she is as big a bastard as you . . .'

My mother concentrated on pouring herself another whisky.

'Gran's illegitimate too,' I said, replacing the ugly word. 'She thinks her father may have been the son of the house where old Nana worked in service—so her parents weren't married either,' I said, warming to the subject.

'Neither were Lolo's,' he said triumphantly.

'What?' I said, not believing I understood.

'We 'ad to get your mother's birth certificate before we got married; that's when we found out,' he said.

'But why did . . . ?'

'We just got married, Janie,' interjected my mother sighing—as if she had been drawn into this conversation against her will, 'at the French Embassy in Tripoli. Lolo was our bridesmaid. She didn't know it, of course. She thought it was another party. So she's not a bastard any more as you so charmingly put it, Papa, and now I'm really Madame Lapotaire.'

CHAPTER 26

I wrote a letter to Yves telling him I'd passed my O-levels. In fact I'd failed three, maths and biology and domestic science, but I didn't tell him that. I was now adept at omitting what I didn't like, as long as no one else was party to the information. Gran wouldn't write to tell him. Their dislike was mutual.

I was ashamed that girls like Valerie Plummer, whom I thought dull and insignificant, had passed all eight, and for several days after the results were out, Valerie, the focus of unusual attention, shone.

Delia had passed all hers, Vivienne hadn't. Deirdre, Rita and Annette surprised no one with their few passes.

I was cross with myself. I thought I'd worked hard. I'd learned all my history notes parrot fashion—every single date, treaty and act—so I felt it was Miss Kemp who'd just scraped through with a grade 4.

No one expected me to pass maths, least of all myself. In fact, having failed my mock O-level exam earlier in such a resounding manner I gained (which I suspected I gleaned from drawing a straight margin and for having written my name correctly) in the exam proper a surprising eleven per cent. I think it was Miss Greenham who suggested that I was wasting the one pound ten shillings entrance fee paid by the Suffolk County Council by attempting to take the exam at all.

My failing of domestic science, the obligatory second science subject which those of us who were

366

complete duffers at both physics and chemistry had no choice but to resort to, was a shaming failure. I'd even been tipped for the in-school domestic science prize—which I saw go to a blushing Elizabeth Evans.

I was good at cooking and knew it. I'd picked up many tips from my mother under some duress and Yves's critical eye, and becoming increasingly impatient with Gran's lack of speed and deftness found plenty of opportunity to put them into practice. Once in my continual search for credit I'd listened too carefully to a piece of nonsense uttered by the domestic science teacher, Miss Gregory, flustered by a stream of silly questions during the decorating of shepherd's pie for one session.

'Miss, Miss, how can I hold the piping bag open and put the mashed potato in it at the same time?'

'Miss, my mashed potato's fallen all over the bench.'

'Miss, mine's fallen on the floor'—this accompanied by giggles.

'Oh, goodness me, girls . . .' She hadn't been on the staff of the school long, and was unfamiliar with the various types of teacher-baiting perfected by the different cliques in the class. 'Oh, goodness me, girls, use your common sense. I'm sure the examiner will understand if you ask her to hold the piping bag for you.'

So, ever hungry for approval, I had—and failed resoundingly at one fell swoop.

I felt cross with myself that my exam results allowed me little glory. Five passes were adequate and average. No amount of consolation from Gran would persuade me otherwise.

I was cross with her too. Gran, who'd insisted every morning during exams that I take a disgusting powder mixed in with my milky coffee.

'Now, come on, get this down—it'll help your nerves.' Sanatogen Powder. It was expensive and revolting. It made me gag, but I swallowed it doggedly every morning under Gran's watchful, anxious eye.

Now that proved wasted too.

I couldn't allow myself to dwell on my failures. It was too uncomfortable. It seemed somehow like a confirmation of my worst suspicions about myself. I'd so longed to be included in the group of clever girls with Lorna Mayon-White and Bridget Newson. They weren't leaving school to work in offices at Burton Son and Saunders or Barclays Bank, so neither was I. With no one to discuss my future with, I issued edicts, first to Gran then to the welfare people and last of all to Yves.

As PS to Yves's letter I wrote: 'Please find enclosed ten nail clippings of some considerable length—just to prove to you that I could do it. PPS I *will* be staying on to do A-levels.'

'What, again this joke?' Gran's voice came from behind me. I was hot and irritable from blackleading the grate, warm work at the best of times, but especially difficult with a fire burning.

'Oh, Gran, shut up, you always complain about my not helping with the housework . . .'

'Yes, but thass a fine time to be doin' it now, at huppast six of an evening. I s'pose you're ashamed of my house like you were when that whatsiname bloke called, that bloke who brought you the gramophone he'd made.'

'Record player.'

368

'You never use it.'

'Well, I've only got one record . . .' I made a mental note to get it out to impress Barry with the similarity of our musical tastes.

'Oh, poor you—I s'pose your mother's got hundreds.'

'. . . The one he gave me for Christmas last year in Tripoli.'

'And who's he when he's at home?'

'Michael Bloody Drew. If I've told you his name once, Gran, I've told you—'

'Umpteen bloody times—I know, I'm just a stupid old woman who can't remember anything. I'm gettin' on, you know, I won't always be here and 'at'll be a happy release . . .'

'Oh, don't start.'

'Thass you thass started, my girl. The home help only came two days ago. I don't know why you're making all this fuss.'

'I just want it to look nice, Gran. It's the first time he's been here properly.'

'Well, who do Barry Cunnell think he is? He in't no one. His mother and father used to go Old Time dancin' in Holywells Park, his father only work in an office down at the foundry, don't he?'

'Move your feet, Gran, so I can move the fender back.'

'I s'pose you're goin' to Brasso that now too?'

'No, I've done that.'

'Now watch what you're doin' or you'll have that black lead polish on the lino and then you'll traipse it everywhere, and listen to me when I'm talkin' to you, Jane. I in't agoin' to sit in that cold front room all evenin', you know.'

'I never said you had to.'

'Anyway 'at in't right to leave you two on your own.'

'You complain when we talk in the passage outside, because you say it disturbs the Kerridges, and you moan when we stand in the hall because you say we make greasy marks where we lean up against the wallpaper, and now I've invited him for supper and that's not right either.'

'Well it's a bit early for all this palaver, in't it? You're a bit young to be startin' all this courting lark?'

'Oh, Gran, I'll be sixteen this Christmas. I'm in the Lower Sixth—and I'll be leaving school in just two years.'

'I s'pose you'll be glad to see the back of me.'

'Annette Macro and Rita Nelson had boyfriends in the *fourth* form.'

'Common as muck they were, that lot, I never liked them.'

'Well, they've left Northgate now.'

'Good riddance to bad rubbish, that's what I say.'

'Me too,' I muttered with heartfelt relief, thinking of Annette and Deirdre, Rita and Sylvia's departure and glad at last that we agreed about something.

'It's lovely, school, now, apart from having to sit biology again. I love it—just doing the subjects I enjoy: English and French A-level and O-level Spanish. Why couldn't it always be like that?'

'You want everything too much your own way, my girl.'

'Gran, he'll be here in an hour, don't stand there jawing.'

'Well, what do you want me to do—put the flags

370

out?'

'Have you buttered the bread?'

'Yes, I have, Lady Muck. What did your last servant die of?'

'Is the draining-board full of washing-up?'

'No it in't—but he in't goin' in my kitchen is he? I've got my vest and corsets drying on the oven door.'

'Oh, take them off, Gran, please—and *hurry*.'

'You're like all young people nowadays, rush here, rush there, you in't got time to breathe—boyfriends at sixteen, I don't know what the world's a comin' to. I don't know what your mother'd say; still, she'd be the wrong person to ask knowin' her and men—I 'spect you take after her.'

'Gran, we're not *doing* anything; he's just coming round for coffee and something to eat.'

'I s'pose you want the top brick of the chimney to put in them there sandwiches—I in't got no more money till pension day, you know.'

'Oh, don't worry. I'll ask Fowlers to put it on tick.'

'' 'At mount up, you know. I in't made o' money, 'at don't grow on trees. We thought we'd be better off with Yves's money; strikes me, we're a damn sight worse—and I s'pose with another one on the way now we'll get even less . . .'

It shocked me that Gran remembered it so often. I wished I'd never told her. I'd almost managed to forget it. If I thought about it at all I could hear my mother shouting still, shouting and screaming from inside the locked bathroom of the villa in Gargaresch, threatening to take every pill in the medicine cabinet to get rid of it. Lolo, fortunately, was spending the night with Bob and

371

Gwen Yates-Earl and their adopted daughter Mandy. Yves in his usual way had shrugged his shoulders, worn down by yet another crisis, and had said, 'You deal with it, Janie, she'll listen to you.' It seemed ironic that it should be me she relied upon. I'd begged and pleaded with her to come out and she'd just shouted more, then turned on me.

'I don't know why *you're* crying, Janie. It's never mattered to you what I've felt before. Why does it matter now? You'll go back to Nana and get on with your life. You're a hypocrite, you don't care what happens to me. You don't really love me. You've never loved me.' I shook and trembled at her accurate assessment of the truth but no words came that could deny it. I would have given up then but for Yves gesturing me to go on pleading with her.

She did come out eventually, tear-stained, blotchy-faced and swollen-eyed. She walked with some difficulty and I had to hold on to her to stop her bumping into walls and furniture. Bebop cowered and slunk for cover underneath the table. Little Girl was in her usual place. Buster Brown had been killed on the Tripoli road. She pined for him, spending most of her time in a corner of the patio, body inert, eyes never leaving the door to the garden.

Yves met my anxious look with a quiet, 'She's not taken anything—it's whisky make 'er like that.'

Having persuaded Yves to sleep on the divan in the *salon*, we eventually managed to get her into bed and I undressed her. She'd put her hand against my face as I bent to kiss her and pushed me away saying, '*Va t'en, va t'en, je ne veux plus te voir.*'

372

I'd returned to the *salle à manger* shocked and shaking. Yves lit me a cigarette and offered a glass of whisky. I shuddered at the prospect and poured myself some wine instead with trembling hands. '*Ouf!*' he'd said, placing a well-manicured hand on mine, its wedding ring glistening in the light. 'Forget it, *c'est de la comédie*—'ow you say in English?'

Comedy seemed such an inappropriate description of what we'd just witnessed. 'Play-acting,' I said after some reflection, topping up my wine with bottled water.

'I don't know why it's such a problem for her,' Yves mused. 'We 'ave money, Lolo is going to school in France, she 'ave Ahmed to help in the 'ouse—she always say she'd like a boy because I'm the last Lapotaire and all that shit; she make problems because she like problems.' He sighed. 'She is crazy. Mad.'

I'd got him a spare blanket from the wardrobe in their room where my mother was asleep, her hands crossed over her chest as if she were in a coffin, and her mouth wide open. I stopped for a while to watch her breathe. After several more whiskies Yves padded off to the *salon* going through the patio door so's not to wake her, and I clicked out the light and made to go to bed.

'Janie!' Her voice came thickly from the bedroom through the open door.

I hesitated, fearing another onslaught, not knowing whether to pretend I'd already left the *salle à manger*. I stopped still, hardly breathing.

'Janie,' came again, a more plaintive cry this time. Maybe she *had* taken pills and was frightened that they were taking hold. I put the overflowing ashtrays down and rushed into the darkened musty-smelling room.

'Get me some water, darling,' she said, slurring her words.

When I returned she gestured me to sit down on the bed.

'Est-ce qu'il fait dodo dans le salon, Papa?'

'Mais oui,' I said. She looked reassured.

I held the glass for her as she gulped the contents like a thirsty child. I wiped her face where the water had run down her chin. I was used to looking after Gran, but this felt wrong.

'I can't tell Lolo,' she said, her head bobbing against her chest as she struggled to sit up. 'She's so naughty at school. Les Soeurs de l'Assomption, they are good, Janie, not like nuns, they ride *vélos*, you know, and have degrees in child psychology.' She concentrated hard and made a determined effort to get the words out.

I didn't want to hear another saga of Lolo's escapades and unwillingness to work, and I didn't want to be reminded of how wonderful her boarding school in the Seine et Marne was; Northgate paled by comparison.

'And Papa,' she said, lowering her voice into a whisper. 'I can't tell him. Papa and me . . . *foutu.*'

She made a decisive scissor-like gesture with her hands and let them fall on the bed beside her.

'Sorry?'

'Foutu—finito—kaput.'

'Oh, no, don't say that. You've not long been married,' I said, trying to jolly her along.

'Janie,' she said with an edge to her voice, 'I know what I'm saying.'

'Ssh, don't wake Yves.'

I was frightened by how quickly her moods seemed to change.

'No, no,' she said, nodding her head in confirmation, *'C'est fini—fichu . . .'*

'Mummy . . .'

'Sandy,' she said. 'You know Sandy, Janie . . .'

I vaguely remembered the tall good-looking Englishman who called at the house sometimes, along with all the other visitors. Papa often pulled my leg about the young geologists who called in 'more often' now that I was there on holiday, and I'd been flattered, though not entirely convinced, that it was me they came to see.

'What about Sandy?' I prompted, sure her mind had wandered off the subject.

'I can tell *you*, darling,' she said, searching out my hand across the bedclothes, conspiratorially lowering her voice even more. 'I can tell you, Janie darling, but don't tell him, you mustn't tell him. It's not his child, it's Sandy's.'

* * *

'It's not his child,' echoed in my brain. I stopped cleaning and listened to it, frightened.

'Thought you said we had to hurry,' said Gran.

I collected up the rags and the brushes and made to move the hearth-rug back into place.

'Now look, I'd said you'd do it and I'll be jiggered if you haven't.'

'What?'

'Blacklead polish on my lino. I'll go and get the dwile—oh.' She stopped and looked back at me. 'Oh, I suppose I'd better call it a floor cloth, or I'll get told off again,' she muttered as she disappeared into the kitchen.

'No, it's all right,' I said, sheepishly trying unsuccessfully to rub some blacklead polish off my gym slip.

'What is?'

'I didn't tell you—we're doing Chaucer's *Canterbury Tales* for English A-level, "The Franklin's Tale".'

'Oh, yes,' she said, in that particular way she had when she wasn't interested.

'Chaucer uses the word dwile,' I shouted.

'Oh, yes,' she said, coming back into the living-room.

'The word dwile, Gran, it means floor cloth in *Middle* English. Just fancy—you were talking Middle English without knowing it. I was wrong, you were right and I beg your pardon,' I said, giving a mock curtsy.

'Oh, put a cross up,' she said with a hint of a smile. 'Put a blinkin' cross up, I got something right at last.'

*   *   *

'And who's going on to university?' asked Miss Freeman during one of her needlework classes.

Our group chatted easily now. There were only a few of us who went because we enjoyed it, not because we had to. We were all more relaxed, about most things. Privileges helped too. The Lower Sixth didn't have to wear berets any more and we could walk across the grass in the two quadrangles like members of staff. I made several pointless journeys even in the rain, when more sensible people scuttled about under the shelter of the roof that edged the quadrangle, just to relish my new-found freedom, also partly out of disbelief that no one would complain or try to stop me.

We didn't even bother to relate the question to Lorna Mayon-White or Brigid Newson, nine O-levels each; everyone knew they'd be going to Oxford or Cambridge.

They'd been chosen as sub-prefects already; they wore badges on their V-neck sweaters and pale blue braid decorated the edges and the pockets of their blazers. I wanted to be a sub-prefect more than anything else in the world. I'd show them I could be responsible, that I could be looked up to, that I could be one of the good girls. I felt new-born now that Annette, Deirdre and Rita had gone.

Along with my new outlook I had new friends. Marilyn Oldfield who was going to be a nurse and Elizabeth Fish who was going to be a teacher. I didn't want to be either. I'd done well in English and I held on to that, but when Miss Freeman, noticing that I was unusually reticent about my plans, singled me out for special attention with a 'And you, Jane, what are your future plans? University?', no one was more surprised than I when I heard myself answer, 'Oh, no, Miss, I don't think so—I want to be a journalist.'

'A journalist?' she mused, surprised. 'A journalist indeed.' She turned the word over again, her long neck bulging as she spoke. 'A journalist.'

I began to wish I'd never mentioned it.

'Yes, you'd make a good journalist.'

I beamed and returned to my smocking and its ever-diminishing row of grubby herringbone stitch.

'Yes, you'd make a good journalist, Jane, you're

pushy enough.'

*   *   *

We heard that Miss Carter, the red-faced history teacher who punctuated all her sentences with a 'd'you see?', was doing a play.

A play?

We were incredulous.

A school production. 'D'you see?' Unheard of.

'With the boys' school?'

'No such luck.' It was unspoken law to have no dealings with the boys. We thought this law an ass as we waited at the same bus stops, cycled the same route and had our break-time in adjoining fields. The boys were clearly visible as much of the fence that divided the two schools had been surreptitiously removed.

'*Toad of Toad Hall.*'

'We dare you to go to the audition,' said Liz and Lyn.

Never one to refuse a dare, I conveniently forgot about my resolve to be one of the good girls and went to the audition in the school hall, surrounded by a clutch of giggling girls. My brief, to cause havoc.

Delia went too, of course. She'd won a prize for verse-speaking nearly every year in spite of her buck teeth which made her spit a lot. Perfect for a toad we all agreed.

Once on the stage of the assembly hall, usually graced only by Miss Atkinson the headmistress and senior members of staff, with slightly wobbling knees I warmed to my purpose and overdid it dreadfully, eliciting giggles from several of the

378

juniors who had been press-ganged into playing stoats and weasels. I loved *The Wind in the Willows* especially Mole and Ratty. I thought Toad a pompous bore. Liz and Lyn, who'd crept quietly into the back of the hall to watch, clutched each other, silently convulsed.

'Thank you, Jane,' bellowed Miss Carter in her usual manner as she propelled her bulky frame down the aisle between the rows of wooden chairs where we sang hymns with more gusto than conviction and prayed reluctantly every morning. 'Thank you, that'll do, d'you see,' she said, demanding the book with an outstretched chubby hand.

I found it difficult to stand upright after I'd bent down to give it her back. For some unaccountable reason my legs had turned to jelly.

She turned her ample back on me and, addressing the two front rows of expectant faces from the Fourth and Lower Fifth, said, 'Now that we've found our Toad, d'you see, who wants to read for Mole and Ratty?'

*   *   *

'You can rant and rave all you like,' said Gran, 'you can shout till the cows come home, you're ill, and I don't care what you say you in't goin' to school, someone else will have to do it. They all know you've got German measles thass bin goin' round the school. I don't care how many weeks you've bin rehearsin', anyone can see you're ill. Look at the state of your face—covered in spots.'

'But they won't show, Gran,' I begged and pleaded. 'They won't show—I have to wear green

379

make-up on my face, they won't show.'

'No,' said Gran, and she meant it.

I lay there in Gran's bed in the front room, utterly miserable, hot and spotty. No Toad, and no Barry. At least until the spots disappeared.

'I don't suppose I can go to Youth Club either,' I moaned.

'No, you can't. What'll people think of me lettin' you go back to school afore you're ready; s'posin' you give it to other people because you're contagious.'

'Infectious.'

'Well, thass as maybe—you in't well, and you in't a goin' out and you in't doin' that there play, and that, my girl, is that.'

*   *   *

Lionel Guy Lapotaire smiled at me and clutched my finger and I smiled back.

I'd given him his *biberon*; I never thought of it as a bottle, and had changed his diapers; we never called them nappies. I'd rocked him in his *berceau*, and sung him 'Rock-a-bye baby' until he closed his eyes and slept. I turned the air-conditioning down and closed the door of Lolo's old bedroom gently behind me. She now shared my bedroom but I almost didn't mind.

'How is he?' said Yves quietly.

'Sleeping,' I said proudly.

' 'e is handsome, *n'est-ce pas*?'

'Oh, yes,' I said, quite genuinely, 'he's beautiful.'

'Like 'is father,' said Yves beaming.

I concentrated hard on rubbing some dried milk off my knuckles.

380

'He doesn't know who his *mother* is,' I joked feebly.

'Huh?' said Yves.

'I look after him so much, he thinks it's me.'

He smiled.

'How's Mummy?'

'Sleeping,' he said happily. 'She need 'er rest.'

'And Lolo . . .'

' 'appy that you are 'ere to do all this instead of 'er—she's out somewhere.'

I sat down, took two Gitanes from his packet. I lit them both and passed one to him. A habit I'd acquired when accompanying him on outings during my mother's pregnancy. I poured myself another glass of wine.

'You want some more cheese now?' he said.

'No, thanks.'

'*Raisins? Melon?* Or a *digestif*?' he said.

'No, thanks,' I said. 'I don't think so.'

'So what *do* you want, you terrible girl?' he said, pinching my light brown arm not quite as hard as usual. I didn't have much time to sunbathe now. Lionel occupied me all his waking moments.

'Do you know,' I said, inhaling deeply on my cigarette, giving the matter mock consideration, 'I don't want *anything*, anything at all.'

'And why is that, *ma fille*?' he said, pushing his chair away from the table, tilting it on its two back legs.

I felt pleased. I'd found a place. Pleased too at last that all of them were glad to have me here.

'I don't want anything,' I said, 'because I'm happy.'

*   *   *

381

Barry decided I was too much of a distraction. He wanted, he informed me, to concentrate on his A-levels, as he was planning to go to Loughborough College to train to be a PE teacher. I couldn't see why A-levels were that important in teaching games. I inflicted all the suffering of my broken heart on Gran.

I wasn't convinced by his explanation. He seemed to be spending increasing amounts of time in the company of the Reverend John Blamey who was, admittedly, teaching him to drive, but who I felt had been instrumental in Barry's decision. My attitude to the Reverend John Blamey changed my attitude to Alan Road. Having persuaded Lyn to come to church and Youth Club with me, I then bullied her into changing her mind. We pocketed our collection money and went on Sunday evenings to the most exciting place we knew, the Gondolier coffee bar. We spent the money on a Coca-Cola or a frothy coffee which had to last us the entire evening. It was dark and smoky and loud. Elvis Presley sang almost continuously on the juke box 'Don't you step on my blue suede shoes', interspersed with Cliff Richard's 'Shrine on the Second Floor' and an unexpected song in French. It was chosen quite a lot too. It was called *'Milord'* and sung by a woman with a croaky rasping voice and an odd name, Piaf. I pretended I knew all the words. I didn't have to swap keys when I sang along with her. My voice was as low as hers.

I'd time my arrival home to match the time that Sunday evening Youth Club meetings finished and I'd recount to Gran in great detail the sermon I hadn't heard the Reverend John Blamey preach.

382

*   *   *

The church was dark and smelled of incense. It was small and narrow and had dark alcoves at either side, all of which contained sombre paintings and statues of various saints in stained white marble. The bag of silvered sugared almonds in my hand felt sticky. The priest's voice echoed in the empty church around me. I understood little of the service except the words 'Lionel Guy Marie Lapotaire'.

'Why is he called Marie?' I whispered to my mother. 'It's a girl's name!'

'Because, Janie,' said my mother condescendingly, as if I should have known, 'he's been dedicated to the Virgin Mary.'

'And that cost me an extra forty francs,' Yves said wryly. 'Did you see the priest waiting for his tip?'

I hadn't. I'd been too absorbed by the golden ornaments. Christ on the cross with rivulets of blood running from His feet and side, His whole body wracked in agony. In comparison with the plain undecorated wooden cross at Alan Road I thought it grotesque, morbid and mesmerising.

'The Roman Catholic Church is shit,' muttered Yves. 'All that Virgin Mary crap.'

'Ssh, Papa. Celia will hear you . . .' I thought it just as well that Celia Gallou who, as Lionel's godmother, had held the baby throughout the service, had been the one who was asked if she would dedicate Lionel's life to Christ and the Catholic Church. I feared the answer the priest would have received if Yves had been asked.

I sat in the back with the baby as the car, a

405 Peugeot that Papa had a right to as Chef de Transport, sped southwards from Paris to Marseilles where we were to catch the boat to their new home in Tunisia. New at least to me. I fed Lionel and changed him while Lolo looked out of the window and said little. She was in disgrace as she'd been expelled from the convent school.

'Janie she pass all her exams,' Yves said from time to time. I'd change this rather uncomfortable subject by asking Mummy for some Kleenex to wipe the dribble off Lionel's mouth. 'She don't think of clothes and cinema,' he went on. 'You are going to be *bonne à rien*, my *fille, tu gaspilles ta vie.*'

'What's *gaspiller*?' I asked unthinkingly, ever eager to improve my French.

'To waste, Janie,' Lolo said, glowering at me.

'Anyway, I'm going to be rich when I grow up,' she mumbled under the noise of the car, and a radio advertisement for Shampooing Dop-tonic. 'I won't have to work.'

I thought that faintly shocking. Everyone in the Lower Sixth wanted a career, that's why we were at grammar school.

At passport control in Tunis we were separated. With my British passport I was forced to join a long queue while the Lapotaires went in another direction where there was no queue at all.

I think the man asked me where I was going and why.

'*Avec ma famille*,' I managed and pointed over where I could see Yves waiting impatiently and Mummy jiggling an irritable, overtired Lionel up and down in an attempt to stop him grizzling.

'*Ils sont français?*' he asked, checking that they had a right to be where they were.

384

'*Mais oui*,' I smiled emptily, and searched for the explanation that would resolve the uncertainty. '*C'est mon beau-père*,' I said triumphantly.

He stamped my well-worn passport and waved me through.

'*C'est bête le langue français.*'

'La *langue française*,' said Yves. 'And why is that?'

'Fancy the word for stepfather being the same as father-in-law,' I said crossly.

'Just say I'm your father,' he said. 'There's no need to *cherche du midi à quatorze*.'

'What?'

'No need to look from midday to two o'clock,' said my mother with her usual flair for translation.

'I can't say you're my father. We don't even have the same name,' I protested.

'Daddy's always calling you his daughter,' said my mother irritably, wiping off some of Lionel's vomit from her shoulder. 'All the company in Tripoli knew you as Janie Lapotaire. Papa had to claim you as his daughter so they'd pay your air fares home.'

'But it says Burgess on my passport,' I insisted.

'Well, change it when you get a new one,' said Yves. 'Let's go and get the car. We've a long drive ahead of us.'

'But it's not as simple as that,' I whined under my breath. I felt dirty and tired, and the vomit that Lionel had deposited on my shoulder smelled rancid in the heat.

And I missed Jean-Michel.

They'd introduced me to him after all. They'd giggled like schoolchildren with his mother and stepfather about the friendship that had grown so

385

rapidly between us. He talked to me of Jean-Paul Sartre and existentialism as if I understood it. Then he'd played me jazz and John Coltrane which I pretended that I understood and didn't. I found his intelligence and Frenchness dauntingly attractive.

'He's a Jew,' Yves had whispered, as if that made him different. He didn't look different, though now I could barely summon up his face. But I could vividly recall the way my stomach fluttered when he'd held my hand in the darkness of the cinema, to which we'd been dispatched one afternoon, consigned the care of Gérard, his younger brother, and Lolo. The initial embarrassment of having to sit through their childish choice of film, *101 Dalmatians*, had been obliterated by the surge of very adult feelings his stroking of my hand produced. I sighed.

'Oh, Janie, you're so complicated,' said my mother. 'Here, take Lionel. I need to find the pee-pee room and repair my make-up.'

I shot an arrow of dislike into her painted face. *Cruella de Vil*, I thought and smiled for the first time that day.

I looked at Lionel and thought it odd that he had no more right to the name Lapotaire than I had.

'*Ne boude pas, Janie,*' said my mother, picking up her handbag and turning to go. 'Don't sulk. Next time just put Lapotaire in brackets.'

*   *   *

Sfax was different from Tripoli in every way—small and not so humid. Elf Aquitaine's pipelines from the desert ended here and the oil was distributed to

386

tankers in the port.

The new '*chez nous*' was the top floor of a two-storey apartment block with spacious gardens below that we shared with the Belgian girl, Nicole, who lived on the ground floor. 'She was married to an Arab,' said my mother, disposing of her in one sentence.

All the rooms gave on to a long corridor which ran the entire length of the apartment. The covered patio outside was protected from the sun by a high white wall which curved in the middle and rose to the roof in a tower dotted with panels of brightly coloured glass which shed prisms of rainbow lights on to the patio floor. Here Lionel could crawl and play and after the siesta my mother and I would have tea and sew, an occupation Lolo despised and shunned.

Lolo and I shared a bedroom here too. I didn't mind except for her eternal chant of how rich she was going to be when she grew up and her absorption with what *Elle* magazine declared to be the latest fashion in clothes, colours and hairstyles.

When I wasn't occupied with Lionel, Papa would send one of his drivers and Lolo and I would go to the beach. A large stretch of sand, rock-free, unlike Tripoli. Several cafés with brightly coloured parasols and roofs made of dried reed edged the water. They all served a thin crispy pancake with an egg trapped in the middle, called a *brique à l'oeuf*, which we devoured with delight, to the accompaniment of a stringy Spanish pop song, '*Quando Caliente el Sol*', that was played everywhere that summer.

The beach's other main attraction was the gangs of teenage boys who'd roam the sands teasing the girls or indulging in horseplay at the water's edge. All of them good swimmers—all of them as bronzed as the models in Lolo's *Elle* magazine.

'Now remember who you are,' my mother warned.

'And who do she think *she* is?' Gran asked inside my head.

'You're *les filles* Lapotaire and they're North African Jews. Most of them would give their eye-teeth to be married to a European girl. So just remember it's not Tripoli, and Sfax is small. Whatever you get up to will get back to us. Janie, you're in charge. Here's a few dinars for lunch, and don't let Lolo bully you into spending it on trash.'

Lolo was very popular and would often wander off, leaving me alone. I didn't mind too much, having been introduced as her *'grande soeur qui habite en Angleterre'* and after much shaking of hands they'd back away to a respectful distance and I felt safe knowing my difference protected me from the danger of being carried protesting to the water's edge and ducked beneath the waves.

Yves had a small boat fitted with an outboard motor, which he kept in the port and used when he wasn't working down at the rig in the desert. He'd go fishing *'à la traine'*. Reducing the boat's speed to a slow guttural chug, he'd haul a length of nylon wire behind it to which was attached a small silver spoon-like hook, baited with a wriggling grub. Sometimes my mother would go with him, but mostly she'd sit in the shade by the port under a makeshift awning put up by the fishermen, the sturdy brown baby playing at her feet.

I loved swimming in the deep blue water when the boat was anchored far beyond the port, out of reach of the odour of yesterday's fish which was gutted and sometimes cooked and eaten on the quayside, and far beyond the whorls of oil left by the tankers that darkened the waters of the port into sludgy rainbows and left a sickly smell hanging heavily in the still hot air. The salt would dry on my skin, leaving a fine film of white dust that clung to the hairs on my arm. When Yves wasn't looking I'd lick it off. I'd help him with his catch and often held the line myself as it trailed through the azure water. I knew he expected me to shy away from the seething mass of maggots stowed safely in the box in the bottom of the boat. So I'd swallow hard and brace myself as I'd hook one into the spikes that curved out from the bottom of the spoon.

We'd chat and smoke and fish and I'd begin to like him. Till he'd jeer at me for not daring to go swimming in the nude or if I did he'd never fail to comment that I'd been unlucky to be given my mother's stick-like legs and tiny breasts.

'You are still a virgin?'

It was my turn to squirm. 'Oh, Papa.'

'That's no answer. You are what now?'

'Nearly seventeen.'

'Most French girls . . .'

'Well, I'm not completely French.'

'Ah ha, you *are* French when it suits you, like your mother.'

'Not when you talk about Napoleon I'm not.'

'*Ouf*, the *sacré* Duke of Wellington,' he'd say and smile. 'So they don't believe in sex, les Méthodistes . . .'

'Of course they do, but I don't go to church any more.'

'Does Nana know?' He had an unfailing way of

389

worming out the truth.

'Well . . . not exactly.'

'Ah ha.' He seemed almost pleased to know I cheated on her. 'Deceitful, like your mother. So you didn't do it with this Barry or with Jean-Michel?'

'No, I didn't.'

'So you don't 'ave a boyfriend any more?'

'No, no, I don't,' I said with some regret.

I'd noticed a boy head and shoulders above the rest of his gang with striking auburn hair, trim beard and pale blue eyes, and best of all I'd seen him notice me.

'Oh, that's Nanou,' Lolo had answered when I pointed him out.

'Nanou?'

'Daniel Zagdoun.'

'What an odd name.'

'Oh, he's Jewish, Janie. He's at university in Grenoble. He comes home for the holidays too.'

Yves chuckled and resumed: 'Well, I'm sure you'll do it soon, and when you do make sure you choose a Frenchman, not an Arab or a Jew.'

His interest in my virginity I found invasive and unsettling. There was something in it I couldn't quite locate. I'd been indecisive up till then. Now I knew I'd chosen.

CHAPTER 27

I was made a prefect and head of Chaucer House. Gran was impressed and so was I. School had never felt better. I was passionate about English lessons.

We were studying *Richard II* and *Macbeth*. I loved deciphering all the difficult Elizabethan words, unravelling the complicated phrases. We read the plays out loud, taking each speech in turn around the class. I hated that. I wanted to read all of *Richard* and *Macbeth* myself, not just the odd speech every other page.

I joined the English Literary and Debating Society. We met after school in the library or, better, in the library of the boys' school.

A tall gangly boy with glasses called Peter Cochran suggested a joint school production of *Romeo and Juliet*. He was going to direct it and play Romeo.

Even that didn't deter me.

I was going to play Juliet.

Gran wasn't impressed and neither was Miss Atkinson, the headmistress, a tall distant woman with sharp features and glasses whom none of us much liked. I was summoned to the presence.

'I suppose you realise that no one will take responsibility, not *if* but *when* you fail your A-levels, which you undoubtedly will, spending all this time rehearsing with the boys instead of studying. I wonder how you propose to go to university when you've failed.'

'But I don't want to go to university, Miss Atkinson,' I said smugly.

'But you want to be a journalist, don't you? Most journalists read English at university.'

'I don't want to be a journalist, Miss Atkinson. I want to be an actress.'

*   *   *

'You must do what you want, dear,' said Gran.

'I should stay here in Ipswich and look after you.'

She spotted my insincerity in a flash.

'Don't be so daft—you've got your whole life ahead of you.'

'Well, if it hadn't been for you I'd have been put in a Home.'

'I've had my life. You've done your share of looking after me. If you want to go to drama school you go. There's only one thing that worries me. Where's all the money coming from?'

'Well, if I get good A-level results the Suffolk County Council will pay. I'll get a grant.'

'More charity,' said Gran.

*   *   *

'Stupid idea,' said Yves. 'There must be 'undreds of girls more attractive and more talented than you; you'll never make it. Go to university.'

'But I want to go to drama school.'

'I'm your father. You do what I say,' he said, not liking to be crossed.

You're not and I won't, I thought.

*   *   *

'Well, I daren't open it,' said Gran. 'Telegrams don't bring good news.'

'Oh, don't be silly,' I said grumpily, annoyed that she'd woken me early on a Saturday, my only chance for a lie-in as I paid the rates now once a month. I worked late each night revising for my A-levels. I was determined to do well to prove Miss

392

Atkinson wrong.

I coughed, sat down and rubbed my eyes and took the telegram from her shaking hands. 'It's freezing in here, Gran. Why haven't you lit a fire?' I shivered in my pyjamas and coughed again.

'Shouldn't need a fire this time o' year. Thass nearly Easter. Strikes me your cough's got worse since you've been smokin'. You'll get asthma again afore you know it. Smokin' them there Capstan Full Strength.'

'Oh, Gran, I smoke Park Drive and they've got filter tips.'

'You lend Woodbines off Mr Kerridge and Doug.'

'*Borrow*, Gran, not *lend*.'

'Coffin nails everyone call 'em. Well, are you going to open it or not? I can't stand here all morning, I've got work to do.'

I read the telegram out loud. It said:

LIONEL DEAD. FUNERAL PARIS TUESDAY.

It was unsigned.

'Oh, God Almighty,' said Gran and sat down abruptly.

'I can't believe it,' I said. 'It's got to be a joke. We were never allowed to let him out of our sight. It has to be some sort of awful joke.'

* * *

The two black cars waited outside the cargo department of Orly airport while the four pall-bearers went inside to get the coffin.

Lolo and I, silent, followed them in. Mummy in

393

the car in front, unable to walk, was slumped between Tonton Guy and René Marcou. There were boxes and crates stacked high to the ceiling of the dark hangar-like building. There was a smell of rotten fruit. Some of the boxes were stamped 'Bananes'.

Papers changed hands and a man in blue overalls with a beret on his head pointed to a corner where a small white coffin stood alone, alone in a space on the ground half lit by a shaft of sunlight. Planes roared nearby.

The four men hesitated over it, not knowing what to do. Lolo and I clutched hands, and watched.

Two of them bent down to pick it up, and placed it uneasily between their shoulders while the other two marched solemnly behind.

It was a joke. One of them could have carried it easily under one arm.

The last man turned towards us. 'Cimetière de Thiais?' he enquired, much like a taxi driver ascertaining his destination.

'Oui,' we muttered quietly in unison. 'Oui, s'il vous plaît.'

*   *   *

René Marcou and Tonton Guy Latourette supported Mummy between them. She moaned as the little white box was lowered into the grave. Her body jerked as if she were about to fall in after it. Lolo and I, standing behind her, moved as one to catch her. They straightened her up and she moaned again.

A woman placing brightly coloured flowers on a

grave a few rows away turned and stared.

The mound of earth beside the hole was covered in white flowers of every kind.

'Why are they all white?' I whispered.

'Because he is, he *was* a baby,' said Lolo, beginning to cry.

I put my arm around her and held her tight.

'They haven't even spelled his name right,' Lolo sniffed.

A small stone slab lay beside the pile of earth. LYONEL LAPOTAIRE was all it said.

'I wish Papa was here,' I whispered quietly, mostly to myself, as we sat alone in the big black car speeding through the streets of Paris.

'I'm glad he's not,' said Lolo.

'Why?'

'They row all the time now. He says it was her fault, and she says it was mine.'

I didn't think it right to ask her why. I held her close and hugged her.

'I wish you didn't live in England. Can't you come and live with us in Sfax?'

'*Chérie*, I can't. I've got my A-levels to do in just a few months.'

'I hate our stupid family,' she said and cried again.

The Latourettes fussed round Mummy who sat propped up in a chair, her face white under its tan, her gaze fixed nowhere in particular, her movements slow and jerky like a marionette.

She ate nothing but held on tightly to a glass of whisky in her trembling hand.

They fussed even more when she bent awkwardly to get some pills out from her handbag.

'*Mais non, Louise, mais non; ça ne sert à rien.*'

'Uncle' Guy took the tablets from her and, looking around the seven of us gathered in their formal sitting-room, passed them to me for safe keeping.

'*Guy, je t'en prie,*' said my mother, stretching out her hand towards him, her words tumbling over each other as if she were drunk.

'*Mais non, Louise chérie,*' said Ghislaine Marcou gently, kneeling down beside her chair. '*Il ne faut pas. Il faut prier pour le petit—il est avec le bon dieu.*'

'There isn't a *bon dieu,*' said my mother, brusquely waving her away. 'How can there be? He let my Lionel drown.' Her voice was broken with a sob.

'Janie,' she said, turning slowly towards me, her eyes glazed and dead. 'They don't know what it's like, they've never lost a child. They've never even had one. Now give me back those pills. I've had enough.'

*　　　*　　　*

'I even prayed,' said Yves, drinking his whisky in the *salle à manger* in Sfax. He tried to smile. 'I said I'd give my money to the Virgin Mary if he lived. He came to, you see. When Louise found him floating face downward she gave him mouth to mouth and he came to. We thought he'd be all right.'

He poured another whisky.

'Bloody Arabs.'

'Why didn't the fishermen in the port help? They always seemed so friendly.'

'Oh, yes, they 'elped 'er look for him. 'E'd been playing with Lolo and 'er gang on that strip of sand behind the port, remember? And Louise 'ad been

396

sitting in the shade knitting, near where we keep the boat. She packed 'er things together and went to tell them both it was time to go 'ome. 'E wasn't there. Lolo said 'e'd wandered off to find Louise. 'E must have walked down that concrete slope where all the boats are kept. Maybe a big tanker went by and *pouf*—the boats knocked together in the waves, and 'e fell down.' He paused. 'Bloody Arabs.'

'Why?'

'I telephoned to Tunis for some special oxygen equipment to be flown to us in Sfax. It didn't arrive. I could get no one to move their ass. It was Friday—they were all in the bloody mosque.'

*   *   *

'The orchard walls are high and hard to climb.'

I loved that line. Couldn't understand why people said Shakespeare was difficult. What was difficult about that line?

A shaft of light brightened the darkened assembly hall. My attention was caught by it. I saw Gran get up and make her way slowly through the row of chairs.

There must be something wrong.

Silence on stage.

I realised it was my turn to speak.

*   *   *

'But what was wrong? I saw you leave, you know.'

'I'm sorry, dear. I felt so bad. It's so long since I've been out. I can't be in crowds now any more. I felt flustered and got terrible blood pressure.'

'But you didn't see me do it. You left so near the beginning.'

'Oh, no, dear, I saw quite a lot.'

'So what do you think?'

'About what, dear?'

'About my acting,' I said, getting heated. 'About my being an actress.'

'Like I said, dear, you must do as you see fit.'

'But what about my *acting*, Gran?'

'Oh, very nice, dear. I've said before. You're not broad Suffolk like some of 'em. You always said those verses nice at Sunday School. You always did speak nice.'

*   *   *

I started ironing costumes and running errands for Ipswich repertory theatre. I'd met the stage manager Paul Ciani through a boyfriend who replaced Barry, and he and Geoffrey, all enthusiasm for my future, managed to wangle me a job backstage.

Gran didn't mind my disappearing every night. A-levels were over. It was just the dreaded waiting for results.

I'd watched almost every performance of *The Boyfriend*, knew most of the songs by heart. I'd almost become a fixture of the theatre front of house, so moving into the backstage life of cramped dressing-rooms, dark stairways and much laughter wasn't that much of a leap.

Somehow, because they got so used to me hanging around, I slid into the part of Sophie, David Copperfield's friend's wife. A part. Two words. 'Saturday night,' I had to say in answer to a question about my wedding day.

I felt so proud to be on a real stage at last.

And prouder still to be wearing a yellow silk costume that bore the impressive label 'Doctor's Dilemma—Lesley Caron'.

When Lyn and Liz and several friends from school came to a matinée David Copperfield (Ian McKellen) cut my cue. So I had no reason to speak at all.

*   *   *

Geoffrey and Paul encouraged me to try for drama school. I sent off my completed forms for RADA and worked on a speech from Juliet and, as I was told I had to do a modern piece as well, I chose for some unaccountable reason a piece of Dodo from Christopher Fry's play *A Phoenix Too Frequent*.

I knew nothing about the play. I'd never seen it and I don't think I even read the rest of it, but I thought I was terribly funny and was doing very well when a voice from the darkened auditorium shouted a 'thank you' before I was even halfway through the speech.

When the letter came telling me I'd failed I cried non-stop for two days. Gran cried too.

Geoffrey and Paul, ever ready with encouragement, urged me to try once again. The Bristol Old Vic Theatre School was suggested as an alternative and in a half-hearted last-ditch attempt, along with the ubiquitous Juliet speech I practised one of Argia's from a Hugo Betti play, *The Queen and the Rebels*. My choice was dictated simply by the fact that it was the only play in my bedroom at the time, stolen from the school library.

Nat Brenner, the then principal of the school and a man of more integrity and taste than RADA, in Gran's eyes, had the foresight to offer me a place. I walked on air.

Gran worried still about where the money was coming from.

'Grants are based on father's earnings,' I said, making every effort to placate her fears.

'But you in't got one,' she said anxiously.

'Exactly!' I said smiling.

Leaving school was painless. I was given the first and only prize I'd ever won at school. The English prize, shared jointly with Lorna Mayon-White. Things were looking up. I'd never moved in such exalted circles before.

I chose a complete works of Shakespeare on to which was stamped the school crest with its motto *Labor omnia vincit* and inside a label declaring that: 'The VIth Form Prize for English was awarded to Jane Burgess by the Old Girls Association.' I amended it with a 'Lapotaire'; Lorna wasn't the only one with a double-barrelled name.

I was sorry to say goodbye to Miss Reid. Smart, sprightly Miss Reid who'd weeded out Yves's slang from my French essays for years, with many a patient, 'No, Jane, the GCE examiner will *not* be impressed by your frequent use of *cassepied* and please call a sardine a *sardine* and not a *sardoche*. Shoes are *chaussures* and not *godasses*. Only *clochards* use such vocabulary. Now, you surely didn't spend your time in Paris under a bridge.'

Yves laughed when I told him and reminded me of much stronger alternatives I could've used. He refused to be impressed by any of my studies, even though I now could relate with a clear conscience that I had seven O-levels, having passed at a second attempt biology, and having added Spanish to my list. It was, as far as I was concerned, simply French words with a lot of 'o's and 'a's tagged on to the end. And my accounts of how hard I had worked were dismissed with a renewed insistence that the *baccalauréat* was a far superior exam to anything the GCE A-level could demand, and that my results would be the final test.

'Then university,' he said.

'Drama school,' I insisted politely. 'I've got a place—at Bristol.' I thought (but didn't dare say), You're not my father. How dare you dictate my future to me.

'No, Jane, university,' he said in a tone which put paid to any further discussion. 'And until you decide which one to go to, you can work in my office with Nicole.'

He picked Lolo and me up from the beach one day, and casually tossed an opened brown envelope to me in the back seat. All our mail went to a PO box number, so he saw it first.

My hands shook with apprehension, and not a little anger, as I took the paper from the envelope. He had dared to open something addressed to mc. It would never have crossed Gran's mind.

'French—grade 4,' I said with a shaking voice. 'I passed.'

'Not very well,' he said. 'What's that? Sixty per cent?'

'Thereabouts, I suppose.'

'Stupid English system,' he muttered.

'English grade 1! Grade 1—I can't believe it.'

'*Ouf,*' he said. 'What's so surprising? You've

spoken English for eighteen years—you should be good at it by now.'

My only sadness was not being able to flaunt my result—rehearsals having indeed permitted—in Miss Atkinson's face.

*　　　*　　　*

Nanou and I were going to the cinema until I felt his arm on mine, gently but insistently preventing me from following his group of friends into the air-conditioned coolness of the lobby. The late summer heat was fierce outside, and I could feel the damp patches of sweat under my arms and between my breasts beginning to soak through my dress. He looked at me intently and beads of perspiration broke out on my upper lip. I licked them away. Then wished I hadn't. 'Not a very ladylike thing to do,' my mother's voice upbraided me. Then I dismissed it, not without a tinge of pleasure.

He commandeered me into the street again and held my sticky hand. The siesta was over. Sfax was stirring. People were drifting back to work again. A confused tumult of feelings rose inside me. I was pleased to be walking along with him, proud that he'd chosen me. He was by far the most handsome boy in all the groups that beachcombed Sfax. Apart from that I knew little about him. Panic overtook the pleasure. If someone saw us it would only be a matter of hours before it got back to Yves. Or, worst of all, Yves could drive by and see us for himself. My hand, drenched now, slipped against his palm. I used this as an excuse to remove it from his grasp, and with a great to-do in dumbshow mimed my excuse for not returning it, and wiped it on my dress. Another unladylike gesture.

He led me down a cool back alley where rows of washing strung above my head stirred in a breeze that rustled through geraniums in terracotta pots, bright red and orange against the dingy whiteness of the old apartment buildings. I didn't know this corner of the town. The Jewish quarter, I supposed it was. Several times I stumbled on the uneven paving and blushed, embarrassed by my clumsiness. I hoped he hadn't seen. His gaze was fixed ahead of him until a *deux chevaux* making its trundling way along the narrow street passed us with much klaxoning and waving through the open roof. He took my elbow and guided me protectively away from the kerb while waving silently with his other arm. This time I didn't move away from him. I didn't dare.

He led me through a darkened entrance hall complete with dusty dark green plants. Smells of couscous and spices that were unfamiliar hung in the air. Muffled voices and the chink of distant crockery broke the silence.

We crept silently up the sombre wooden stairs, hand in sweating hand. We said little. He spoke no English at all and I was frightened by the inappropriateness of the only words I knew for love-making which were Yves's gross slang. I understood his unspoken intention and my acquiescence was evident from the way I meekly followed him across the hallway into his darkened room.

I knew this virginity was something I had to get rid of soon. After all I was eighteen, and I was going to drama school in spite of what Yves said.

403

Fumbles with Barry always stopped short of the crucial gesture, undoubtedly restrained by Methodism, and Jean-Michel had probably felt inhibited by our parents' ribald encouragement. It had seemed wrong to have their approval. I wouldn't have it now, I knew. That added to the swells and swoops of excitement jockeying for precedence in my churning stomach. This was something to be done without their knowing, in the dark.

Thin shafts of afternoon sun filtered through the shutters on to the unmade bed. The clutter in the room embarrassed me. I pretended not to notice.

Silently he turned me round and, tilting my chin so that I could no longer gaze intently at the floor, made to undress me. Ever eager to be helpful I overrode his hands and struggled with the difficult buttons on my mother's dress myself. Firmly he placed my trembling hands down by my sides. I stood there helplessly, not knowing what to do nor where to look, wishing I'd borrowed my mother's lacy underwear.

He didn't seem at all hurried or embarrassed by standing there in front of me with no clothes on. I looked admiringly at his suntanned chest but allowed my gaze to look no further.

I sat obligingly on the rumpled bed while he began to kiss my feet, which shocked me. They'd been encased in my mother's high heels all afternoon and must smell dreadfully of sweat, I thought. Besides I had an ugly bunion on my left foot which I preferred him not to see. I moved it slowly away from him and hid it under a corner of the sheet while he made his way silently up my body towards my breasts, a startling white against the tanned flesh of my chest. I'd only once been touched like this before. Squashed in the back of a car heading home from a party a boy had stretched across and cupped his hand around my breast. I'd frozen at the strangeness of another touching that part of me and couldn't understand the reason for it. I didn't know what I was supposed to do, if anything. I'd never given it a thought with Barry. We just followed the aches and surges of our bodies.

My body now was being unobligingly remote and unaffected. I watched his shoulder muscles flex as he moved above me and looked down at my body underneath him as if it belonged to someone else. Silently I watched and didn't move. Silently he moved and went on moving.

*   *   *

'I've done it,' I said triumphantly to Lolo later that afternoon. She put down the latest edition of *Elle* magazine and looked up at me.

'What?' she said.

'It,' I answered meaningfully.

'Oh, Janie,' she said gasping, her eyes wide. 'He's Jewish. You mustn't tell Papa. What was it like? What was it like?'

'I cried at first.'

'Why, did it hurt?'

'No, not at all, that was half the trouble.' Odd that such a Gran-like phrase should come into my mind. Her reaction didn't bear thinking about. 'He didn't believe I was a virgin. At least I think that's what he said. I told him I'd been wearing Tampax a long time. I don't think he believed me. He got quite cross at one point. My verbs came out all muddled.'

She laughed. I didn't tell her how upset I'd been trying to justify the truth again.

'So?'

'I was bored. I couldn't wait for him to finish. I should have taken some knitting.'

She clasped her hand over her mouth to muffle the noise of her snorts of laughter. Mother was still unconscious in one of her ever-lengthening siestas.

'I don't know what all the fuss is about. I can't believe that's what they've told me not to do all these years at Alan Road.'

*   *   *

August 30th came and went. The end of the season. No more going to the beach. Now *that's* a silly system, I thought. The sun could be as bright on September 1st but the beach was deserted. Summer was over. Official.

September 12th came and went too, the date for starting drama school.

I worked at Yves's insistence in his office sorting Kardex systems into rattling metal filing cabinets under the drone of an overhead fan. Nicole, from downstairs, did the typing while my days were occupied with sorting cards that read '¼ mm drill and 2" bores'. I wasn't bored. Unknown to Yves I was saving money to pay my air fare back to England.

Somehow I managed to juggle a visit from Greg, the current boyfriend in England and a Cambridge Hockey Blue, with my surreptitious visits to Nanou's house.

Greg had been on a sponsored expedition to the newly opened Aswan dam with a group of friends who were also reading geography at Cambridge University. They arrived in Sfax with blistered lips, a battered sand-eroded jeep, almost devoid of provisions and one of their members dicing with insanity. They'd had to tie him to the jeep at night to stop him wandering off into the desert. Yves supervised his transfer to the local hospital, where he waited for the wheels of British Consular bureaucracy to grind slowly into action. They hired a private plane to fly him home to England. No regular airline would take him. He wandered vaguely about the apartment, eyes vacant, in a weird assortment of clothes. The only person he didn't look out of place beside was my mother. *'Voilà les fous,'* said Yves, pointing to where they sat side by side on the terrace, staring into space. We'd got used to her aimless misery. His presence jarred us into realising how she couldn't shock us any more.

'We 'ave to hide the pills from her,' said Yves.

'She hides the whisky,' Lolo interrupted. 'I found a bottle yesterday stuck right behind the fridge. If she takes pills *and* whisky that's serious, isn't it, Papa?' asked Lolo trying not to yawn.

It was late. We'd sat up many nights like this talking randomly all of us, not quite knowing what to do but not wanting to go to bed. Fatima cleared up noiselessly around us.

Mummy slept most of the day or wandered purposelessly, dressed only in her soiled nightgown, leaving cigarettes burning on the edge of tables. Yves would shrug his shoulders and point at her behind her back. 'The walking dead,' he'd say.

407

'You'll have to talk to her, Janie, she won't listen to me.'

'And she pushes me away,' said Lolo. 'When she's feeling really nasty she says she'll tell us something about Lionel that none of us know . . .'

'*Ouf*,' said Yves. 'I know.'

I held my breath.

'I know what she mean,' he went on. 'When Lionel came to, she put a needle in his foot to test his reflexes. He didn't move. He'd have been a cabbage if he'd lived. That's her big secret.'

*   *   *

October 15th came and went. The French officially evacuated Bizerte. I was envious of their leaving. I didn't share Yves's concern about the Tunisians increasing the percentage of locals employed by every foreign company. It was only a matter of time, he said, until all the French would go. I wanted more than ever to be French.

Momentarily I forgot my secret pile of money and my obsession to get back to England, Bristol in particular, the day a well-dressed, quietly spoken Tunisian turned up at the apartment. We had barely finished lunch. We didn't do the siesta during what they called the autumn. They had no Arab friends so I was curious to find out why he had come. He spoke in muted tones to Yves that made it hard to eavesdrop, but as I stood up to leave the dining-table to prepare myself for the afternoon's Kardex session, I saw that he was crying.

Later in the car Yves told me: '\'E will have my job, when it's my turn to leave. \'E said Tunisia won't be the same without the French. 'E don't want us to go.'

*　　　　*　　　　*

November came and with it enough money earned to buy my air ticket back to England.

Lolo was sad to see me go. I did feel bad about leaving her to cope with Mummy's pain but I reminded her that while Gran lived *she* was my first responsibility. Yves merely shrugged his shoulders and insisted, '*Tu es folle*—you'll never make it.' My new passport, acquired after several exchanges of official forms, now read Jane Burgess-Lapotaire, and was safely hidden with my ticket well out of his grasp.

As a final act of defiance, instead of catching a connecting flight from Paris to London, I stopped off and spent a night in Paris with Nanou who'd travelled up from Grenoble by train.

*　　　　*　　　　*

He took me to a restaurant near a flat he'd borrowed for the night. We still conversed little. His use of English hadn't increased, and my slightly improved French, uttered in terror of a slap from Yves for so long, was still hesitant and shaky.

'*Chez les Grecques?*' That at least I understood.

'*Ça te plaira?*'

'*Oh, oui*,' I said. I wasn't difficult to please. Away from all that misery at last and free to go to drama school, albeit two months late. I was in Paris with my lover. I felt grown-up, sophisticated and almost chic.

The restaurant was full and noisy. Greek music jangled in the background. I stared in horror at the menu, all in Greek and equally confusing French.

My eyes alighted on one familiar word. *Steack*.

'*Steak, s'il te plaît*,' I said. I was unsure whether I should vousvoie him or not. Although it seemed silly to be that formal with someone who made love to me. I was still non-active in this pastime.

My choice was greeted with such surprise that I stared hard at the grubby table-cloth. I muttered my insistence, lacking courage and vocabulary to explain my need for the familiar.

A large white plate arrived. A mound of red raw meat occupied the centre. Beside it lay a pile of chopped raw onions and dark green pellets which I realised were capers. Resplendent in the middle of the meat was half an eggshell which contained a raw egg. I stared at it in horror and bewilderment. Nanou tucked into something called moussaka. I stared desperately about me longing for a clue as to what I should do with this unpalatable assortment of food. Of course no one ate steak tartare in Greek restaurants. Only pretend sophisticates like me. I didn't know how to begin to eat it. Not that I was hungry any longer. Did I dip the fork into the meat? And then into the egg? I blushed, not knowing what to do and being unable to voice my need for help. Finally he noticed. Deftly he upturned the egg into the meat and mixed the whole raw mess together. I smiled wanly and ate slowly, finding it impossible to swallow if I thought about it.

* * *

410

'But 'at's nearly Christmas,' Gran said as I took my summer clothes out from the suitcase and replaced bikinis with pullovers and my complete works of Shakespeare. 'You can't start school this late.'

'Mr Brenner said he'd keep my place open for me till I got there, Gran. He knew Yves tried to stop me.'

'You're right pig-headed! I've always said so— once you make your mind up to do something . . .'

'I damn well go and do it, don't I?'

I laughed and hugged her. 'Now, you'll be all right, won't you?'

'Oh, of course I will. You hurry up and get that there train or you'll be even later than you said. As a matter of fact, I thought you was due back yesterday. I'm getting old and forgetful I suppose.'

'You're not old,' I started.

'Now, don't you stand there jawin' here to me.'

'Can't wait to see the back of me?'

'That's right,' she said, putting on her apron. 'Now, come on, get a move on. I've got Russell comin' in for dinner any minute now—and there's nothin' on the table.'

'Take care of yourself now, won't you, without me here . . .'

'Oh, of course I will. I've managed all right without you so far when you in't been here. Stop worryguttin'. You always were a worryguts.'

'Well, g'bye, then.'

Somehow it seemed more final than any goodbye we'd said before. I was leaving home for good, and we both knew it.

'Well, goodbye again, then.' I turned to look at her one last time. 'Now don't you dare die while I'm gone! I need you.'

'Die?' she said incredulously in her broad Suffolk accent. 'I got no intention a dyin'. Don't be so daft, I'm good for a few more years yet—you mark my words.'